GHOST
PLATOON

Praise for *Ghost Platoon*

'Walker, and others like him, are doing their country a great service by bringing both the bad and good of deeds of Aussie diggers out of the shadows and into the light'
Sunday Age

'His findings are a shocking indictment of the long-term effect of war'
Sunday Examiner

Praise for *Maralinga*

'An original and compelling account that succeeds in exposing the subterfuge and myopia of both British and Australian governments'
Saturday Paper

'Demonstrates powerfully why, regardless of the context in which the testing took place, the emotional legacy of Maralinga will linger in the Australian psyche'
Weekend Australian

'[An] excellent examination of a dark chapter in Australian history'
Australian Defence Magazine

Praise for *The Tiger Man of Vietnam*

'One of those great untold stories . . . Walker tells it with verve and excitement and with meticulous attention to detail'
Sydney Morning Herald

'Walker's finely researched book goes beyond the biographical account of an Australian war hero'
Sun-Herald

'It's been suggested Petersen was the model for the character of Colonel Kurtz in the film Apocalypse Now. But this remarkable true story is much richer and more compelling than anything Hollywood could conjure'
West Australian

GHOST PLATOON

FRANK WALKER

hachette
AUSTRALIA

Note to readers: This book contains photographs which some readers may find distressing. To Aboriginal readers, please also note that some of these images feature people who are deceased or who may now be deceased. The photographs are relevant to the text and have not been included lightly. The author and the publisher believe that they are an important part of telling the story of the Ghost Platoon.

hachette
AUSTRALIA

First published in Australia and New Zealand in 2011
by Hachette Australia
(an imprint of Hachette Australia Pty Limited)
Level 17, 207 Kent Street, Sydney NSW 2000
www.hachette.com.au

This edition published in 2015

10 9 8 7 6 5 4 3 2 1

National Library of Australia
Cataloguing-in-Publication data:

Walker, Frank, author.
Ghost platoon/Frank Walker.

978 0 7336 3460 4 (pbk.)

Riddle, Jim.
Australia. Army. Defence and Employment Platoon, 2nd – History.
Vietnam War, 1961–1975 – Veterans – Australia.
Vietnam War, 1961–1975 – Pyschological aspects.

959.70438

Cover design and illustration by Luke Causby
Picture section, map and diagram design by Christabella Designs
Ambush diagram based on original illustration by Clare Belshaw
Text design by Simon Paterson, Bookhouse
Typeset in Simoncini Garamond by Bookhouse, Sydney
Printed and bound in Australia by Griffin Press, Adelaide, an Accredited ISO
AS/NZS 14001:2004 Environmental Management System printer

'In war, truth is the first casualty'

AESCHYLUS, 525–456 BC

CONTENTS

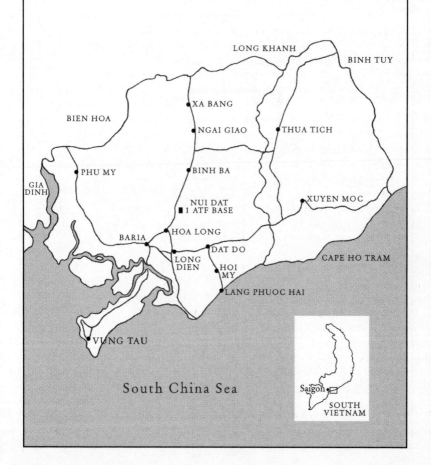

PHUOC TUY PROVINCE

SOUTH VIETNAM, 1969

LONG KHANH

BINH TUY

BIEN HOA

XA BANG

NGAI GIAO

THUA TICH

PHU MY

BINH BA

GIA DINH

NUI DAT
1 ATF BASE

XUYEN MOC

BARIA

HOA LONG

LONG DIEN

DAT DO

HOI MY

CAPE HO TRAM

LANG PHUOC HAI

VUNG TAU

South China Sea

Saigon

SOUTH VIETNAM

THUA TICH AMBUSH

29 MAY, 1969

KEY

•   men

▭   APC

⊶   M-60 gun

Three groups of APCs in case of attack from the north.

1 KM

1 KM

Captain Arrowsmith's command post with four APCs.

THUA TICH GATEWAY

North Vietnamese regular army and Viet Cong column.

500 M

Riddle's section.

PROLOGUE

During the Vietnam War he'd been a photographer in the army's public relations unit. He'd captured some of the worst moments of the war, snapping photos of Australians in action and dead enemy bodies, recording all the horror and destruction that comes with any conflict.

Bending down, he picked up the box full of pictures he'd taken during the war and carried them to a bonfire he'd started in his backyard.

He waited as the flames steadily built up. He'd risked his life getting these photos. Now the burden of what they revealed was too heavy. For more than 40 years he'd kept the pictures tucked away in a box in a back room of his home. There were hundreds of them. He rarely looked at them; in fact, he'd got them out just once in the past few decades when an old friend, a former army public relations journalist he'd worked with during the war, had visited him. After dozens of beers, he'd surprised his old mate by disappearing and coming back with the box of photographs.

They'd pored over the pictures for a while, remembering war stories and having a few laughs about their old comrades and some of the crazy situations they'd all found themselves in. But after 20 minutes the laughter dried up. They couldn't look at the images any longer; particularly the ones of mangled bodies, of Aussie soldiers doing things they shouldn't have. Images that could have turned the public against the war if they'd ever seen the light of day. It was too close, too painful. He'd put the pictures back in their box and had never looked at them again – until a few days ago.

Army photographers weren't supposed to keep copies of the pictures they'd taken during the war. As he'd been attached to the Army Public Relations Unit he was supposed to hand over all of his work to the Defence Department. In his 12 months in Vietnam he'd taken some of the most iconic images of the war, pictures that have been reproduced in newspapers, magazines and books. Several are still proudly displayed at the Australian War Memorial in Canberra.

But unknown to his superiors, he'd kept copies of every one. Many were so gruesome and so ugly that the Canberra headquarters of the busy military propaganda outfit never allowed them to be seen. Some had been destroyed by censors among the top brass; some had been officially marked 'Not for Release'. Some were to prove so controversial that attempts were still being made, decades after the war, to suppress the story they told.

In the last few days, the damned photographs had begun to haunt him. There was fresh interest in the secrets they contained. For so long he'd managed to expunge memories of the war from his mind. Now it was all flooding back. The war had reached out and found him once again, shaking the peaceful life of gardening and golf he'd carved for himself in one of the most remote parts of Australia.

He couldn't bear that. He believed nothing good could come of dredging up events that had happened so long ago and now couldn't be changed. People would get hurt. He dreaded being dragged back into the conflict surrounding events he'd witnessed and photographed. Now in his 60s, he felt he was winning the fight to stay fit and healthy, but since it became apparent that the long buried story behind the photographs was about to come out, the nightmares had returned. For so long he'd managed to stay beyond the reach of the beast lurking in his dreams. Now the beast was back: just out of sight, but lurching closer.

He'd decided to put an end to it for good. He reached down and picked up a pile of the old prints from the box and, one by one, started feeding them into the bonfire. He watched the edges curl. Images he'd taken, revealing the truth of what happened in Vietnam, blackened and burst into flames.

He added more to the fire. The intense heat drove embers up into the air, where they caught the breeze and floated towards the vast waters of the ocean. They were gone.

Yet despite the photographer's efforts to erase the past, the answers to some of the mysteries of the Vietnam War would still be sought. The secrets surrounding the Ghost Platoon – as it came to be known – weren't all ash. There were still some old soldiers who were ready to look back and reveal what they knew. Nothing could remove the images in their heads; not time, not therapy, not alcohol.

They just needed someone to ask. Many thought it best to remain silent, even after all this time. Some talked, and then retracted what they said as pressure was applied to silence them. But there were some who faced their nightmares and told their story, believing only the truth could wipe the memory clean.

This is the story of the men of the Ghost Platoon – a ragtag unit the army said never existed.

1

AMBUSH AT THUA TICH

VIETNAM: 29 MAY 1969

There was no moon, no suggestion of wind. The jungle behind the small group of Australian soldiers was still, as though holding its breath, anticipating the agony and death that was about to be unleashed. Even the flickering red lights of fireflies that sometimes bounce around the darkness of Vietnam's forests were absent this night.

Dim starlight allowed Acting Corporal Jim Riddle to make out the line of the dirt road 15 metres ahead of him through the knee-high grass that covered the open space. Riddle and the six Australian soldiers around him were on a slight ridge overlooking a dirt track called Route 328. They were 130 kilometres east of Saigon and 25 kilometres north-east of the Australian base at Nui Dat.

The seven men were braced in their positions, manning their guns, careful not to make a sound. Silence was not only the key to the coming ambush, it was essential if they wanted to survive this night.

Riddle was a natural leader. A tough, nuggety former sergeant in the British Royal Marines, he was a man held in something close to awe by the younger Australian diggers. He spoke with a thick Geordie accent undiminished by six months in the Australian army. He'd joined up from his home in northern England's Newcastle upon Tyne. His accent didn't worry his new Aussie mates; they were ready to follow him wherever he led.

Acting Corporal Riddle certainly looked like he could rip anybody apart. He had a rugged moustache and his tough wiry frame was constantly wound up like a spring. They way he moved lightly on his feet in quick darting movements hinted that he was a fighter. His scars confirmed he'd been in many a scrap. He always carried an M-16, a big semi-automatic rifle that held 30 round magazines. In the early years of the war Americans had trouble with the gun jamming because they didn't keep it clean. Riddle knew better. The gun was his ticket to survival and he kept it spotless. It fired 5.56 millimetre bullets at a very high velocity. The bullets were designed to wound rather than kill as a wounded enemy soldier was far more burdensome on enemy resources than a dead one. Riddle and his men knew that to make sure they killed an enemy with an M-16 they had to hit them several times.

Along with the rifle, slung over his shoulder was a stocky wide-barrelled M-79 blooper gun, a grenade launcher that had the aggressive look of a sawn-off shotgun. It fired 40 millimetre explosive rounds. They could be high explosive grenades, heavy buckshot or small arrow-like projectiles that spread out in an arc. It was a fearsome weapon, particularly in close combat or in jungle fighting where targets were hard to line up quickly. Strapped to his thigh was a large K-bar knife, a vicious 18 centimetre blade that resembled the more famous Bowie knife. It had been issued to US marines and was designed for close combat. Riddle didn't like feeling defenceless if his guns ran out of bullets. In his pack was extra ammo, two Claymore mines and several hand grenades. Hanging off his belt were half a dozen bottles of water. He was a man who believed in preparing for the worst.

Chances were Riddle would have had three stripes on his arm if he hadn't been in so many drunken brawls, or had the unfortunate tendency to inform officers rather too bluntly of their many shortcomings. Truth was, at that moment he was a lowly private with only a temporary rank of corporal.

Thirty-nine men, including Riddle, all regular infantry privates with not a conscript among them, had been left behind when the 4th Battalion had returned to Australia a few days earlier. Riddle and the rest of these men had arrived in Vietnam as reinforcements and hadn't yet fulfilled their 12-month stint in the country. Just three days before they'd been thrown together in a temporary Headquarters unit dubbed the 2nd D&E Platoon. D&E stood for Defence and Employment. It was usually a general dogsbody role, providing escorts or guards for visiting VIPs and drivers, and also providing security around the base at Nui Dat. There was already an existing D&E Platoon under a lieutenant, so the surplus men from the 4th Royal Australian Regiment (4RAR) were formed into a second, separate makeshift unit.

It was a ramshackle arrangement. They had no sergeant, not even a corporal. They hadn't seen their lieutenant since the first day. They had no clear duties; no one seemed to be in charge. Someone had to step up, so Riddle simply took control of the ragtag platoon. Senior officers at the base noticed the way Riddle was respected by the other privates, saw his bearing and obvious experience and recognised that he was a soldier ready to fight. They saw no reason to rail against the natural order established in the ranks, so Riddle was put in charge.

Riddle would have loved to have those sergeant stripes, even a corporal's two stripes. He was a tough professional soldier who didn't cop shit from anybody. But he loved a drink. He loved it too much for his own good. However, out here in the combat zone his mind was clear and sharp. At the age of 29 he was eight or nine years older than most of the other men in the platoon, and they saw him as almost a father figure, confident he would protect them in the coming fight and get them through alive.

As he looked around him in the dark, Riddle knew he and the seven men in his section were in an extremely vulnerable position. They were the forward listening post, around 500 metres in advance of the rest of the platoon and the protection of the Armoured Personnel Carriers (APCs) that were hidden in a clump of trees to the north.

Riddle raised himself on his knees and looked to his left. Far in the distance he could just see the ghostly outline of the old stone gate that stood over the road. Four metres high and standing upright like football goalposts, it was a battered and crumbling concrete and stone arch decorated with Vietnamese writing. A hole in one side of the arch looked as though a tank shell had gone right through it. This gate had once marked the entrance to the village of Thua Tich.

The village had been eradicated years ago; burned, razed to the ground, wiped off the face of the earth. Its people had been forcibly moved to other settlements or detention camps. The villagers had been deemed too sympathetic to the Viet Cong, a danger that needed to be removed. Now all that was left were a few mounds of earth marking where rice paddies and thatch houses had once been. The ground was covered in tufts of grass. The jungle was slowly claiming it back, but the land was still open and clear for 50 metres east of the road and for another 30 metres on the west side where Riddle and his men had set up their position.

•

The Australians had arrived earlier in the day to set up for an attempted ambush of a unit of North Vietnamese and Viet Cong troops expected to come from the south during the night. Intelligence reports suggested a large enemy force was gathering about five kilometres north of the Australians' position. The column they were to ambush was bringing supplies up to this larger force, arms and equipment that had been smuggled all the way down the coast from North Vietnam and as far inland as possible on the countless canals and creeks.

The clear space along the road at the site of Thua Tich was a perfect spot to set the trap. Captain Tom Arrowsmith, cavalry commander of 2 Troop, B Squadron, 3rd Cavalry, with 13 APCs had taken temporary charge of the hastily formed second D&E platoon. Most of the 39 men in the platoon had been sent with him as infantrymen from Headquarters for this mission.

Arrowsmith deployed his troops before nightfall. The APCs were divided into four groups of three vehicles, with each APC carrying a crew of two – a driver and commander at the machine gun – with the exception of Arrowsmith's command vehicle which carried a radio operator as well. Each group of three APCs also had six to eight infantrymen attached to it. On this mission, an extra APC accompanied Arrowsmith at his command post. It had an 81 millimetre mortar fixed in the cargo area, a welcome bit of extra armament.

The Australian unit was in a dangerous position. They were out of range of the covering fire of artillery. Within striking distance was a far larger enemy force. Effectively they were alone, isolated and surrounded.

Arrowsmith positioned three groups of the APCs well to the north of the Thua Tich gateway on either side of the road. The nine APCs and 25 or so infantrymen with them there were to prevent any surprise attack coming from that direction. Then he positioned the remaining three APCs, the vehicle outfitted with the mortar, and a section of infantrymen under the cover of a group of trees and bushes 12 metres west of the Thua Tich gate. Arrowsmith would command from this post. The dirt road came straight up to the gate, then veered slightly to the east. Three of the APCs with Arrowsmith were positioned so they could fire straight down the dirt road. One vehicle was behind them with its guns pointing to their rear in case of a surprise attack from that direction. The APCs were equipped with powerful 50 calibre machine guns. They had a clear line of fire for more than 500 metres straight down the road. They'd have to be careful not to shoot at Riddle and his men sent forward to act as spotters.

Riddle knew they were in a tight spot. All day he'd had a gut feeling it was going to be a far bigger action than the brass seemed to anticipate. He trusted his sixth sense on these things. It had worked well for him in the past, both in Vietnam and in his time with the Royal Marines in conflicts including Aden, Sarawak and Cyprus.

Christ, we're isolated down here, Riddle thought as he looked over his position. His task was to spot the enemy column coming up the road from the south and radio it through to Arrowsmith. His section would let the Viet Cong go past and hold their fire until the enemy were in the middle of the kill zone for the APCs and troops hidden on the roadside up near the gate. Once Arrowsmith ordered his APCs to open fire, Riddle's section would follow suit and hope like buggery the VC didn't overrun their post.

Before dark, Riddle and his men laid Claymore mines all around their little ridge. He went for a walk down the road with Dennis 'Snow' Manski, one of the soldiers he'd known in the 4th Battalion, named for his shock of white hair. He looked back at their position where he could see his men laying the mines and digging in their two machine guns. It was more of a bump than a ridge. *Shit, they can run right over us here*, he thought. They were dangerously exposed.

In his mind he could see exactly how the enemy would spread out once Arrowsmith gave the order to fire. If the VC tried to outflank Arrowsmith and his APCs they would come up through the grass and bushes on the left side of the road and run right over his position. His section would have to shoot like hell and create a big noise to make themselves look like a much larger force to confuse the enemy so they didn't come their way.

He left his men on the ridge and walked back along the road toward the gate. The dirt road went slightly downhill from his position to where Arrowsmith had backed his APCs into some tree cover near the old stone pillars. Riddle wanted to report that his forward position was set up and ready. As he walked, he looked over the killing ground and thought that from Arrowsmith's point of view it was like a long cricket pitch, with his section stuck way up at the bowler's end. *Fookin' hell, they can have us for breakfast out there,* he thought. *If that force is as big as I feel it's gonna be, then we're stuffed.*

Riddle didn't let his concerns show. Back on the ridge he had his men take cover on the far side of the rise, away from the ACP's line of fire. In the dark, you were just as likely to be killed by a wayward 50 calibre bullet as a carefully aimed shot from the enemy. The men were spread out in a horseshoe shape. They didn't dig in deeply so that they could move around in the firefight to make themselves look like twice the number of men. VC fired at gunflashes, so it wasn't good to stay in one position for too long. Riddle checked in with each of his men, making sure their weapons were primed and ready, giving last-minute instructions.

Most had been in Vietnam for only a few months. Private Edward 'Ted' Colmer, his head swathed in his preferred green bandana, was just 19 years old and had only four months' war experience behind him. He settled behind his M-60 machine gun, the gun's barrel held up on a folding bipod. The stocky Colmer had been involved in a deadly attack on an enemy bunker just weeks after arriving in Vietnam. Within arm's reach to his right, 24-year-old Private John Arnold from Innisfail, Queensland, carefully placed his own M-60 into position. The .308 calibre guns could fire 550 rounds a minute, but good gunners fired around 100 rounds a minute at a sustained rate. Fire more than that and the weapon got too hot to handle and could even destroy the barrel. The M-60s were much treasured weapons and were given to the more skilled and experienced soldiers in a section.

The two machine gunners would direct their own individual arcs of fire over the road. Former timber cutter Don Moss and Snow Manski were beside them to assist with the belt feeds. Lanky Queenslander David Simpson manned the clackers, the triggers to fire the Claymores that would each blast 750 ball bearings towards the enemy. Behind them was Peter 'Pedro' Allen, a quiet 20-year-old from Tasmania. His task was to guard against attackers sneaking in from the rear or flanking them. They settled down to wait for dark.

The radio crackled. Arrowsmith was sending someone down to join the forward post and wanted an escort for him. Roger that. Riddle was surprised when a white-haired bloke aged about 50 arrived. He was Ernie Hayden, an English-born veteran of the British 8th Army desert campaign of World War Two. Although Hayden was officially designated a Warrant Officer Class 2 in the Australian infantry attached to Headquarters, he insisted he was present only as an observer, not to act in any combat or command role. Hayden told Riddle he was part of a civil aid group who'd come to see what the fighting was like.

Riddle didn't believe a word of it. He was sure Hayden had come to the front for a day to try and earn himself a combat medal. Or maybe he was a spook of some kind. There were lots of strange folk in Vietnam with secret missions who had been given military ranks to help them get around. But Hayden was an easy-going bloke, and Riddle was glad for the chance to chat with a fellow Englishman to pass the time. They talked about Tobruk and the desert. Riddle had been there when he was in the Royal Marines. Hayden was happy to help out when Riddle asked him to hold the radio while he checked on the men.

But Hayden quickly showed his combat skills were lacking when he settled back, reached into a pocket and pulled out a cigar. The soldiers watched in disbelief as he lit the fat stinking object. The smell alone would travel for miles, let alone its glowing end acting as the crosshairs on a target. 'Put it out, you fuckin' idiot!' someone yelled. Hayden did so immediately, looking rather sheepish.

As night fell around 7pm, the men lay down in the slight depressions in the ground they had scraped for themselves. It was now a tense wait, ears and eyes straining to catch the first sign of Viet Cong coming up the road. Darkness was their greatest friend but they had to be on high alert. Riddle's bad feeling just got worse and worse. In his mind's eye he could see all his men butchered and splayed out like dog meat from enemy machine-gun fire. The VC did that, spraying bullets into the bodies of fallen Americans and Australians so that they had to be scraped up into buckets and plastic bags and taken home in little chunks. Shaking off the horrific image,

Riddle settled himself behind Manski and Colmer and their M-60s and kept a constant watch down the road.

•

An hour went by excruciatingly slowly. Riddle was convinced the enemy would come an hour after nightfall. Eight o'clock went by. Nothing. Was his sixth sense wrong? Another half an hour ticked by, the entire section peering intently into the darkness, ears straining for the slightest sound.

Suddenly John Arnold leaned back and nudged Riddle. He'd heard something in the distance. Arnold turned his thumb down – the sign for enemy close by – and pointed down the road. Riddle strained his eyes but couldn't see a thing. Then he heard it, too, just a faint sound, like the shuffling of feet. Then, a voice in the distance. An answering laugh. The VC weren't being careful. They had no idea what they were walking into.

Through the gloom about 20 metres down the road, Riddle could finally make out the faint silhouette of a man. He was walking well ahead of the others. Another figure was about four metres behind him. Then another. Riddle reckoned these scouts must know they would have no chance in an ambush. His first thought was that they must be on some sort of punishment detail. He'd told his men not to open fire until he gave the order. Riddle wasn't going to do that until Arrowsmith and the APCs further up the road unleashed their heavier firepower on the killing ground in front of them.

The first VC drew level with his position. Riddle let him walk by, a dark shape against the brighter reflection of the dirt road, his AK-47 slung casually over his shoulder. Two more advance scouts came level with his position on the ridge. Then Riddle turned and looked down the road, and his heart leaped into his mouth. *Oh shit, there are hundreds of them. The road's full of the fuckers*. A tightly packed column of the enemy filled the road as far as he could see. Most were in the black pyjamas and conical straw hats typical of the Viet Cong, but he could also see tan uniforms and pith helmets on some of them, indicating they were regular North Vietnamese Army. This was a proper military battalion – far outnumbering the 20-odd men of Arrowsmith and Riddle's combined sections waiting to ambush them.

To hit them hard Riddle knew they'd have to let the advance scouts go right through before the main body of the enemy column would be in the kill zone. He calculated that if the APCs opened fire as soon as they saw the scouts, the bulk of the column would be right next to his position – and probably flee straight over the top of him and his men.

Riddle got on the radio, lowering his voice as much as he could. 'Two Zero Alpha, this is 63,' he whispered, giving their respective call signs. 'Enemy coming, enemy coming.' Arrowsmith's radio operator clicked an acknowledgement.

Riddle knew it wasn't proper procedure, but he clicked the radio again and whispered: 'Let them through, let them through. Don't shoot the first three. There's a whole fookin' army coming behind 'em.'

He heard Arrowsmith reply coolly: 'Wait . . . wait . . . wait . . . Do not fire until my order . . . Wait . . . wait.'

Just metres away the head of the enemy column started to walk past Riddle and his men. Among them was Squad Leader Do Van Minh. He was a respected hero in the D440 Battalion of the National Front for the Liberation of South Vietnam. Ten months earlier he'd volunteered to launch the first rocket-propelled grenade for his squad in an attack that destroyed the enemy post at Bao Chanh. He was extremely proud of the special printed bravery certificate he'd been awarded by the local deputy political cadre Nguyen Thanh Can and kept it in his breast pocket. The column was heading towards his home at Cam My village and he hoped to see his family again after years of fighting the enemy.

Minh didn't differentiate between Australians and Americans. To him they were all Yankee invaders, and he was determined to push them out of his country. He was a scout and proud to have been chosen to be at the head of the column, the most dangerous post in any large troop movement like this. But all seemed quiet as they marched through the night into the empty space where the old village of Thua Tich used to stand. So much of his country had been destroyed, but he was determined to keep on fighting until victory.

To Minh's left, just 15 metres through the darkness, Riddle and his section watched as the Vietnamese walked past their position. The road was elevated slightly above the surrounding grassland with a small ditch running along each side and the

Vietnamese soldiers were exposed. Lying in wait, Private Don Moss felt his heart thumping *boompa boompa*, so loud he was convinced the VC must be able to hear it. His younger brother Ron had fought at the celebrated Battle of Long Tan three years earlier. Don was determined he would give as good an account of himself in this coming action, but he was scared as hell, holding his breath as the VC moved past just in front of him.

As the main column of VC reached them their footsteps sounded like rustling leaves. One or two were talking quietly. Riddle guessed that the leaders were tucked away in the middle of the mass somewhere, certainly not stuck out in the front like sacrificial lambs. He could hear a low rumbling noise from further down the road. It sounded like they were pulling carts. The VC had 50 calibre weapons they had pulled off destroyed American APCs and downed choppers. If they got those weapons into operation against the Aussies they would be cut to pieces.

Riddle calculated that, by now, the advance scouts must be just about level with Arrowsmith's hidden position. Since they'd passed his position, more than 50 VC had reached the kill zone behind the scouts, but the bulk of the enemy column was still coming up the road towards him. *Jesus, I hope they open fire soon. If not we'll have hundreds of the buggers right on top of us.* He couldn't understand why the VC didn't have men walking the flanks, off the road and up against the trees. *They must be bloody confident.* He could see they were well armed with AK-47s and grenade launchers. More seconds ticked by. Now more than 150 VC were in range of the machine guns waiting to open fire on them, with still many more coming up the road.

Suddenly Arrowsmith barked into his radio microphone: 'Fire, fire, fire!' Hearing the order crackling through their headsets, the APC crewmen opened fire with everything they had. Arrowsmith's driver, Allan Stanton, pushed the levers on two switches for the Claymores, exploding flames and thousands of ball bearings across the road. Illuminated by the flash of the explosion Stanton saw bodies blasted two metres into the air, twisting head over heels, while others spun in a bizarre dance of death. One of the APCs fired up a flare which spread an eerie light over the road.

Stanton jumped up and took his place beside Arrowsmith, who was on the APC's 50 calibre machine gun. Stanton linked belts of the bullets together to save Arrowsmith reloading. Arrowsmith hammered out a deadly rain of fire at the dark figures on the road and grass. The advance scouts had escaped the initial Claymore blasts as Arrowsmith had waited until more of the enemy column was caught in the kill zone. The scouts dived into the long grass and opened fire on the APCs, identified now by their gunflashes. Several shots hitting the metal of the APCs demonstrated the scouts knew exactly where they were. At least 50 rounds hit the APCs and the cover around them.

The barrel of the APC's gun became white hot and started smoking as it continued to belch fire down the road. Stanton dropped down into the belly of the APC to pick up a new barrel for the gun and a pair of asbestos gloves. He leapt up beside Arrowsmith, who nodded and pointed to the gun barrel. Stanton put the gloves on and unscrewed it, and twisted in the new barrel. Arrowsmith poured out fire once again.

In the APC to their left, Peter Board was behind another of the big guns. His father had been one of the famous RAF dam-busters in World War Two so he'd grown up on heroic war stories. *Why am I so shit scared? This can't be normal,* he thought. Board was a mechanic who'd been conscripted into the army and posted to the cavalry. He'd been in Vietnam just five weeks and this was the 20-year-old's first patrol outside the base, his very first taste of action. All through the afternoon and night he'd jumped at the slightest noise in the bush. He'd shared a brew with Riddle before dark and was impressed with the seasoned soldier's calm. He'd also noted the giant knife strapped to Riddle's thigh and the myriad weapons hanging off him. He knew Riddle was down the road somewhere in the heart of the firefight. He silently thanked Christ it wasn't him down there.

Board didn't want to be there, but he had a job to do. Over the radio mike in his helmet he'd heard Riddle telling Arrowsmith the VC were coming, and then the words: 'There's a whole fookin' army'. Board's heart was in his mouth, every nerve as tight as a bow. But he was totally focused on his weapon and what he had to do. He was extremely diligent in cleaning and maintaining his 50 cal. He knew the gun would keep him alive. And he was well trained: kill the enemy before they can kill you.

When he heard the order to open fire, Board pulled down the trigger with his thumbs and the machine gun spat out its barrage of death. He swept his designated area across the road with an arc of fire. In the flashes of light, Board could see bodies falling. He hated it; he was shit scared; but he fired his gun since his life and those of his mates depended on it. Following the line of his bullets from the gun's tracers, Board saw one hit a VC and watched in amazement as the man's head exploded.

Board heard loud pings on the heavy metal shields of the APC. *They are fucking shooting at me!* He intensified his shooting. It was the only way to survive. *Ouch, what's that?* Board felt a nasty sting in his left foot, as though he'd been bitten. *Ignore it. Keep firing. Kill them before they can kill me.*

•

Half a kilometre down the road, Riddle called out to his men, 'Hold your fire!' There was no point in staying silent now that the APCs had opened fire. Riddle expected the column to bulge out from the road as those at the front stepped back from the machine-gun fire ripping into them and those in the rear kept coming forward. Riddle had positioned himself under a small tree. It offered little protection against enemy bullets, but it gave his men a central reference point.

'Wait for it . . . wait for it.' Riddle wanted the VC bunched together in front of their position. By the light of the flares he could see them duck and hesitate, unsure at first where the firing was coming from and where to take cover. In front of him he could see a group of men hedge towards their position 15 metres away, now 12 . . . 10 . . . 8 . . .

'Fire, fire, fire!' he yelled, and he fired his M-79 at the bulging enemy force. A grenade exploded over the VC, raining down death. At the same time, Simpson tugged the clacker which set off the Claymores in front of them and enemy soldiers evaporated in a roar of fire. Riddle saw one man thrown three metres into the air, his arms and legs flailing like a rag doll. Every man in the seven-strong section gave it all they had, straight into the mass of enemy soldiers in front of them. Among the Vietnamese cut down in the first hail of lead from the Australians was the proud scout Do Van Minh, bullets slamming into his slim body and spinning him to the dirt.

Shadowy figures were running everywhere and Riddle's section tried to mow them down. The noise was deafening as Arnold and Colmer let rip with the M-60 machine guns, firing at anything that looked like a human being. The others fired their M-16s in bursts at the silhouettes that darted in and out of the light.

Riddle crouched, turned to his right and fired a flare over the column. He hoped to sow confusion and temporarily blind the enemy. The APC carrying the mortar launched another flare and as the area lit up, Riddle was shocked at what he saw. The road to the south was packed with men. Hundreds of them. Most were in the brown uniform of the North Vietnamese Army. These weren't VC guerillas, they were well trained regular soldiers, many with bushes stuck in their helmets for camouflage. They were ready for combat. He could see the surprise and anger on their faces as they looked straight at his position.

Riddle knew that, if they rallied and charged his position, they would completely overrun him and his men. The Aussies poured more gunfire into the mass of men as fast as they could. It was kill or be killed. In the flashes of light, Riddle could see that there were women among the enemy soldiers. He thought he could even see a few kids in the pack of humans struggling to get away from the hail of bullets. He saw one man's face ripped off by the gunfire, leaving a black bloody pulp.

Red and yellow tracers from the 50 calibre guns fired from Arrowsmith's APC lit up the road in bizarre arcs. Some whizzed only metres over the top of Riddle's section. He was glad he'd positioned his men on the other side of the rise, away from the APCs line of fire. But that put them square in the firing line of the enemy column. The VC had recovered from the shock of the ambush and were firing back, picking out the gun flashes to determine where the Australians were hidden. Green and orange tracers whipped out from the VC column towards Riddle's position and he could feel the bullets whizzing over their heads and thudding into the ground around them. The lightshow was like a bizarre fireworks display, the tracers bouncing off at crazy angles.

Bullets came at them from every direction. Machine gunner Colmer burrowed further into the dirt, but that left the muzzle of his gun pointing up into the air.

Manski yelled at him, 'You're firing too high, Ted!'

Colmer wriggled back and dropped the muzzle down so his fire resumed its assault on the killing ground, its flashes lighting up the enemy. Riddle saw another face simply ripped off as he fired into the column.

Suddenly Riddle was struck by the crazy notion that if he stood up and fired, the VC would see his muzzle flash and train their sights on him, not at his men on the ground. He got to his feet and did just that, moving back and forth across the ridge to keep himself a mobile target. *If I can save the lads I am doing my job. If they shoot at me, they are not shooting at the lads. Come on – here I am. Come and fookin' get me!* He fired a burst, moved, fired again, moved, fired and moved again. He watched as a rocket-propelled grenade whizzed towards their position. It hit the dirt in front of the M-60s and threw dirt up in the air. Some of it went straight up Riddle's nose. He shook his head and kept firing, kept moving. He was convinced they were all about to die. *Ah shit, I've pissed myself.* He could feel the warm liquid spread across his crotch and down his legs. It was something he'd never admit to his mates. Still he fired and moved, fired and moved.

Why aren't they coming? Riddle was puzzled. The enemy wasn't advancing on his section's position as he expected. If they charged, they'd easily take out his isolated Aussie section. He could see the VC dropping dead or wounded. He could hear them scream. He could see some of them trying to crawl away into the darkness. Riddle dropped to the ground to reload his M-79. He was most worried about enemy soldiers who had dropped out of sight among the grass tussocks on the far side of the road. If they rallied and launched a charge his section had little chance. From the cover of his tree, Riddle fired grenades over the road to explode among those enemy troops.

Some of the enemy were getting closer. They were only shadows now that the light from the flares had gone so Riddle and his men fired at the shadows, no matter if they were wounded and trying to crawl away. No mercy was given.

The heavy firing seemed to go on for almost an hour . . . At least, that's what it seemed to the men. In reality the heavy barrage of machine-gun fire and Claymore blasts probably lasted between just 10 and 15 minutes. There were simply no more VC to shoot at after that. They were dead, or they'd cleared out. The shooting slackened off. Riddle did a quick calculation and realised his section was fast running out of ammunition. But somewhere in the dark, the main body of the VC column was still out there. He'd seen hundreds of faces in the light of the flares, explosions and gunfire. Riddle feared they were rallying just out of sight to the south, maybe working their way up through the forest on either side of the road, possibly behind them. It wasn't over.

Riddle felt a tug on his shirt and almost jumped out of his skin. He spun around with his gun, ready to kill.

It was Hayden, holding up the radio. The old veteran had been sitting up at the back of the section throughout the fighting. Riddle had forgotten all about him.

'Arrowsmith for you,' Hayden said.

'Get down, you crazy bastard!' yelled Riddle.

He grabbed the radio. Arrowsmith told him to keep their heads down. A Spooky was coming. It was due in about 15 minutes. A Spooky was an AC-47 United States Air Force gunship, a converted DC-3 with three ferocious 7.62 millimetre Gatling guns on the port side, each capable of pouring out 100 rounds per second – 6000 rounds per minute for each gun. They were formidable weapons; they literally rained death from the sky.

The tactic was simple and deadly: the gunship banked to the left as it flew at 120 knots in circles over its target, the pilot aimed the guns and fired, keeping the bullets pouring into the enemy. The USAF Spooky squadron had been operating for four years and had built up a fearsome reputation with its high hit-rate accuracy. No base had ever been taken while a Spooky was protecting it. The Vietnamese so feared the gunships they at first believed they were fire-breathing dragons. American and Australian soldiers loved them, giving the chunky planes the more affectionate names of Puff the Magic Dragon and Snoopy.

Riddle just hoped the Spooky pilot knew where they were. The VC fired a few potshots at Riddle's position, but hit no one. He was surprised and relieved no one in his section had been hit in the firefight so far but the Spooky could wipe them out in seconds if its firestream strayed their way. If the old plane hit an air pocket its bullets could go anywhere. Then he heard the plane coming from the south. It would arrive in seconds. There was no time to dig in. He warned his men what was coming and they wriggled themselves deeper into the dirt and pulled their skulls in.

The Spooky flew in low, using the road to navigate. The pilot radioed to Arrowsmith's call sign: 'Tango Alpha Two – this is Snoopy,' he drawled in his American accent. 'Am approaching your position coming up the road. Require you to shine red flashlights directly into the air to mark your position. Do you copy? Over.'

'Snoopy, Tango Alpha Two. Message understood,' crackled Arrowsmith over the radio. 'We are all west of the road. Shining lights now. Charlie east of the road and south of our position.'

The drivers of each APC got out torches with red filters and shone them straight into the night air to mark their position. The last thing they wanted was for Snoopy to wander their way. If the VC saw their position by the red lights then the fire from the Spooky would keep their heads down.

At his listening post, Riddle heard the American pilot over the radio. He hoped the Yank knew he was well to the south of the groups of APCs. *Shit, a light. We need a light.* Riddle got on the radio. 'We are south of command. Wait for our light.'

'How close is Charlie?' asked the pilot. *Too bloody close,* thought Riddle. He had to signal his position to the pilot, and fast. He scrambled up the rise and rummaged in his backpack. He pulled out a torch, along with a transparent bit of red plastic he'd packed for just this kind of situation. He positioned the red plastic over the torch and stuck it into the ground pointing straight up.

'OK, I can see you now,' called back the pilot. *Thank Christ for that*, thought Riddle.

The pilot knew the Australians were all positioned to the west of the road so he lined up his guns on the eastern side. As he flew in, he banked the plane and pulled the trigger, unleashing the terrifying firepower of the Gatling guns on the cleared land and forest to the south and east of the road. Down poured the incredible firestorm of bullets and red tracers. It was easy to see why the VC saw it as a fire-breathing dragon.

Riddle watched in awe as the bullets rained down on the other side of the road. As each bullet slammed into the earth it kicked a tower of dirt into the air, as if a forest of trees was springing up from the cleared ground. Like the others, Riddle was trying to bury his face in the dirt. The noise was terrifying, like a giant grinder cutting through steel. *It's like a T-Rex roaring*, thought Riddle. There was no margin for error. With the slightest shift in the plane's flight path they could be carved into minced meat. For 45 long glorious minutes the Spooky hailed its fire down on the forest and the road. Then the pilot radioed he was going back to base to reload and would return.

A couple of hours later the Spooky came back for its second run, this time heading south down the road. The pilot opened up his guns again as he approached Riddle's position, still marked by the red light. The pilot's accuracy was incredible.

For a brief second the volley of fire came within five metres of Riddle and his men's position, before veering off into the scrub and jungle down the west side of the road, heading south in the direction the enemy had fled. It flew in circles over the jungle on either side of the road, laying down its devastating gunfire. There was no way the enemy column was going to mount a counterattack after that. After half an hour the Spooky flew away back to Saigon, taking its deadly fire breath with it.

Silence descended over the clearing. *Fookin' hell, nothing could live through that,* Riddle said to himself. But then he had a second thought. The VC were tough, and they kept on coming no matter what overwhelming firepower was thrown at them. Some might have escaped the Spooky and were coming looking for revenge. He told his men to lay low and not attract attention.

Then he heard them. Off in the darkness was the faint sound of feet scraping on gravel. Weapons and equipment clinked as they were picked up. Soft moans drifted in the night from down the road along with the sound of bodies being dragged away. The noises were getting closer and closer, first from the south and on the road in front of them, then on the left and the right. *Christ, they're all around us. If they come up this ridge they'll walk right over us.*

Riddle motioned to his men not to fire unless the VC were right on top of them. From the sound of it there were enough VC around to easily mount a charge and kill them all. No quarter would be given after they had lost so many of their people. But Riddle couldn't see them. They were staying 20 or 30 metres away. They must have known where the Aussies were, but just seemed intent on gathering their weapons and fallen comrades and getting out of there.

One of the wounded VC cried out. He'd been moaning softly ever since the shooting had stopped. He was about ten metres away. He must have heard his comrades shuffling around in the darkness and, in a whimper, called out for help. Riddle stood up and peered around, looking for the man. In the faint light he saw a body in the dirt move an arm. Riddle quickly took aim and fired a burst at the figure. He didn't want him attracting more VC to their position.

Suddenly he saw a figure stand up in the grass about 15 metres away. From the outline of the silhouette he could see it was a woman. She was holding an AK-47 in front of her. She fired a quick burst in his direction. Riddle brought up his gun and fired back. He was sure he hit her in the chest. Her body was thrown back into the grass.

Riddle squatted down again and the entire section remained still and quiet for the rest of the night. The sound of the VC moving around stopped after a while. They'd retrieved all the bodies they could safely reach, and had now fallen back. But the Australians stayed on full alert until the first rays of dawn began to light up the scene of devastation around them. The seven men of the forward lookout post looked around, nodding to each other, smiling. They were all alive. They had made it through the longest night of their lives.

2

AN ENGINEER'S BURIAL

30 MAY 1969

At the first hint of daylight, Arrowsmith was on the radio to the APC crews who had been stationed to the north of the gate all night. They hadn't been involved in any of the fighting and had watched on safely from a distance as if it had been a fireworks display at a carnival. He told them to come down and sweep the open ground to the east of the road where enemy soldiers could still be hiding in the tall grass and jungle.

The APCs roared through the grass, but didn't find any VC there. They fired their machine guns into the tall vegetation and the edge of the forest just in case, but they had no way of knowing if they hit anything. They saw a number of blood trails from where the enemy had carted off their dead and wounded during the night, but no bodies were found apart from the dozen or so they could see on the road. Then the APCs formed a protective position and the remainder of the 2nd D&E Platoon jumped out. They were keen to see their mates who had been stuck out front in the listening post.

Once the area was secured, Riddle stood up cautiously and looked around. He could see bodies on the road in front of him, but it wasn't the dead he was worried about. He was more concerned about what was lurking in the forest 100 metres away on the other side of the road and south of their position. *Where'd that bloody column go? Are they just waiting for us to pop our heads up to shoot them off?* Riddle told his machine gunners to keep their weapons trained on the forest and to the south, then moved forward with the rest of his section.

The first body he came to was the woman he'd shot right at the end of the firefight. She was in the black pyjama-style uniform of the Viet Cong. Riddle had indeed got her in the chest. Her body was covered in blood but, strangely, her face was untouched. *She's so young, just a girl. Pretty, too. Ah shit. I hate this.* Riddle knelt down. He had to search her clothing and pack for intelligence.

He reached into her shirt pocket and pulled out a black and white photo. It was the young woman with two boys – maybe aged nine or ten – all three smiling at the camera. The boys were dressed as cowboys with black hats held on with string and toggles under their chins. From the look of it, the picture had been taken around the bars of Vung Tau, the coastal town where Australian troops and their allies went for rest and convalescence. *They're probably her brothers,* he thought. *She's too young to be their mother.*

Riddle knew Intelligence would love to get a hold of this picture, especially if it proved she had been a VC living in Vung Tau, which was regarded as a safe zone for allied troops. Riddle slipped the photo into his pocket to destroy later. *If those fookin' South Vietnamese police get hold of it, they'll hunt down the kids and arrest and torture her family. She's dead. That's enough killing.* Riddle cut the straps of the girl's backpack and slid it out from beneath her. It contained a full surgical kit with knives, bandages and medicine. *She must've been a trainee doctor or nurse.*

Snow Manski stood guard next to Riddle, his gun pointing at the body. Riddle had told his men to always have someone watching their back when they searched a body in case the enemy was still alive and ready with a gun or grenade when they were turned over. There was also the chance that a sniper was waiting for them to be still, which was long enough to take a bead on them while their attention was on the search. He'd only had to tell them once.

Manski was ready for anything but he was very uneasy. 'Fuck,' he snarled, 'What is this?' he snarled. 'I didn't come here to shoot fucking women.'

Riddle said nothing. He felt no shock or guilt. *It was me or her,* he thought. *That's war. It's just fookin' war.* He got up and walked the few metres to the next body. It was the wounded man he'd shot to stop him crying out in the night. Again, he cut the straps of the man's backpack in order to get it out from underneath the body. He wasn't worried about it being booby trapped. He knew the VC hadn't had time to do it over the course of the night and, in any case, his sixth sense wasn't tingling. He knew the area was clear.

The soldier had been shot in the stomach and, as Riddle rolled him to his side to pull the backpack free, his guts opened up, disgorging black blood and intestines into the dirt, making a terrible sound as the air raced into the man's stomach cavity. It sounded like a big bottle being emptied – glug, glug, glug. Riddle gritted his teeth. *I wish I'd killed him quicker, poor bastard. What the hell. He doesn't know my name. He can't come after me.*

Riddle dug into the man's pockets. According to protocol, everything they found on the dead should be handed to officers, who should in turn pass it on to military intelligence to assess for potentially useful information about the enemy. But Riddle knew it didn't work like that. He'd seen sergeants and officers keep interesting looking objects for themselves as trophies. He didn't judge anyone who had been part of a battle for pocketing something but he felt no one had the right to trophies if they hadn't been involved in the fight. Enemy weapons and personal effects often ended up being sold for cash back at base, bought and traded by men who hadn't participated. But Riddle didn't have any qualms about keeping some of the things he'd found on bodies – as far as he was concerned they were the spoils of war. Like a warrior taking the spirit of the enemy he'd killed, it was a sign of respect; a way of honouring the dead. As he bent over to search the body, Riddle was consciously looking for booty as much as useful intelligence.

Riddle found a yellow paper card with Vietnamese official stamps on it. It appeared to be some sort of certificate. Later, after it had circulated among members of the platoon, it was translated. It was the bravery citation of Comrade Do Van Minh, scout squad leader of D440 Battalion, awarded to him for his voluntary lead of the attack on the enemy post at Bao Chanh on the night of 26 June, 1968 – just under a year earlier. Minh's luck had finally run out, never to see his dream of the foreign invaders being defeated come true.

As Riddle emptied the soldier's pockets, in his mind he replayed what had happened during the night. The man had been wounded in the opening seconds of the ambush and his comrades had tried to reach him later. *His mates couldn't get to him 'cos he was too close to our position. I made sure of that. The girl, the medic, was probably trying to reach him. She would'a heard him moanin'. I'd'a let her go if she hadn't shot at me. They weren't really looking for us. They were thinking the same as us, just glad to have survived that fookin' onslaught. They were just looking for the bodies of their own people, just as we do.*

Arrowsmith roared up in his APC. He was beaming. He saw Riddle stooped over the body and called out, laughing: 'What's wrong with you, you big bastard! Couldn't you handle it?'

Arrowsmith was obviously pleased, but his attitude pissed Riddle off. *It was all right for you,* he thought, *sitting back there behind your bloody armour-plating while we were stuck down here in the open facing hundreds of the buggers.* Riddle was physically exhausted from the night's fighting and his body was reacting strongly to the release of the tension. *I'm fookin' shagged – blotto, or whatever it is the medics call it.* He had no patience for bullshit and no time for any officer who claimed credit for the efforts of rank squaddies while they sat safely behind the barricades.

Riddle knew the ambush had been a total success and was relieved his section had got through it intact, but he was angry that he and his men had been put in that situation. *They must'a known we were facing a far bigger force than a dozen or so VC,* he fumed to himself. *The bloody SAS was out there spotting these blokes and if they knew they were coming up the road, they must have known there were hundreds of 'em. What a fuck-up! We're bloody lucky we're not going home in body bags. Did they put us out here expecting us to be killed?*

Riddle looked down the road to the south. There were no bodies in sight in that direction. If there had been any, the VC had carted them away during the night. He'd heard them dragging bodies, but now there was simply no evidence of the hundreds of enemy soldiers he'd witnessed coming up the road towards them. The Spooky had undoubtedly saved their lives, scaring off and dispersing the rest of the enemy column. Riddle knew he couldn't prove the size of the force so he kept his mouth shut. But his sixth sense warned him that a pile of shit was coming his way.

Captain Arrowsmith was cock-a-hoop. He'd pulled off a textbook ambush against vastly superior forces. The operation had been a huge success. No one on his side had been killed and a dozen enemy bodies lay on the road. The rest of the enemy column was nowhere to be seen. A force of 20-odd Australians under his command had taken hundreds of VC by surprise and thrashed them. He'd already radioed the success of the mission to HQ and the commander of the Australian task force, Brigadier Sandy Pearson, was on his way to congratulate them.

Arrowsmith ordered that once all the bodies had been properly searched they were to be dragged together into a bomb crater just beside the road. It was a dirty, unpleasant job. The bodies were all mangled and broken up; there was blood and gore everywhere. Riddle was pissed off that the work fell to the grunts, the infantrymen of the 2nd D&E Platoon. *Fookin' cavalry don't want to get their hands dirty.*

It turned out that one Aussie had been hit. The sharp pain that cavalryman Peter Board had felt in his foot had been a bullet ricocheting off the armoured plating of his APC and going right through his boot into his ankle. By morning, blood had drenched his sock but Board was still pumped full of adrenaline and could hobble around. He told Arrowsmith he would cope.

Board had a small Super 8 movie camera with him in his APC. He'd used it to film scenes around the base camp at Nui Dat, mostly of his cavalry mates skylarking and some vision of their pet monkey. He'd been struck by the pathetic sight of starving local Vietnamese scrambling through the rubbish the Australians tipped into pits outside the base and had filmed the kids grabbing food scraps and junk as the bulldozers unloaded it. Now Board retrieved the camera from his APC and filmed what he saw on the road that morning.

First he filmed the dents in his APC's armour plating from enemy AK-47 bullets. He focused on one in particular on the crane, close to where he had manned the 50 calibre gun, which he reckoned had been left by the bullet that bounced off and then hit him. A few inches either way and the bullet would have got him in the head. He didn't dwell on the thought and, with his foot starting to seriously hurt, he limped on to film the stone gate to the old village, capturing the blast hole in the centre where an artillery shell had hit it in the past. Then he panned down the road in front of the archway and lingered on the bodies littering the ground. They were twisted and broken, ripped apart by heavy machine-gun fire. Thick white lines in the dirt nearby marked where rice had spilled out of enemy backpacks as they were dragged away.

When Board heard that Brigadier Pearson and some other commanders were about to fly in to see for themselves what had happened during the night, he limped over to where a plastic orange sheet had been laid down to mark a safe landing spot for the VIP chopper. From 20 metres away he filmed the Huey approaching and kept rolling as the chopper landed, capturing Sandy Pearson stepping out with one foot on the landing strut and pulling on his trademark olive-coloured giggle hat. From the other side of the chopper two protective force soldiers fanned out and took up guard.

Out next was Major Ron Rooks in a black beret, the commanding officer of the Third Cavalry Regiment; then two photographers – army photographer Sergeant Christopher Bellis and experienced war correspondent Denis Gibbons. Gibbons was filing for United Press International at the time but he'd been in Vietnam covering the war since 1966. He'd started out doing soft features on the troops for Fairfax magazines like *People*, *Pix* and *Woman's Day*. Three years on, he'd seen it all; probably far too much. A former soldier, Gibbons got on well with the troops, and their commanders – like Pearson, whom Gibbons was travelling with. He insisted on covering the war from the front line rather than from the bars in Saigon and was a respected and battle-hardened reporter. The sight of dead bodies didn't faze him, but he was anxious to try and capture the Aussie soldiers' reactions to the carnage.

While Pearson and Rooks inspected the weapons captured after the ambush, Board filmed Gibbons taking photos of the scene. Then he focused in on a single body. The dead soldier was lying on his side, his back to the camera, and when Board moved to get a different angle he captured a horrific sight: the back of the man's head was missing. The bone of his empty skull flared out like a blossoming white flower. When he zoomed in for an even closer shot, Board realised with a jolt that it must have been his bullet that had killed him. He had seen his head explode in the firefight. *Only a 50 cal could do that kind of damage*, he thought. *Jesus, what a fucking mess.*

Board felt no pride, no shame, no horror, and no sense of accomplishment in the killing of an enemy soldier. Decades later, he still feels absolutely nothing, and that realisation shocks him even more than the awful image that, in the dark of the night, is always there, seared into his mind.

There were 11 bodies on the road and Board filmed them all, moving slowly from one to the next. They had been stripped of their packs and weapons and some lay in impossible positions, with limbs broken or blown off. The bottom half of a torso lay by the side of the road; Board couldn't see the top half. One or two lay on their backs, their arms folded over their chests, a sign of humanity and respect from the Aussies who had killed them. The bodies lay in a line all the way up the road to the shadow of the shellpocked old gate to Thua Tich, the town that no longer existed. The archway stood like some kind of battered monument, a silent witness to the horror that had occurred only hours earlier.

Board didn't film close-ups of the women killed. According to later accounts of the men involved in the ambush there could have been two. They were soldiers, certainly, and there was no reason to feel guilt over their killing but Board was uncomfortable about recording their grisly deaths. Before Gibbons flew out with the brass, who left in the Huey to inspect other Australian troops in the field, Board filmed the war correspondent taking photos of the bloodied road and the young Aussie diggers. The photos Gibbons took that day took do not tell of victory or triumph – he captured the deep shock and sorrow of the Aussie soldiers, their shoulders slumped as they take in the awful scene in the aftermath of the ambush.

While Gibbons was an independent journalist trying to record an accurate and real story of the war, Sergeant Bellis was a soldier armed with a camera. His role was to supply the army public relations unit back in Canberra with pictures they could hand out to civilian news outlets – images of heroic soldiers, wholesome folksy soldiers, Anzacs of the legend. Bellis's pictures were used to enhance the war effort, not to reveal the horror and carnage of combat. But before Bellis had been conscripted, he'd been a newspaper photographer and his instincts had never left him. He had a strong drive to keep a diligent record of the scene at Thua Tich for military history. He didn't flinch at the torn bodies, but he doubted his photographs would ever get past his seniors at Canberra HQ. Bellis shot his pictures from a distance, and when he saw two diggers dragging bodies up the road to a central point where they were being dumped in a pit he recorded the scene for posterity. Privates Richard 'Barney' Bigwood and Terry Slattery were the soldiers doing the dragging, each man gripping a foot of the body in one hand, their weapons in the other.

In the humidity of Vietnam and the heat of an already strong morning sun the bodies had begun to decompose. It was horrific to see flesh starting to break off in the soldiers' hands as they pulled the bodies along the road; most preferred to grip the trousers as the clothing was all that was keeping the bodies together. Private Don Moss, who'd been at the listening post with Riddle, saw a girl's body just about break in half as she was dragged towards the rapidly filling crater. Moss did his bit searching the bodies. Inside one of the men's pockets he found a black-and-white photo of a baby girl sitting in a small plastic bowl gazing happily in wonder at the world around her. The baby's mother was beside her, smiling into the camera. The image seared itself into Moss's memory for life. *A father and husband who isn't coming home.*

Arrowsmith wasn't focusing on the state of the bodies. Word had come through by radio that South Vietnamese Army officer and local police chief of the nearby village of Xuyen Moc, Major Le Van Que, had asked that some of the dead be brought to his village to be displayed as a warning to Viet Cong sympathisers. Que wanted to slam home the message that this was what happened to you if you joined up with the VC.

It might have seemed a good idea to the Vietnamese major but the Australians weren't keen. Nobody liked carting enemy bodies around the countryside. Normally they were buried where they fell. But it was important to back up the local police chief. It was suspected that intelligence for the successful ambush had probably come from him, and now it was payback time. Major Que could show how powerful he was by displaying the bodies in the village square, and he, like most South Vietnamese government officials, drew power from fear.

Arrowsmith received his orders from HQ and it was up to him to ensure they were carried out. Three of the most intact bodies were kept out of the crater. Another chopper flew in with fresh ammunition and loaded up Peter Board, whose foot had swollen terribly. Blood was now seeping out of his boot. As the helicopter took off, Board's precious Super 8 camera buried deep in his pocket, the adrenaline had worn off and he was in agony.

Once the cavalrymen were told what they had to do, they protested: they didn't want the mangled, rotting bodies stinking up their APCs. According to accounts from the soldiers present, including Riddle, Bigwood and Arrowsmith's driver, Allan Stanton, they were hung from the back of Arrowsmith's APC for the 20-kilometre trip to Xuyen Moc. They were tied together and hung upside down by their ankles from the rear ramp. The grim task fell to infantrymen Bigwood and Slattery.

Riddle, still fuming over the ambush tactics, was furious when he heard of the decision. *You want more people to head off and join the VC?* he thought. *Then just storm in, draggin' the bodies of their husbands, brothers and fathers into their village. That'll make them think Aussies are their friends. It's*

*fookin' stupid. All we're doing is creating another generation
of kids to hate our guts.*

Several members of the platoon came over and told Riddle
they weren't comfortable with the order. After a long night
of feeling that he and his section had been badly exposed,
this was the last straw for Riddle. He respected Arrowsmith
and thought him a good officer, which was a rare thought for
the former Royal Marine, but this felt completely wrong. He
respected Arrowsmith enough to decide he had to tell him.

Riddle was filled with resentment as he strode over to
Arrowsmith, determined to give him a piece of his mind. *I'll
probably be in the shit for it, but what's new?* He felt he had
to speak up for his men. They'd been stuck out in the open
with thousands of rounds whizzing around their heads while
Arrowsmith and the cavalry sat at a comfortable distance
shooting from behind thick armour plates. *It's always us infantry
who have to do the dirty work. We go through the bodies while
they sit up there like Lord Muck. It's the same in every bloody
army. The footslogger gets the shit jobs while the cavalry rides.*

Arrowsmith was on the radio when Riddle reached him
and he had to cool his heels until the captain had finished.
The wait settled Riddle down a bit and by the time he spoke
he was relatively civil.

'Sir, the men aren't happy about what you are doing with
the bodies,' Riddle told Arrowsmith.

The cavalry captain appreciated what Riddle had done
during the ambush but he wasn't going to debate with him on

the issue. It was well known among Australians that the Americans frequently used APCs to drag enemy bodies. It was an obscene demonstration of superior power, but it had its uses. It wasn't unheard of being done by Australians, but it wasn't something that was openly talked about.

Arrowsmith had other concerns. He told Riddle they would be leaving in a few minutes and ordered him to get his men ready to go. There was some sheet lightning in the distant sky; if it got closer it could set off the explosive charges now being positioned under the bodies in the crater, which included plastic explosives, a few gallons of petrol and a long fuse cord.

Ideally, enemy bodies were buried and the locations of the graves marked and recorded on a map. Army rule books say the location of the graves should then to be passed on to the Red Cross, along with any personal effects found on the bodies. At some point in the future these would be passed on to the enemy so they could recover the bodies and give them a proper burial with full military and religious customs. That was the official line, and that was the way it was supposed to happen. Mostly it did.

According to Riddle and other soldiers who were at Thua Tich, burying the bodies in the crater would take too long. The enemy was all around and could mount a counterattack at any moment and so the dead would be given what was known as an 'engineer's burial'. Sappers placed explosives under the pile of bodies and simply blew them up. It sure wasn't in the training manual, but the troops knew it sometimes happened.

Riddle says he then went back to his men, but first he strode over to the pile of bodies in the crater and looked them over. They were definitely all very dead. They wouldn't know any difference. Bigwood and Slattery followed their orders and dragged three of the more intact bodies over to one of the APCs and tied them by their ankles to the top of the rear door. When the door was raised the bodies went up with it, hanging upside down. Infantryman Private Bob Secrett was shocked at the sight. He'd missed the night's action as he was at the northern position with the APCs, but he thought this was beyond gruesome. One of the bodies was a big Chinese-looking bloke. *What was he doing here?* he wondered. *Is he Vietnamese?*

Riddle says Arrowsmith then ordered all the troops saddle up in the APCs and they set off at high speed, heading south down Route 328 towards Xuyen Moc, the three bodies bouncing grotesquely against the rear door of the captain's APC. As the vehicles left, engineers lit the fuse for the explosives under the bodies, and when the last of the noisy machines joined the convoy, the explosives went up.

Allan Stanton, Arrowsmith's driver, heard the noise, but he didn't look back; neither did Arrowsmith. Don Moss, on top of one of the rear APCs, looked back at the sound of the blast. He saw bits of bodies blasted six metres into the air and quickly turned away, unable to watch as they fell back to earth.

3

AMBUSHING THE AMBUSHERS

30 MAY 1969

As the 13 APCs started trundling south along Route 328, Riddle knew they were heading straight into the area where hundreds of VC had fled after the ambush. Only his section in the listening post had seen the size of the enemy force on the road south of their position and he didn't think anyone in authority was taking the numbers into account.

Riddle had a bad feeling. His internal radar was registering danger ahead. *Bloody Arrowsmith didn't see them packed down that road*, he thought. *He's got no idea how many of them there are. We're heading right into Indian country just like General Custer. They'll be in the trees and bushes all around us, waiting for the right moment.*

As far as Riddle was concerned, the best place to be when there was a chance of enemy fire was in the bowels of an APC, surrounded by plate metal. If you sat on top you were vulnerable to being shot. But despite knowing this, Riddle and his men chose to ride up top, ready to jump off if trouble came. Being inside an APC had its good points, but if a mine went off it was the worst possible place as you were thrown around like a peanut in a tin. Before they'd left the ambush site Riddle told his platoon to check their weapons and ammunition. 'It's not over,' he told them. 'This time we're the target. They've had time to lay an ambush out for us.'

Riddle felt the cavalry could stick their necks out for a change. The men in his platoon were all tired and exhausted. No one had slept during the night, and the long hours of tension of waiting for the counterattack had definitely taken a lot out of them. Searching the mangled bodies, dragging them to the pit and then stringing up three of them added to their feeling of being deflated and fed up. Riddle detested the sight of those bodies banging away on the back of the APC and the part the platoon had been forced to play in it.

Army photographer Sergeant Christopher Bellis had hitched a ride with the APCs and was perched on the back of the APC with Captain Arrowsmith and his driver Private Allan Stanton. Bellis wanted to get back to the base at Nui Dat via Xuyen Moc, and he knew these men were a good story. He would send the photos he'd taken at the ambush site back to Army Public Relations in Canberra for release to the media as soon as possible. He reckoned his photos of the successful operation at Thua Tich would appear in newspapers across Australia. What he didn't know was that he was about to have one hell of a ride.

Five minutes after the APCs left Thua Tich the forest crowded in around the road – the perfect place for a VC ambush. A two-man spotter helicopter had flown in from the Australian base to scout ahead for the APC column. Arrowsmith must have listened to Riddle's warning about the size of the enemy force more closely than he'd appreciated.

About halfway to Xuyen Moc the crew in the chopper suddenly spotted enemy moving among the trees and bush a short distance ahead of the column. 'Two Zero Alpha – Possum One. You are right in the middle of them. They are on both sides of the road.'

Seconds later bullets crashed into the APCs from the surrounding jungle. A rocket-propelled grenade (RPG) slammed into the side of one APC but, luckily, failed to go off. The enemy was so close that the grenade hadn't had time to arm itself as it flew toward the vehicle.

Arrowsmith immediately ordered a Herringbone attack, a classic attack manoeuvre and well-rehearsed cavalry tactic. The first APC peeled off to the right and drove into the forest with its guns blazing, the second to the left, the third to the right, the fourth to the left, and so on right down the line.

Figures darted everywhere as the APCs burst into the forest, their 50 calibre guns sweeping the bush at full blast and all soldiers on board firing at every shadow. One Viet

Cong raised his launcher and fired another RPG straight at a charging APC but it bounced off, leaving only a dent. Again it had been fired far too close to its target. By speeding straight towards the enemy shooting the grenade, the APC driver had saved all those on board.

The firing intensified as the VC broke cover to flee the APCs rampaging through the tangled undergrowth. Enemy AK-47 fire poured onto the split convoys of carriers. The Aussies had only one thought in this moment of madness: *Keep moving. Don't remain still long enough to become a target. Fire at everything that moves. And hang on like buggery!* Fall off and you could be shot by the VC or run over by your own APC.

Riddle could see enemy soldiers running around each APC, trying to shoot the Aussies behind the big guns. In return, the Aussies crouching on top of the carriers had their guns on full automatic, spraying bullets blindly into the surrounding jungle. Lance Corporal Len Ellcombe of Riddle's platoon couldn't get a clear shot at the figures firing from the bush so he stood up, firing his M-60 machine gun from his hip down into the thick undergrowth where VC were trying to get close and climb on board. It was as though he was standing on a giant metallic surfboard trying to keep his balance as he fired the heavy gun. When the ammunition belt ran out, Ellcombe dropped the M-60, picked up his M-16 and kept firing into the bush.

The dramatic moment was photographed by Bellis from his position on the APC behind. It would be one of the great action shots of the war: Ellcombe is captured with his feet planted wide, oblivious to the target he made of himself, the smoke pouring from his gun muzzle frozen in time forever. Ellcombe gunned down one VC officer who had a pistol in his hand, trying to climb aboard the APC, and then another enemy soldier who tried to follow his leader in the attack.

Minutes later the APCs broke through the thick bush and emerged into open grassland. They picked up speed and thrashed along the tree-line, the big 50 and 30 calibre guns firing continuously. The Aussies' fighting fury was up, and they weren't going to stop now. A handful of VC were flushed out and fled into the open, going down in a hail of bullets from the APCs. It was intense shooting on the run – ideal fighting for the cavalry, something to be relished. The infantry on board were glad not to be doing this on foot.

As the firing from the VC came to an end, Arrowsmith ordered the infantry down off the APCs to pick up all enemy weapons. Riddle wasn't happy about his men leaving the relative safety of the APCs. The VC were only one of the risks they faced – anyone running around out in the open at this point was as likely to be shot by the adrenaline-pumped cavalry as they were by the VC hiding in the bushes. *If anyone's gotta get out there to pick up souvenirs, it'd better be me. At least they all know what I look like . . .*

Riddle slid off his carrier and picked up an RPG lying on the ground near the body of a dead Viet Cong. It was still loaded with the grenade inside. He pulled out the round and dropped the launcher into the back of the APC. Then he bent to pick up the body, but its head literally fell off. The young soldier had been shot through the neck by a couple of 50 calibre bullets. *Fuck,* thought Riddle. *He's just a kid by the look of 'im. Poor bugger.*

He looked around. A few of his men were picking up rifles and rockets and conducting quick searches of the bodies that were near their APCs. Someone found a Chinese-made pistol, most likely that of the officer killed by Ellcombe during the attack on his carrier. He would have to have been fairly senior officer to have such a prized weapon. Arrowsmith took the pistol for himself as a trophy.

As they continued the search, Riddle was uneasy. *This isn't good*, he thought. *How many more of them are around here? Time to get out.* He and the men got back on board with whatever weapons and papers they'd managed to grab. The APCs revved up and were on the move once again.

The enemy body count was officially put at five, but from what Riddle had witnessed he was sure it had to be at least triple that figure. Some had probably been crushed by the tracks of the APCs as they crashed through the thick undergrowth, but it was too thick and dangerous to search too closely for enemy bodies. Once again the Aussies had again come through the action without a single casualty. Arrowsmith and his squad had done well. It was textbook combat leadership.

The APCs fell back into single convoy formation on the road and revved up to full speed. High on adrenaline and driven by the fear of another ambush they continued to pour heavy calibre machine-gun fire into the bush on both sides of the road. The Australians fired into the trees, gullies and thickets where shooters and RPGs could come from at any second. They'd been under fire and had survived – they weren't taking any chances of being killed now after what they had just been through. It was only a few more kilometres to Xuyen Moc. There they could relax and get their breath back. But in the meantime – fuck it – they'd just keep firing to keep the buggers away; maybe even kill a few more.

Suddenly the heavy forest opened up on both sides of the road and the speeding APC column burst into the open, roaring through clear land and rice paddies being worked by a few local farmers – farmers who wore the traditional black peasants' garb also favoured by the Viet Cong. And to this day, what happened next is hotly disputed among veterans of the action.

Recalling the scene decades later, Acting Corporal Jim Riddle swears that the machine guns in several of the lead APCs continued to fire as they emerged from the jungle. He has vivid memories of bullets ripping into a youth leading a water buffalo on the far side of the first rice paddy. He remembers seeing a woman carrying a baby knocked flat as bullets slammed into her, and the infant flying through the air. 'I was in the APC behind them and I screamed at the machine gunner in our APC not to fire,' he explains. 'They stopped firing up front within seconds but it was too late. It was a mistake, but they were so wound up from the fighting. We were all exhausted and shit scared. We expected the enemy to be everywhere, ready to fire at us if we didn't kill them first. Shit happens in war. There was no intent. It was just fear and exhaustion. It was bad, but it did happen. The firing stopped within seconds and the APCs kept barrelling along the road to Xuyen Moc. We didn't stop and we never talked about it. But I can see it today as clearly as I did four decades ago. It's never left me.'

Only one other veteran has since publicly stated he remembers the killing of the civilians, but he admits he has memory problems. There are no photos of the incident that have seen the light of day. One cavalryman admits the lead APCs did fire towards the civilians when the speeding convoy emerged from the jungle, but insists they didn't hit anybody. Several acknowledge the men fired continuously all the way along the road, but claim the shooting stopped as soon as they emerged into the open. Some are adamant there was no firing into the bush at all after the successful herringbone manoeuvre, and others simply refuse to talk about it.

Many are angry Riddle makes the allegation, and are extremely hostile to anybody who raises it in public. Whether it happened is an open question. There is no proof either way. But what is not disputed is that for every man, their harrowing experience was not quite at an end.

•

The APCs rolled into Xuyen Moc and Bellis snapped a photo of children from the village running up to look at the Australian warriors returning from battle. It captures the horror on their faces as they saw the bodies of the dead VC. During the mad scramble through the bush, the three bodies had come loose in their ties and were dragging on the ground behind Arrowsmith's APC. They were shockingly bashed and battered from the bumpy ride. Driver Allan Stanton remembers in his 2009 memoir *Before I Forget* that Bellis was sitting right behind him on the hatch cover as they drove into the village. The photographer's face was pale and he had a handkerchief planted firmly over his nose and mouth to cover the stench of decay.[1]

The lead APCs rolled right into the market square in the centre of the village. Soldiers from one of the APCs laid down a circle of barbed wire and the bodies were dumped inside the ring. Hundreds of villagers gathered around, looking on in revulsion at the state of the bodies. Major Que strode to the front of the crowd and harangued the locals, warning them that this was what would happen to anyone who joined the Viet Cong. Riddle didn't think the villagers looked too impressed. In his memoir, Stanton recalls that, a few days later, he heard that relatives of the dead had come forward to claim the bodies of their brothers, fathers, sons or husbands and buried them in the local cemetery. However, local Vietnamese in Xuyen Moc dispute this. Nguyen Van Sang, who was security chief in Xuyen Moc in 1969, said in 2010 that no one dared to claim the bodies and they were buried in unmarked graves outside the town. Like Riddle, Stanton thought the whole exercise of bringing the bodies to the village was counter-productive.

Arrowsmith was invited by a pleased Major Que to come for a beer and a talk at his house. Riddle recalls that Arrowsmith told him to come along. It was unusual for an officer to invite along an NCO, let alone a private, but it was a courtesy from the commander of the operation to the de facto leader of the infantry platoon that had been so vital to the success of the operation. Riddle had earned respect and this gesture acknowledged his own creditable action in the fighting. At the house were an Australian army captain and an American marine major. Recounting his story more than forty years later, Riddle can't remember the officers' names, but he is sure they were advisers attached to Major Que's outfit.

Que's men came in with beer and a bucket of ice. Riddle watched aghast as the South Vietnamese army orderly dropped ice into his glass of beer. The ice was filthy, with dirt and charcoal clearly visible. *If the gooks don't get me, this beer will,* he thought grimly. Meanwhile, the American major had quickly ascertained from Riddle's accent that he was a Brit in an Australian uniform – and a dirty uniform at that. He asked Riddle how an Englishman came to be fighting in Vietnam.

'I love this sort of thing. The Royal Marines weren't doing too much so I came out here,' Riddle explained, not offering too much to this stranger.

'You mad bastard,' said the marine.

You have no idea how right you are, thought Riddle.

The American raised his glass and offered cheers, whispering confidentially that the only way to drink the contaminated beer was to get it down fast. Not being one to resist a challenge, Riddle settled into a bout of serious drinking with the marine. Riddle didn't usually like officers, but this Yank seemed OK to him. After the third or fourth beer the major confided to Riddle that the Thua Tich action was the talk of HQ and there were bound to be medals for Riddle and his unit, possibly even a field promotion.

Maybe in your army, mate, thought Riddle. *Your lot get medals for wanking before breakfast. Not ours. The officers collect all the gongs and we mug privates get fuck all.* While Riddle liked the sound of medals and a possible promotion, he had a growing suspicion that something stank about the whole operation. Even with the beer working its way into his weary body, he had many questions that needed answering: why were they were sent into an exposed position against a vastly superior force beyond the protection of artillery? The treatment of the enemy bodies wouldn't go down well in the newspapers if it ever got out – and then there was what happened in the rice paddies near Xuyen Moc after they emerged from the forest . . . But no one was talking about that. Riddle knew that incident was never to be mentioned. *It simply never happened.*

As Riddle and the American swapped war stories and laughed, a few more beers went down. After a while the Australian captain advising Que, who Riddle didn't know, strolled over to see why the two were getting on so well. He was mortified when he heard Riddle addressing the marine major as 'mate'.

He pulled Riddle aside and dressed him down. 'You do not call him "mate" – he's "Sir" to you!'

The admonishment completely knocked the wind out of Riddle's sails. After all he'd just been through, to have this young officer – who'd probably never been outside HQ and had probably never seen a battle like the one he'd just been in – berate him was the last straw.

'Fuck the pair of you!' Riddle told the Australian.

'You've just blown your chance of a medal,' the captain replied.

'Is that all it takes?' Riddle said. Then he left, removing himself before he did any more damage. *They can stick their bloody medal where the sun don't shine.*

Riddle joined his platoon for a few more drinks. There was no dirty ice in the beer this time. *Warm beer, no problem. I'm a Pom, after all,* he thought. As the exhausted men relaxed, things deteriorated. One of the infantrymen recklessly fired a bullet from his M-16 which hit the ground near Riddle's feet. After hearing the shot, an officer ran over and wanted the private charged. Riddle took the officer aside and strongly suggested he leave him to sort it out.

'They've been through a lot, Sir. Let this one go,' Riddle said. Sensibly the officer decided to allow Riddle to handle it in his own way.

The next day the clumsy private was nursing a black eye. But they were all carrying wounds from the past 24 hours – they just weren't scars that could be seen with the naked eye.

4

ANIMALS RUN BY A FOUL-MOUTHED MERCENARY

After a hugely successful action like the Thua Tich ambush and the subsequent APC herringbone manouvre, the army brass and Defence public relations machine should have been lauding Riddle and the men of his platoon as well as Arrowsmith and his cavalry unit.

The next day glowing stories about the action appeared in Australian newspapers. 'Australians kill 16 Viet Cong' said *The Sydney Morning Herald*. 'Australians surprise Viet Cong' raved *The Daily Telegraph*. The story had been distributed by the Australian Associated Press newswire in Saigon after a briefing from Australian army officials. It gave a bare outline of the action:

Saigon – Friday: Australian troops last night clashed with a Viet Cong unit in a three-hour battle 12 miles north-east of Nui Dat.

Armoured personnel carriers and infantry surprised about 50 Viet Cong on a road in a clearing and killed at least 11. No Australians were hurt.

The same troops late today killed another five Viet Cong in another clash as they were on their way to make temporary camp at a village 14 miles away.

The Viet Cong are believed to be from the D445 Battalion, a longstanding enemy of the Australians in Phuoc Tuy Province.

Only two armoured personnel carriers opened up on the main body of the Viet Cong company after the Australians had let four scouts through their position.

About 650 yards further up the road hidden in thick scrub were 10 infantry of the defence platoon of the Task Force Headquarters.

The ambush was opened up by two carriers of 2 Troop, B Squadron, 3rd Cavalry Regiment commanded by Captain Arrowsmith, 26, married, of Campbelltown, NSW, and 2nd Lieutenant Dallas Mills, 22, married, of Liverpool, NSW.

At one stage during the action a US DC-3 gunship droned up and down likely withdrawal routes pumping thousands of 7.62 mini gun rounds into the area.

The news reports added one interesting fact – the Australian ambush on 29 May was carried out during a 48-hour Viet

Cong ceasefire held to mark Buddha's birthday. Allied forces only recognised the birthday ceasefire for 24 hours, beginning on 31 May, so this may explain the Viet Cong unit's casual and relaxed mood as they wandered into the ambush at Thua Tich. Certainly Riddle and his platoon knew nothing of a VC ceasefire. During a ceasefire, troops are not supposed to resupply or manoeuvre to better tactical positions. However, in the past, the North Vietnamese had used ceasefires to extensively resupply their troops. In 1968 they launched a major attack during the traditional Tet truce, which is now known widely as the Tet Offensive. US military leaders felt the ceasefires announced by the North Vietnamese for occasions such as Buddha's birthday and Christmas were simply a ruse to build up forces.

But Allied forces weren't exactly sitting idle during their own declared 24-hour ceasefire. During that day waves of US B-52 bombers carried out the heaviest air raids of the war on neighbouring Laos to attack the Ho Chi Minh Trail, a complex string of jungle paths used by North Vietnam to send soldiers and supplies down to South Vietnam. United Press International reported that two million pounds of bombs were dropped by eight B-52s on the trail during the ceasefire.

On 3 June *The Australian* newspaper carried the story of that bombing raid, and positioned the headline 'American B-52s use Viet truce for big raids on Laos' under Denis Gibbons's photo of an Australian soldier standing over a road full of dead bodies. The caption didn't state when it had been taken, nor that it was taken at Thua Tich during the Buddha's birthday ceasefire declared by the Viet Cong. It also failed to identify the soldier, even though Gibbons had identified him as trooper Peter Board in the photo he filed to United Press International.

The image has impact: the bodies on the road appear small, almost childlike. The body closest in the shot is a young man dressed in shorts. Lying on his back with one leg twisted over the other, his face is to the camera, his mouth wide open. Board stands side-on to the camera, his head bowed, his gun held loosely in his left hand. He's looking away from the camera at another dead man who is curled up lying on his side, his head resting on his arm as though he's simply sleeping. It is not a triumphant picture. It is one of great resignation and sadness.

Under the headline 'Digger Counts the Dead' the newspaper's caption said: 'An Australian soldier stands beside bodies of Viet Cong who were killed in an ambush by Australian troops 80 miles east of Saigon. Eleven bodies were counted. In weekend battles in South Vietnam the Communists lost nearly 100 dead. The American death toll was 22. In Saigon two civilians were killed and 25 wounded when Communist gunners fired two 122 mm rockets into the city.'

But in Canberra at Army HQ the shit was just starting to hit the fan. Word had filtered back from Vietnam about the engineer's burial at Thua Tich. That was unsavoury enough, but far more controversial was the matter of soldiers careening around the countryside with dead enemy bodies hanging upside down from the back of an APC. And to do that in front of a journalist and a photographer! The spin doctors in Defence PR were furious. If the story got out it could do real damage to the war effort. Bellis didn't know it at the time, but his photos taken at Thua Tich caused a huge stink when they reached Canberra and many fell victim to the censor's red pen.

It couldn't have come at a worse time for those trying to keep the image of the Vietnam War squeaky clean and unruffled by preventing any hint of misbehaviour or atrocities reaching the public. Opposition to the war and, in particular, to conscription had been building throughout 1968 and was gathering powerful momentum in 1969. Anti-war protesters had clashed violently with police several times and plans were afoot to mobilise massive anti-war demonstrations of hundreds of thousands of people in the big cities. In the early years of the war two-thirds of Australians had supported troops being sent to Vietnam. But after four years of fighting and 250 Australians killed so far with little apparent progress, the tide was turning.

Some young conscriptees were copying American protesters and publicly burning their draft cards. Prominent Australians, some of them conservatives, were starting to back the protesters and religious leaders were beginning to speak out against continuing the war. The Catholic church had long been a strong supporter of the war as its leaders saw South Vietnam as a Catholic fortress in South East Asia. But as the death toll of young Australians rose into the hundreds and horrific images of the war appeared nightly on TV screens, pressure was growing fast to bring the troops home.

The Australian newspaper became a voice for the anti-war movement. It carried notices advertising anti-war demonstrations and published open letters against the war signed by well-known citizens. By 1969, for the first time, opinion polls were showing that more than 50 per cent of Australians wanted the troops out of Vietnam. The Liberal government faced an election by the end of the year, and there was a very real prospect of losing power to the Labor Party which had vowed to end the war.

In Australia most of the television coverage of the war was coming from US networks and, compared to the uncensored footage of American troops, the image of Australian troops was still relatively positive. Generally, the Australian military kept a tight hold on media access to their troops, and kept a close eye on journalists, particularly those who might write something critical. Army PR officials supervised nearly all contact journalists might have with Australian troops, and reporters known as troublesome found it difficult to get the credentials they needed to enter Australian bases.

So alarm bells were ringing in military HQ over the Thua Tich operation. Not only had there been mistreatment of enemy bodies, but it had been carried out while journalists with cameras were present. One of them was from Army PR, and his pictures could be suppressed. But the other one would have to be watched. Repercussions came thundering down the line. Captain Arrowsmith was told he would now only receive a Mention in Dispatches for the action – a significant downgrade to the medal he could reasonably have expected to receive for leading such a successful military operation. Also, within days of returning to base, Arrowsmith was removed from command of his cavalry troop and shunted to the backroom position of Squadron Technical Officer. It was a hefty demotion.

Arrowsmith's driver, Allan Stanton, was shocked when his captain told him he was leaving the unit. 'You could have knocked me over with a budgie feather,' he wrote later in his memoir *Before I Forget*. He felt he didn't have the right to ask if Arrowsmith was going voluntarily, and he never really found out. He had his theories, but he kept them to himself at the time.

It was quickly becoming clear to the men of the 2nd D&E Platoon that they were in the doghouse, too. They'd expected to be feted for their bravery in combat. Jim Riddle had secretly hoped he would get a promotion – maybe even get those sergeant stripes he'd always craved. When they were relaxing in Xuyen Moc after the action, Riddle told Arrowsmith and other officers that several members of his platoon deserved to be promoted and commended for their part in the ambush. Indeed, the photographic evidence of Ellcombe's courage in firing while standing on the APC should have been enough for a bravery medal alone. Riddle believed the makeshift platoon had proved itself in battle, and its position as a rapid deployment assault unit would be formalised. Instead they found themselves being shunned.

After a day at Xuyen Moc, Riddle's platoon was suddenly separated from Arrowsmith's cavalry unit and handed on to another cavalry squad that had arrived in the village. The new squad and their officer in charge seemed to resent the infantrymen they would now have to carry in their APCs and animosity quickly sprang up between the two units.

Bugger them, thought Riddle. The men from the platoon got hold of a couple of dozen cans of beer and settled down to another round of serious drinking. In the new cavalry unit was Trooper Normie Rowe, a popular singer who'd been conscripted into the army six months earlier. That night in Xuyen Moc he put on an impromptu concert. While it went down well with the villagers, there was considerable grumbling among the platoon men. Several tried to take the pop star down a few pegs and catcalled during the performance. Some thought, rightly or wrongly, that because of Rowe's high profile in Australia he was getting special treatment and was protected from real danger by the brass. If Rowe came to harm it would be a huge story back home.

A few days later the platoon was on a night patrol with the new cavalry troop. In the dark, something – or someone – set off some Claymore mines. Before the unit moved out at first light, Riddle grabbed a few of his men and went out into the bush to check what had happened. He walked alone along a clear track in the direction of the explosion, telling his men to cover him. It was important to stick to well-trodden paths as it was easier to spot mines that had been dug in overnight.

Further up the track where the Claymores had gone off, Riddle found four very dead Viet Cong. They had taken the full blast of the mines in their bellies, almost chopping them in half, and their weapons had been hit so hard by the explosion that they were embedded deep inside their remains. Riddle retrieved two AK-47s and two bolt-action rifles covered in gore and returned with his men to the unit waiting in their APCs.

He whistled as he walked as he didn't want the unit to shoot him by mistake, thinking he was some crazed, blood-soaked Viet Cong on a suicide mission. The men looked at him in horror as he walked past them, his grisly trophies still dripping blood. Riddle walked up to the cavalry captain sitting atop his APC and dumped the weapons in front of him, blood spreading over the armoured plate of the carrier.

'Here you are,' Riddle said cheerily.

'Where are they from?' demanded the officer.

'There were some kills last night up the path. These used to belong to them.'

The officer ordered the men to saddle up, and Riddle climbed on board one of the APCs. The carriers roared off in two groups. One went straight up the track and the other up a parallel road. Riddle immediately got on the radio and put out a call to all the other APCs, warning them not to continue straight up the track as they would drive right over the bodies.

'Fuck the bodies, keep going straight,' ordered the officer. He was pissed off at the infantry private who had dropped blood-soaked weapons on his APC and had the audacity to speak on his cavalry radio.

'Hang on, if you drive over the bodies and then come back to search them they'll be mashed to a pulp from the tracks,' radioed Riddle. 'It'll have to be your men who search them then, not mine.'

As angry as the officer was at this upstart private telling him what to do, he knew Riddle was right. He ordered his APC drivers to avoid the bodies and pull the carriers into a defensive circle. Riddle and a couple of his men searched the bodies. He surreptitiously slipped a roll of cash he found on one VC into his shirt, and he and his men dragged the bodies into a ditch. Then they started pushing soil from the side of the road down over the bodies.

When one of the men threw a shovel full of dirt on the face of one of the bodies Riddle reprimanded him. 'C'mon, for Christ's sake – he's got his eyes open.'

The soldier looked at Riddle as though he was mad. The VC was dead, what did it matter? But then he saw the expression on Riddle's face and backed down. 'Sorry mate,' he said, and buried the dead Vietnamese with a little more delicacy.

Riddle had a thing about the eyes of dead bodies. He'd once taken cover in a fire fight next to a mate of his. As the bloke's eyes were wide open, Riddle thought he was keeping still so he wouldn't draw enemy fire. Then Riddle watched in horror as a fly landed on the man's open eyeball and crawled around. His mate didn't flinch. Only then did Riddle realise he was dead.

When the unit returned to Xuyen Moc, Riddle and a group of his men walked into a bar and ordered beers all round. Everyone in the bar stopped talking and looked at them. *It's like some fookin' cowboy movie when the bad guys walk into the saloon and the piano stops playing.* After more than a few drinks Riddle stumbled outside to have a pee. Rain was pouring down but Riddle spied a bit of shelter at a bus stop near the road and headed there to relieve himself.

As Riddle pissed onto the road, the cavalry commander he'd been with that day spied him and strode over. 'You are disgusting,' he snarled.

'Have to be to kill people like this,' Riddle replied, without breaking his stream. The officer stalked off.

The cavalry transported the platoon back to the Nui Dat base and the two units were glad to part company. But word had got around that the 2nd D&E Platoon was to be disbanded as soon as they returned to HQ, and the infantrymen were unhappy about it. They could see recognition for their achievement at Thua Tich slipping away. The stink caused by the way the enemy bodies had been treated was smothering everything else they had achieved. Riddle and the rest of the platoon were mightily pissed off.

The final nail in the coffin came when the cavalry officer stormed into the command post and complained bitterly to the second-in-command, Major George Pratt, about Riddle and the platoon's behaviour. 'That platoon's a bunch of animals run by a foul-mouthed mercenary,' he told Pratt. However, Pratt had a soft spot for Riddle. He appreciated the soldier's tenacity and admired the way he'd stepped up to take responsibility for the platoon when they were short of officers. Pratt later told Riddle what the cavalry officer had said. Riddle laughed, but he suspected the sergeant's stripes he had his eye on were now out of his grasp.

Once they were back in Nui Dat the platoon had a bit of downtime before it was finally broken up and sent to new posts. They got a ride in a couple of trucks to the bars of Vung Tau. Fronting one, Riddle pulled out the thick roll of cash he'd taken, plonked it down and told the barman to keep the beers coming until the money ran out. The cash went a long way before the soldiers, drunk from the proceeds of war, moved to another bar where they proceeded to get into a punch-up with another group of soldiers. American military police turned up, but a soldier with a thick Irish accent from the other group took exception to being told to simmer down by a Yank, and loudly yelled: 'Come on, Yank, I'll fucking kill you!'

The American pulled out his pistol and levelled it at the soldier, then reached for his radio and told his command he'd just had his life threatened. Riddle was sober enough to know the place was about to be swamped by heavily armed MPs and hussled his men out a side door. They stumbled across the road to another bar where they grabbed seats on the front porch, ordered a fresh round of drinks and watched in delight as dozens of military police officers stormed the scene, their clubs swinging, bodies flying everywhere.

'Why is it always the bloody Irish?' joked Riddle as he clinked beer bottles with his platoon mates.

That night, Riddle was late getting back to barracks and he was put on a charge. His punishment was to spend the day polishing boots, and cleaning out his tent and his gear. It was a humiliating moment for a man like Riddle. This kind of disciplinary action was normally dished out to fresh young squaddies, not experienced soldiers who had just led their men through combat. As Riddle sat down on the doorstep outside his tent, his boot polish and brush in hand, one by one each member of his platoon walked up and sat down beside him. Without a word they also started polishing the boots. The numbers grew until there were dozens of them, rubbing away. It was a silent gesture of support and solidarity that meant a lot to the embattled veteran.

But Riddle was fed up. He was starting to regret his decision to leave the Royal Marines and join the Australian army. *They fookin' follow me with their clipboards everywhere I go, counting the number of times I fart and spit,* he thought. *I thought Aussies were supposed to be rebels. They're supposed to hate authority and the stupid British upper class way of running an army. It's bullshit. They're just the fookin' same.*

But he liked the troops, the ordinary young diggers he'd led in action and through the bars and brawls of Vung Tau. Some were gangly, easygoing kids from the Australian bush, others were hard nuts from the cities. Some had joined up because they needed a job and a steady income, some had no idea why they'd joined up, maybe just because it was expected of them. Over long talks in the bars and mess halls and around campfires, Riddle found that many had volunteered to escape an abusive family – a bullying father, an overbearing brother. He found very few had enlisted because they believed they were in Vietnam to stop the communists invading Australia. And the few who did believe it had certainly changed their minds after they'd seen a few months of battle. Riddle could see the whole action was a crippling disaster for the men who'd been sent to fight it, and he could see that the methods used to fight it weren't going to win it. Ordinary diggers were being screwed by the army top brass who hadn't a clue how to win this war, even if it could be won.

Riddle wasn't going to desert these diggers. He believed he had a mission – a calling, even – and that was to get these young men through this dirty war alive.

5

FROM GEORDIE TO DIGGER

As Riddle polished boots, he thought back to what had brought him to this godforsaken jungle war. James Bertram Riddle had been born in wartime Britain on 7 February, 1940, in the steel and coal city of Newcastle upon Tyne. Being a local of the Tyne valley made him a Geordie, the nickname given to those of that northern region who speak with a strong sing-song accent and a distinctive dialect that is credited with being the oldest in England.

As a young boy Jim Riddle lived on a street that led to a tank factory, and the first five years of his life reverberated to the sounds of war. As new tanks rumbled down his street, leaving for the front, his home became a target for German bombers who attacked frequently, trying to take out the nearby factory. One of his earliest memories was being out on the street with his mum when a German fighter-bomber suddenly roared up the street, its guns blazing.

One night, his grandmother's house was bombed. She survived, and the women and children of the Riddle family all moved in together to pool their stretched resources. The men were all away in the army or navy. His father, Bertram Riddle, was a senior British army officer and something of a war hero, having been at both Dunkirk and the Normandy landing. He started the war as a corporal and ended as a major. Promotion tended to be swift due to the high death rate among British troops. Young Jim didn't see much of his dad during his first five years, so the strange man in the army officer uniform naturally took on mythical hero status to the young boy.

Bertram Riddle was awarded the Military Cross for pulling one of his men out of a burning tank and when he eventually came home, young Jim gazed in wonder at the medal on his father's chest. After the war the major was appointed secretary of the North East Command, which put him in charge of the exhausted and depleted army in the region. Major Riddle had come through the war physically unscathed, but the long years of fighting had taken a huge psychological toll on him. Young Jim found that once his father was home, the man he had looked up to as a hero for so long became a figure of terror.

'He played squash using me as the ball,' Riddle recalls. 'He was a bastard. He beat the shit out of me. I used to escape the house to watch cowboy movies at the local cinema. Then I'd come home and the punishment would start again. I'd just curl up in a ball, praying it would stop. I'd dream of being Roy Rogers riding across the Wild West, free of this horrible angry man.'

As a boy, Riddle couldn't understand why his father turned on him with such anger and venom. He'd waited all his childhood for his father to come home from war. But the soldier had brought the war home with him. Young James was confused and angry. At the private school his father sent him to, he frequently got into fights and after one too many he was expelled. 'Then I had to go to the local public school, but the kids there thought I had a posh Geordie accent – if there is such a thing – and they quickly picked me out for a bashing. I had to fight back to survive. I knew then and there that I had to get away – away from my father and away from Newcastle.'

As a boy Riddle read everything he could about war and was fascinated by stories of Aussie soldiers. He deeply admired the diggers, so named for their hardy trench digging in World War One: he liked how they had volunteered to come from the other side of the world to fight; how they were dumped on the wrong beach at Gallipoli by the British and yet still fought with tremendous heroism; how they were sent into the face of enemy machine guns in the trenches of France by idiotic allied commanders and died in their thousands. He admired how, even after that abuse and terrible treatment, the diggers quickly volunteered once again when World War Two broke out, fighting side by side with the British.

He was particularly impressed that the Aussies were such a large part of the British Special Forces – commandos and the Special Air Service long-range patrols in the deserts of North Africa. He absorbed everything he could about Australian pilots flying to defend Britain, as well as the Australian navy ships which fought alongside the Royal Navy. 'They all seemed so heroic, so free, so gallant,' Riddle recalls. 'They fought with a great sense of humour in the face of death. I read everything I could about them. I loved their contempt for toffee-nosed British officers and the British class system. I loved that they didn't salute. I loved the way they sent up the spit and polish of the British army and broke down the class system which saw the upper class automatically made officers. I really admired everything about them. The image I had of the Aussies was the light on the hill for me.'

By the age of 16 Riddle had quit school and was working night shifts down a coal mine. His Geordie accent didn't win him any friends among rough-hewn miners either, and Riddle found himself the target of the pit bullies. Determined to get away from his father, at the age of 18 he joined the Royal Marines, deliberately avoiding the army as his father was still a big wig in the army hierarchy in the north east. Riddle feared any promotion he got would be put down to influence from his father.

'It was very tough in the marines, and I got into plenty of fights there, too. When my father heard I'd joined them he came to visit the company commander at my training base.

The sergeants in charge of my squad then discovered my father was a major and a war hero. They figured he was trying to cut me a special deal and they gave me shit for it. If only they'd known.'

After 12 months' training, Riddle volunteered to do the commando course and was awarded the coveted green beret and wings which demonstrated he'd completed parachute training. The marine commandos were a tough unit, and he was proud to be part of them. He was posted to Cyprus where the Greeks were fighting the Turks. Standing in the middle were the British troops, trying to keep the place safe for the British Empire. More than 350 Brits were killed in the crossfire. 'The Cypriots were killing each other in the hundreds. I didn't know for what. I was all for just leaving weapons lying around for them to get on with it. We should have done that in Ireland. But, oh no, they had to have the British squaddie stand in the middle so everyone could shoot at them. I was there a few months, and then asked to join a unit that was being sent to Malaysia.'

By 1963 Riddle was a sergeant. His Royal Marine unit was stationed in the Malaysian province of Sarawak on the island of Borneo, trying to prevent Indonesians crossing the border into the territory, a part of the British Commonwealth. 'We were badly under-equipped, and were often stuck on exposed mountains with not enough ammunition or firepower and with little hope of aid reaching us. I got bad infections in my legs along with two others who died from it. They expected me to die for a while. It was a bit of a stuff-up.

'There was some hot action there. I resented the officers who sat back and ordered us to go in, guns blazing. I got a reputation for being reckless, taking too many risks. I would always get up and go straight at the enemy – maybe I thought they were all my father or something. People thought I was mad, but I thought it was the fastest way to kill the enemy and stop the shooting. I was an experienced soldier and I felt my responsibility was to get my blokes through intact. To me, that's what sergeants should be doing.'

Riddle got to know a few Aussies who were also there to assist in the action, known as the Indonesia–Malaysia Confrontation. 'They were good blokes, very competent soldiers. I liked them. I got into lots of fights after getting on the grog, but never with the Aussies. I respected them and they seemed to respect me. We listened on the radio as US bombers attacked Vietnam. I was positive that's where we would be going next. I could see the domino theory was a reality and the communists were advancing across the region.'

But after 18 months in Sarawak, Riddle was transferred back to England and immediately posted to the Middle Eastern port city of Aden, then a British colony, as part of a commando squad. Local rebels were trying to oust the British and had launched a guerilla war, ambushing British trucks and attacking outposts. 'They were up in the hills and we were in a base in the valley. At night we'd put up a big screen and watch movies.

They'd try and take pot shots at us when the movie was on, but the funny thing was they'd never shoot when there was a John Wayne movie running. They must'a liked John Wayne, and just sat back in their hills watching the film along with us.'

After two years in Aden, Riddle was fed up with desert heat and dust so he volunteered for Arctic training – and hated it. He found he couldn't stand the cold. In late 1966 he found himself back in England, stuck in his barracks, reading about the Aussies fighting communists in Vietnam. The article was about the Battle of Long Tan, where a small number of Australians beat off 2500 North Vietnamese regular troops in an incredible feat of bravery.

'It all came back to me what I had felt as a kid, that the Aussie diggers were something special. I was jealous – they were fighting a real war while we were piddling about in places like Aden. I wished the British were there in Vietnam, I'd 'ave my hand up for it in a flash. In the past, whenever the British were in trouble the Aussies had rushed to fight alongside us. Here were the Aussies fighting the communists and I felt we, the British, should be there supporting them for a change.'

Riddle took a few days' leave and walked into Australia House at The Strand in London. He asked to see someone about joining the Australian army. He was quickly shown in to see the military attaché. Riddle told him he was a sergeant in the Royal Marines just back from Aden, and was keen to join the Australians fighting in Vietnam.

'Do you think you might have room for me?' Riddle asked.

The Australian army officer looked closely at the nuggetty sergeant. He was impressed by the man's service history, particularly his experience in the jungles of Sarawak. But there was something in his military record that bothered him. There seemed to be a lot of disciplinary charges.

'Do you drink?' he asked.

'Yes, Sir, I don't need training for that.'

Riddle was in, but first he had to resign from the Royal Marines. It wasn't a happy departure. The pencil pushers in the British Defence Department told him he'd have to pay £75 to cover his bills and buy out the remaining time he had signed up for. By an incredible coincidence that was exactly the same amount they owed him in salary. After eight years of service, Riddle walked out without a penny in his pocket.

As soon as Riddle's father discovered he'd quit the marines to join the Australian army he travelled down to Plymouth to see him. He said it was for a goodbye beer, but he ended up telling Jim he was very disappointed with him. He laid on the guilt, telling his son he was making his mother very unhappy. Riddle had expected this of his father – he couldn't recall a time his dad was ever happy with anything he did. He told his father he didn't like the way the Brits had left the Aussies in the lurch in Vietnam; that he was going over to do his bit. Riddle suspected he was doing it subconsciously to get even further away from his father. Or perhaps just to prove something to him.

The decision made, Riddle felt free and excited to be starting a new life among the Aussies he'd always admired. He went back to the Australian High Commission and showed his discharge papers to the military attaché. He was given a fitness test, which he passed with flying colours, and told to fill in a questionnaire.

'If this proves I'm an idiot do I still get in?' Riddle asked.

'You go to the front of the queue, mate,' laughed the Aussie official.

Later that day, Riddle was presented to the Commission's sergeant major, who had Riddle swear an oath of allegiance to the Commonwealth of Australia and signed him up as a recruit in the Australian army. He was given an Australian passport and the army number 311589. Riddle insisted it be clear that he was only joining up for the duration of the Vietnam War. The sergeant major smiled and said they could talk about that later. There was no way he was going to let Riddle back out. The Australian army needed experienced soldiers like him. The sergeant major personally drove the new recruit to the airport and escorted him directly onto the Qantas plane that would take him to Sydney. Riddle sat down in his seat, the door closed and the plane took off.

'The plane was called the Waratah,' Riddle remembers. 'The hostie explained it was a big red native Australian flower. I was excited. It was a new life. I was sick of Britain: the unions had taken over, the place was going communist. I'd been fighting communist rebels in one place or another ever since I'd joined the Royal Marines, and I was disgusted Britain hadn't offered to help Australia in its fight against the communists in Vietnam. I thought I was doing the honourable thing. I was paying back the Australians who helped Britain in our hour of need.'

Landing in Sydney, Riddle pinned on the white button he'd been given to identify him at the airport. An army private met Riddle and drove him to the military barracks at Watsons Bay – a pleasant place with breathtaking views across Sydney Harbour. It was a long weekend, so Riddle found himself pretty much alone for a few days. He wandered around the beachside cottages of the picturesque suburb and had a long cold beer or two at the Watsons Bay pub, which sits at the edge of a quiet harbour beach. He watched sailing boats skitting around the harbour, people fishing from the pier, the Manly ferry crossing every so often, and people going about a typical sunny weekend in Sydney. Riddle thought he'd landed in paradise.

But the respite didn't last. After two days Riddle was issued his Australian army kit and put on a train to the army training base at Ingleburn, west of Sydney. He wore a khaki uniform and a brand new slouch hat. Riddle loved the iconic hat, its side pinned up by a badge proudly depicting the famous image of the rising sun. Riddle didn't know whether the pinned up side should go on the right or the left and when he alighted at Ingleburn he put his hat on the wrong way. Several old blokes sitting on the veranda of a pub in shorts and singlets burst out laughing when they saw him. 'What the fuck have they sent us now – he's going backwards!' one called out.

Riddle was embarrassed, but thought to himself, *No, Jim, don't start a fight now. It's too early.* A jeep rolled up and the young private driving threw him a funny look, but said nothing. He drove Riddle into the base where a corporal marched up and glared at him.

'How long have you been in the army, digger?' he demanded, staring at Riddle's hat.

Riddle took a deep breath, stood awkwardly to attention and replied in his thickest Geordie accent: 'All day, Sir!'

The corporal immediate pegged Riddle as a Pommy smart-arse. 'He thought I was taking the piss, but I wasn't really,' said Riddle. 'They looked up my record and saw I already had eight campaign medals and eight years in the Royal Marines with the rank of sergeant. I had more experience than any of them, but there I was starting as a fresh recruit. The military attaché had told me I'd make rank quickly, but I'd have to pass the Australian army promotion tests first. The corporal and his mates looked at me differently once they knew my record. I was put in with a squad of new recruits for training, and I knew they were watching me, to see what I could do.'

Riddle set out to impress the trainers. A rather snooty officer who spoke like an upper-class Brit told Riddle that if he kept his nose clean and did as he was told, he'd earn his sergeant stripes fast, adding that because of his experience he would stay at the base and be used to train young recruits.

Patronising bastard, he thought. *I should be in the fight, that's where I can use my skill and experience to look after the men. Officers don't have a thought for their welfare.*

Riddle held his tongue. He wanted those stripes. But it wasn't long before his fists brought him undone. A corporal with strong republican sentiments thought it would be funny to insult the Queen in front of Riddle, describing the royal couple as 'Phil the Greek and his whore'. It was a stupid thing to say – the Queen is Australia's head of state, and is therefore the official head of the Australian Armed Forces. Australian regiments carry the 'Royal' title and the relationship is symbolised by the image of a crown at the centre of the army's rising sun badge. Riddle went straight up to the corporal and got in his face. 'Don't say that, it's not funny.' The corporal took exception at this newcomer with a funny accent telling him what to do and snarled another insult about the Queen into Riddle's face.

'I tackled him and he went through a window,' Riddle remembers. 'I was in the lockup for that. From that moment on I couldn't fart without them taking note. I'd only been there two months and already I was marked as a troublemaker. I was furious. If you're in the army it's just so wrong to insult the Queen – and it's not just because I'm a Brit.'

After two months of training Riddle asked if he could wear the jump wings he'd earned parachuting in the Royal Marines. He was refused permission since he hadn't earned them in the Australian army. Riddle was disappointed. It wasn't working out as well as the nice man in the Australian High Commission had promised. Riddle reverted to his old ways and got on the grog big time with the new mates he was making among the recruits. Nineteen-year-old Bob Secrett remembers heading out at 6am with Riddle and another recruit on one of their days off to find a pub. They jumped on a train and found an early opener at the wharves, but it was packed and they couldn't even get to the bar. Riddle pulled Secrett and the other recruit into a huddle.

'I couldn't believe it when Jim told us to go outside and start a fight. He said to make it look good – lots of cursing, put on a bit of a show,' Secrett recalls. 'So we did. We started pushing and swearing at each other and threw a few punches. The wharfies quickly came out to watch, egging us on. Jim walked straight up to the empty bar and ordered four beers – and knocked one off while he waited for us to finish the brawl. When we came in, he handed us each a beer and we had a good laugh.'

Riddle was fast becoming a legend among the young recruits. He was ten years older than them, and he had a lot of real combat experience – more than the corporals who were training them. But what impressed them the most was that he didn't cop any shit, even from NCOs and officers. Mention Riddle's name and the recruits quickly tell the same story: they were all rather bemused by the frequency of short-arm parades ordered by one particular middle-aged medical officer. These inspections for sexually transmitted diseases required soldiers to line up and drop their pants to expose their privates while the officer walked along the line using a stick to lift and examine their genitals. The soldiers thought that this dedicated officer seemed a little too enthusiastic, conducting inspections far more often than was necessary.

After about the seventh or eighth inspection in as many weeks, the officer was walking along the line of recruits examining their nether regions in detail. When he got to Riddle he lifted the Geordie's shirt with his stick to discover a most impressive erection waiting for him.

'What's the meaning of this?' shouted the enraged officer.

'Sorry, Sir, I heard it was fish and chips for dinner. It's my favourite, Sir.'

The short-arm inspections came to a hurried end. That was the last they saw of the over-diligent officer.

6

POMMY BASTARD

In December 1968, four days before Christmas, Riddle and
several dozen other new recruits were finally sent to Vietnam
as replacements. Rather than being sent with a unit that they
would stay with throughout their deployment, they would fill
holes in the battalions, companies, platoons or sections already
in country. It was always tough being sent as a replacement
– you hadn't trained with the men, you hadn't gone through
the actions and agonies that they had, you weren't part of the
bonded team. Worse, you were probably replacing somebody
who had been killed or wounded. Rightly or wrongly, that
made his mates resent you.

Riddle and most of the replacements he arrived with were
assigned to the 4th Royal Australian Regiment (4RAR), a

well-oiled fighting regiment that had already distinguished itself in Vietnam. Riddle was taking the place of a man who had been killed just weeks earlier. The new batch of men arrived exactly 12 months after the Tet Offensive, the turning point of the war. The North Vietnamese and Viet Cong had lost around 50,000 fighters, and on paper it was a huge defeat for them. The VC of South Vietnam were decimated, and in Phuoc Tuy province, where the Australians were based, the communist forces had taken a long time to re-emerge from their jungle retreats. However, over the last 12 months the North had steadily bolstered their numbers, working their way down the coast and inland down the Ho Chi Minh Trail.

Despite the heavy losses, the Tet Offensive was a tactical victory for the North. It proved they could mount a massive coordinated attack throughout the country. Their daring raids on the US Embassy in the heart of Saigon shocked the American and Australian public watching as the action unfolded on television. It was a significant contribution towards shifting attitudes against the war as the death toll of US and Allied troops suddenly soared. An increasing number of people back home were questioning whether the war could be won. Also, any confidence that had existed among South Vietnamese troops and villagers that the VC could be suppressed was now shattered.

Despite his lack of rank, on his arrival at Nui Dat, Riddle was immediately made a section leader because of his experience in the Royal Marines. Riddle was still adjusting to the heat of the morning when a young lieutenant took him along a row of 4RAR tents to meet his squad. They had been out all night on patrol; Riddle says he was told the corporal previously in charge hadn't been too keen on leading them out. It was also likely that the men hadn't been too keen on going out with that particular corporal. The lieutenant walked up to a large tent and pulled the tarpaulin back. There were sleeping bodies everywhere, curled up on bunks; even on the floor. As daylight streamed into the tent they began to stir and Riddle stood watching them as the lieutenant told them he was their new section leader. Riddle could see they were exhausted, despondent and fed up. There was no sense in yelling at them like a parade ground sergeant. Besides, that wasn't his way.

Riddle waited patiently outside until they were all up, and then he sat them down in the shade. 'I can see you're an unhappy lot,' he told them. 'You're living like rats in a nest. This has to change if you're going to survive Vietnam. My job is to get you lot through this war alive. The way to do that is to pay attention to what I tell you. Do not argue, do exactly what I tell you – no ifs, buts and doing it too fookin' slow. If I tell you to do something, you do it straight away. That's how you will get through this alive.'

Riddle could see the men were judging him, wondering who the hell he was taking command like this, Pommy accent and all. One of them piped up and asked. Riddle told them he'd served in the Royal Marines for the last ten years and had now joined up with the Aussies to fight in Vietnam. He told them a bit of his experience in Borneo, Cyprus and Aden. Members of the squad began to sit up and take notice, willing to accept that perhaps Riddle did know what he was talking about.

A week later the section was out on patrol with the whole company, heading up a jungle path. Suddenly the company came under machine-gun fire. Riddle ordered his section to lie down under cover and wait for him. He ran on ahead to see what was going on further up the path and could hear the men yelling after him. 'They were shouting at me to get down or I'd be killed,' he recalls. 'Then I heard one voice yell out: "Get down or you'll get me killed!"'

Up ahead, a VC machine gunner had his sights trained on Riddle and bullets whizzed around him as he sprinted to the front of the patrol. All around him men were shouting at him to get down and stop drawing fire on them. Riddle dodged and weaved his way to the head of the line. He dived behind a log, and looked up to see that several Australians in front of him had taken cover in a ditch directly below a well dug-in VC bunker. The Aussies were shooting back as much as they could but they were fast running out of ammunition. In Riddle's mind there was nothing worse than having an empty gun with the enemy coming at you, which is why he always had a big hunting knife strapped to his leg so that he could fight to the end, if necessary. Riddle fired at the enemy bunker and yelled out to the men ahead of him, asking what they needed. They wanted ammunition for the machine guns and the M-16s, and shells for their M-79 grenade launcher.

Riddle got up and ran back down the line, pulling up momentarily to tell the platoon sergeant, who was taking cover behind a tree, that he was going back for ammo. It's always wise to tell those in charge why you are running away from the front line. Bullets chipped the sergeant's tree and the sergeant ducked from side to side, then shouted at Riddle to get away as he was drawing fire. Riddle ran on, bullets zipping around him, and pulled up at a quieter part of the line, well away from the shooting. Going from soldier to soldier, Riddle rounded up bullets and shells, slinging the ammunition belts over his shoulder and filling his packs. He ran back to the front but couldn't get close enough as the firing from the bunker was too intense, so he hurled a belt of M-79 shells and grenades as far as he could. *Shit*, Riddle thought. He could see the belt caught on a vine above the ditch where the men were taking cover.

Riddle and some others gave covering fire as one of the men in the ditch jumped up to grab the belt and dived back down. They lobbed the grenades into the bunker and the machine-gun fire stopped. But it was still too dangerous to break their cover so the troops waited until dark to withdraw. That night artillery bombarded the bunker complex, but it wasn't the end of the action. Next morning Riddle was summoned by the company commander who told him his section would lead a fresh attack on any VC still holed up there.

Standard procedure in an operation like this dictated that a scout be sent out front to investigate and report back, but in this situation the role was one of almost certain death.

The soldiers all knew that if any remaining VC had managed to survive the overnight bombardment by hiding deep in their underground tunnels, they'd be waiting and would spot anyone coming in to scope the site. Riddle couldn't bring himself to tell any one of his young soldiers that his ugly mug was going to be the last one they ever saw in their life. As far as he was concerned there was only one way to approach the bunker, and that was straight up the path, and he would be the one leading them in. He could see the relief on their faces.

'If I hear firing I will run straight at them,' he told them. 'I will run right over the bunker shouting and screaming and firing like buggery and keep on going out the other side. So don't shoot at me. You,' Riddle pointed at a soldier with a machine gun. 'You drop and give me covering fire.' Then he pointed to another soldier. 'You're the spotter. You stay with the machine gunner and point out enemy positions for him.'

Riddle knew he was breaking all the rules. But he figured that as long as the VC were firing at him, they weren't firing at his section. He lit a cigarette. Again, he was breaking the rules as the enemy could smell it on the wind. *Bugger it*, he thought, *they know we're coming up the path. There's no other way to reach them. This could be my last smoke.*

Halfway up the path Riddle heard the crack of an AK-47. He immediately started sprinting to his right through some tall grass. *If they fire at me on the path they'll hit the men behind me, so I'll try and draw their fire to the right.* He ducked and weaved, and then ran straight into his section's scout. As per

Riddle's orders, he'd gone forward to get a clear look to spot the enemy positions for the machine gunner. Riddle realised these young diggers were all right. They weren't shirking the fight. They'd just needed a competent leader.

The bunker had been hit hard overnight by the artillery barrage but a handful of VC had survived. They were dug in and it took some time for the company to outflank the bunker. They lobbed in grenades and blasted it with M-79 and machine-gun fire for hours before the VC guns finally fell silent. When the action was over all the VC had been killed. Three Australians were wounded.

•

Four months after being assigned to 4RAR, Riddle found himself being left behind in Vietnam as his battalion sailed home to Australia. The battalion's 12-month tour of duty was complete; Riddle still had another eight months to go. But Riddle felt good about his time in 4RAR. He'd made some good mates and had cemented his position as section leader. He had won respect among the troops as well as the officers for his combat knowledge.

A total of 39 soldiers from 4RAR were left behind. They had all arrived in Vietnam as reinforcements, and hadn't yet served out their full 12-month deployment. They were all regular soldiers, not a conscript among them, and all had combat experience. For the army they were a useful commodity but despite this, they were in military no-man's-land.

A new battalion had not yet arrived to absorb them and in the meantime they would be formed into a new unit attached to Task Force Headquarters in what was called a Defence and Employment platoon.

Riddle wasn't happy when he was told about the new team. In his mind, defence and employment platoons had a bad reputation since their main duties seemed to entail standing guard, running errands and escorting visiting bigwigs like politicians and armchair generals. *Fookin' waiters and bottlewashers*, he said to himself. *What a waste of good combat troops.*

Riddle and his men thought they'd been dumped on the scrap heap. Their pride and esteem was so low that when they arrived at HQ in Nui Dat they thought they'd be issued bow ties and shown the way to the officers' mess. To add insult to injury, the young officer assigned to command the makeshift group, Lieutenant Barry Parkin, had two jobs. He'd also been directed to organise the departure of the last of the 4RAR, a time-consuming exercise in logistics that frequently took him away from HQ to the port of Vung Tau. Parkin met the 39 men of the 2nd D&E briefly at Nui Dat before he left on one of his many trips to the port town, telling them they would be part of Task Force HQ Defence, and could be called on at any moment to go out with APCs to do whatever they had to do. At that, the men's spirits lifted a little – it sounded a lot better than peeling potatoes.

Parkin looked around the group and saw only privates. It was large enough to form a platoon, but they needed a sergeant and a couple of corporals to be a properly constituted unit. Parkin recognised that Riddle stood out from the others as an experienced soldier. Riddle asked questions and seemed to be the spokesman of the group, a natural leader. Parkin took Riddle to meet Major George Pratt, the second in charge of HQ administration, introducing Riddle as the unit's corporal and senior NCO, even though he was just a private like the other men. As section leader in the 4RAR Riddle had been made acting corporal but he didn't have the two stripes to cement his position.

Pratt told Riddle his unit would be attached to cavalry officer Captain Tom Arrowsmith and be at his disposal. Parkin took Riddle over to report to Arrowsmith, who commanded a troop of armoured personnel carriers. Arrowsmith told Riddle he wanted a section of eight men to report to him immediately as he was about to lead a rescue mission for some Special Air Service reconnaissance men stuck out in the bush. Meanwhile, the men of the newly formed D&E platoon were wondering what was going on; most of them knew Riddle wasn't a senior NCO. Still, for the moment they were happy to have him – after all, he'd been seen talking with the senior officers and they needed a leader. They responded positively to the Geordie as he picked out seven men he'd known in the 4th Battalion to accompany him on the mission.

Arrowsmith headed out with three APCs and the eight soldiers. The SAS men were hiding in tall grass from a VC unit that had spotted them and were closing in. The armoured vehicles were tracking through the tall grass when the cavalry-men spotted one of the SAS men sticking his head up. He had the distinctive olive green bandana over his head that SAS men seemed to like to wear out in the field. *It's their badge of wank*, sneered Riddle, who had the infantryman's natural suspicion of the worth of special forces soldiers.

Over the radio the SAS men told Arrowsmith they were being pursued by VC and had come up against the open ground of a firebreak. If they left the tall grass and ran out to cross the open ground they could be cut down. Riddle told Arrowsmith to drop him and his lads behind the SAS and they would cover them as they got into the APCs. The back door of the APCs rattled down and the eight soldiers scattered into the dry grass, providing cover as the SAS climbed into the carriers. Riddle and the infantrymen reboarded without seeing any sign of VC. Perhaps the sound of the APCs had made them take cover, but Riddle suspected the SAS had just wanted a ride back to base.

They'd just arrived back in Nui Dat when Arrowsmith told Riddle that he'd just received a report that some APCs had come under fire out in the bush. They got back on board and roared out again to link up with the embattled column. A mine had gone off under one of the carriers and the driver's left leg had been blown almost completely off. Riddle dismounted and took his men along the road to clear the area while a chopper came in to pick up the wounded soldier. As he was being lifted onto the stretcher, his leg fell off completely. As the medics pumped him full of morphine, his mates wrapped the leg in a sheet and put it on the stretcher next to him.

Back at base Riddle found the other 38 men of the unit had now fully accepted him as their leader as they'd heard he'd taken command of the section sent out with Captain Arrowsmith to rescue the SAS. Most of them knew him from 4RAR, either personally or by reputation. The fact that he was older and had served actively in the military far longer than them helped to bolster his standing in their eyes. As for Riddle, even though he was only an acting corporal, he was leading a platoon, normally the task of a lieutenant or a sergeant. The responsibility was way above his pay grade, but he was happy to assume command.

Riddle checked in briefly with Major Pratt about where his men were to bunk down. Pratt sent them to a section of the camp where they were given old and worn gear, with shoddy tents and bunks which they'd have to clean up before they could use them. Pratt told Riddle that his lieutenant, Parkin, would be gone from the camp for several days, and told Riddle he could sort out the platoon and appoint section leaders. Three sections of up to 12 men each make up a platoon – usually between 30 and 40 men. A section is usually commanded by a corporal, and a platoon is commanded by a lieutenant with a sergeant to assist him. Riddle would head up one section, and he appointed two men he knew from 4RAR to take command of the other two sections: 24-year-old Glasgow-born Len Ellcombe, and Kevin Lloyd-Thomas, a 20-year-old British-born private who was on his second tour of Vietnam. In Parkin's absence, Riddle would have to fill the role of both lieutenant and sergeant.

It was a highly unorthodox and loose arrangement. Pratt then informed the men that, because there was already an established D&E platoon on the base, they would be set up as a second D&E unit. The major saw the group as only a temporary one lasting a few weeks, and as history would show, there was a big gap in the paperwork regarding the 2nd D&E – something that would have dramatic consequences for the men of the platoon.

From the moment it was formed, the new platoon was left to fend for itself without an officer present. After their initial mission into the bush with Arrowsmith, the platoon did some watermanship training for a few days in preparation for patrolling the rivers and waterways which were being used by the VC to smuggle weapons and supplies into the province. But after a couple of days, the 2nd D&E found themselves kicking their heels, lying around the riverbanks wondering what they were supposed to be doing. Parkin had been gone for days and their role was unclear.

Riddle could see a malaise setting in and decided he had to pull them together. He remembered a trick from his time served in the Royal Marines and got hold of a couple of grenades, told the men to stand back, and lobbed them into a deep part of the still water. A great geyser of water shot up and, one by one, dozens of stunned fish rose to the surface. The men gathered them up, got a barbecue going and had a beachside feast, improving their mood somewhat. Not long afterwards, the platoon's waterways training came to a swift end when Arrowsmith pulled most of them in to accompany his cavalry troop on the ambush at Thua Tich. But little did they know that, many years later, those slow days on the river would play a crucial role for the men of the platoon in proving that their unit had ever existed.

•

Back at base after the action at Thua Tich, the men of the 2nd D&E were once again at a loose end. Frustrated that they had been dumped back at Nui Dat with a dark cloud hanging over their involvement in the mission, drink seemed the logical solution. The men hit the bottle hard. Another week would pass before the men of the ragtag unit were split up and sent to other battalions.

Along with most of his platoon, Riddle was transferred to the 9th Battalion, which had just arrived in Vietnam. While Riddle's men were now seasoned fighters with real combat experience, most of the 9th were on their first tour of duty. Riddle was again made a section leader. He still didn't have the corporal stripes that went with the position, but he wasn't surprised – it seemed his clash with the officer at Xuyen Moc had certainly put the kybosh on his chances of any promotion or medals.

Shortly after joining the battalion, Riddle was sitting with his new section in a bar when one of his men let out a loud laugh. A corporal nearby took offence, thinking the soldier was laughing at him, grabbed the soldier by the scruff of his shirt and belted him. Riddle stepped in to stop the fight, telling the corporal the laugh wasn't directed at him and to piss off. The two men shaped up for a scrap before they were pulled apart, but that night the corporal poked his head into Riddle's tent and told him he was putting him on a charge for insubordination. Riddle had his usual answer: 'Fuck off!' The corporal invited him outside and the two went around the corner of the tent to settle their differences. The corporal had been a boxer in civilian life, but Riddle didn't play by Marquess of Queensbury rules and promptly flattened him.

From that point on Riddle was a marked man with the NCOs of the 9RAR. A few days later, Riddle was consoling one of his young troopers who was crying; he'd just heard a friend of his had been killed in action. A burly sergeant demanded to know what was wrong with him.

'His mate's just been killed,' said Riddle.

'Shit happens,' said the sergeant.

Furious at the sergeant's insensitivity Riddle stood up, ready for a fight.

The sergeant was ready. 'You fucking Pommy bastard,' he snarled into Riddle's face. 'You're just here to get what you can for yourself.'

Riddle was riled. Certainly, he was a Pom, and had no issue with that. He was used to the endearing Aussie insult for an Englishman, which stemmed from the days when Australia was a British penal colony. One explanation for its origin is that it's an acronym for 'Prisoner of Her Majesty'. But that wasn't playing a role here. In Riddle's mind he had right on his side – it was a mistake for a senior NCO to insult one of his own troops.

What was coming was an old-fashioned sting. The NCOs had their trap ready. While Riddle battled to control his temper, the corporal he'd fought with days earlier suddenly stepped in, grabbed Riddle by his arms from behind, and yelled, 'Don't hit him, Riddle!'

The sergeant walked away, returning with several other sergeants and arrested Riddle for threatening assault. Riddle realised he'd been set up good and proper. They marched him to the company commander. The sergeant gave his evidence, saying Riddle had threatened to attack him and would have carried out his threat if he hadn't been restrained by the corporal. The commander asked Riddle if he had anything to say for himself.

'He called me a Pommy bastard, Sir. I took offence. My parents are married.'

The commander tried to keep a straight face. 'Did you try to hit the sergeant?'

'If I'd tried to hit the sergeant, Sir, I would'a hit him, and he would'a stayed hit,' Riddle replied.

Riddle was dismissed and heard nothing more about it, but he knew his time was up in the 9th. He applied for a transfer and was quickly shifted to the 8th Battalion. By now,

Riddle was drinking a lot; he felt that the war would never end. Despite this, when his 12-month tour of duty was up he immediately signed up for a second, and when that was up, a third.

'I felt the war had lasted a lifetime,' he recalls. 'I got so bad that eventually I didn't know or care where I was, who I was with, what I was doing or where I would be tomorrow. It was like being a ghost in a long-running nightmare movie where they kept changing the cast. The odd thing about it was that I didn't ever want to leave. I was a basket case, a dead giveaway.' Riddle had now been on continuous active service for seven years starting with his time in Borneo and Aden with the Royal Marines. 'I think it's possible that I drank too often from the well of courage, and it didn't refill.'

The rough and tumble Geordie was in trouble once again when he discovered something that chilled him to the bone. Riddle had belted a cook who happened to be a sergeant. He and his men had just come back from a patrol and were settling in for a few beers in the mess. The cook had been shooting the stray cats which hung around the kitchen for scraps. This didn't impress the men and they loudly joked the cook would probably get a medal for shooting pussy. The cook wasn't impressed and told them all to get out. True to form, Riddle indelicately advised the cook where to stick his soup ladle.

'You're on a charge!' shouted the cook. It was the charge that broke the camel's back, and Riddle snapped. He punched the cook hard and down he went. This time Riddle couldn't joke his way out and he was sentenced to two weeks in the cells.

As Riddle settled into his cell he was shocked to find Peter 'Pedro' Allen in the cell next to him. Riddle remembered Pedro as one of the young privates who'd been with him in the forward listening post at the Thua Tich ambush. Riddle was surprised to see him in prison as the youngster was one of the quiet kids who kept to himself – a little strange, certainly, but unremarkable. Riddle thought Allen had conducted himself well during the ambush, but he hadn't thought of the young soldier since that day.

Riddle had seen plenty of madness in war. He'd had his own brush with it himself on more than a few occasions. But what Allen told him through the prison bars shocked the battle-hardened soldier to the core.

7

THE FRAGGING OF LIEUTENANT CONVERY

No one was certain as to exactly why, on the night of 23 December 1969, Private Peter 'Pedro' Denzil Allen reached into the tent of his platoon's commanding officer, Lieutenant Robert Convery, carefully placed a grenade under the sleeping man's body and blew him to pieces.

Pedro Allen couldn't explain it, even to himself. Throughout his court martial for murder, the 20-year-old Tasmanian struggled to find a good reason for his action that night. All he could come up with was that he didn't like the 22-year-old lieutenant. Allen, Convery and the 9th Battalion had just finished their 12-month tour and were due to be shipped back to Australia in just six days time. Convery was in high spirits, looking forward to going home to Melbourne. Despite being wounded in the arm in his first contact as a platoon commander, he'd enjoyed his tour of duty in Vietnam. His friends described him as an easygoing chap and a keen officer.

In the few days that Riddle was in the cell next door to Allen, long before the court martial got under way and lawyers and psychiatrists put Allen under the microscope, Riddle got a glimpse into the young soldier's state of mind. 'He told me Convery had always picked on him. I said it was no reason to kill an officer and that maybe he'd got the wrong bloke. He said: "Nah, I got the one I wanted."' Riddle was shocked by the cold-blooded way the young soldier talked about killing his senior officer.

'Fragging' was a term invented during the Vietnam War by American troops. It came from the alarming practice of disaffected soldiers throwing fragmentation hand grenades into the tents and bunkers of officers or NCOs who were unpopular, overzealous or inept. According to Pentagon figures, the total number of US fragging incidents during the Vietnam War was estimated at between 600 and 1000.[1] Not all of them were fatal, but many American combat deaths could also have been deliberate killings from their own side.

Fragging was extremely rare in the Australian army and Allen's court martial for murder was big news in the Australian media when it got under way in early January 1970. It certainly wasn't the kind of publicity the army wanted. Allen was a regular soldier, fit and young. With his handsome face and his ramrod-straight back, he looked every bit the bronzed Anzac. Had the young private been driven mad by the war? Or had the army recruited a psychopath? They were questions that Allen's court-martial would avoid. Neither answer would be good for the army.

The Australian army had already had to contend with two other reported cases of fragging in 1968 and 1969. In the first incident a private placed a Claymore mine near the bed of his sergeant. It wasn't charged, but its intention was clear: it was a warning. A few months later a soldier blew up the unoccupied living quarters of a staff sergeant. Perhaps it was only a matter of time before somebody was murdered.[2]

Riddle knew how it felt to be angered by a superior – and he could understand how Allen had done what he had. In the cells he listened to the young private talk and he felt his anger. 'This sort of thing happens a lot more in war than any army is prepared to admit,' says Riddle today. 'Some blokes just get fed up and direct all their hate at officers and NCOs who force them to go out on futile, virtual suicide missions. I know how they felt. I'd often been put in pointless, dangerous situations by officers who hung back, trying to score medals at the expense of their own men. They'd get airlifted out of tough spots first, and then enjoy all the luxuries back at camp while their men had bugger all. Sure, I could understand why some soldiers tipped over the edge. Some officers were scared stiff of being killed by their own men.'

Lieutenant Convery wasn't the first Australian to be murdered by someone on their own side. In July 1969 a pretty 19-year-old Australian singer called Cathy Wayne was performing on stage in a pale yellow miniskirt for about 75 US marines at an American NCO club at Da Nang. She had just finished her final song and was introducing her fellow performers in her touring group, Sweethearts on Parade, when a shot rang out. A .22 millimetre bullet hit her in the chest and went right through her lungs. She fell down, blood spurting from the wound. Cathy died within seconds in the arms of her fiancé, the group's drummer Clive Cavanagh.

In the immediate commotion marines ran outside searching for the shooter. Was it a VC infiltrator? Was it a pissed-off marine who'd been rebuffed by the girl? Was it a crazed recruit fed up with war? No likely suspect was found. Days later, investigators found a pistol fitted with a makeshift silencer buried in sand about 100 metres from the club.

A week later, US Marine Sergeant James Wayne Killen was charged with the killing. The court martial found the 38-year-old from Birmingham, Alabama, had fired into the club through a window screen of mosquito netting. Killen confessed, saying he had been trying to hit his commanding officer, Major Roger Simmons, who was sitting in the front row. Cathy Wayne had moved into the line of fire just as he pulled the trigger.

Cathy Wayne – whose real name was Catherine Anne Warnes – from Arncliffe in Sydney, was the first Australian woman killed in the Vietnam War. The US marine sergeant, who had been drinking heavily on the night, was convicted of unpremeditated murder, given a dishonourable discharge and sentenced to 20 years hard labour. His court martial failed to reveal why he wanted to kill his commanding officer. It didn't rule whether he was mentally ill, and it didn't supply any motive for his action. It seems the purpose of the court martial was to convict, sentence and get the disgraced soldier out of sight.

•

The court martial of Australian Private Peter Denzil Allen got under way in Vung Tau on 8 January 1970. The president of the court martial was Brigadier G.F. Richardson, sent specially for the trial from army headquarters in Canberra. Three lieutenant-colonels from headquarters, as well as two majors and a captain from the Vietnam deployment, made up the court-martial panel. The judge advocate was Queen's Counsel Colonel J.L. Kelly. Chief prosecutor was Adelaide barrister Colonel Robert Mohr of the Army Legal Corps. Sydney barrister Lieutenant Colonel B.E. Egan was appointed to defend Allen, who had pleaded not guilty.

The seven officers took their place at a long table in front of Australian flags at the head of the packed makeshift military courtroom perched on a hill overlooking the ocean. They wore crisp army greens with decorations, but despite the breeze coming from the South China Sea, they were clearly feeling the heat as it rose towards 32 degrees. Opening the prosecution's case against Allen, Colonel Mohr drew himself up before the crowded gallery, which had several Australian reporters taking notes, and turned to face the row of officers who would decide Private Allen's fate.

'It's a fairly simple story,' Mohr said. 'Private Allen wished to kill the deceased.'

Mohr would provide evidence that Allen had been drinking heavily that night. He would show that shortly before midnight, Convery had gone to the tent where Allen and others were drinking beer and told them to turn the light out and go to sleep. He would also show that Allen then crept over to Convery's tent, waited until he was asleep and slipped an armed grenade next to his body. Mohr said that after the explosion Allen ran back to his own tent, got undressed, climbed into his bed and went to sleep.

Mohr waved a sheet of paper at the court that contained Allen's handwritten and signed statement in which he'd confessed: 'I did it. I killed Mr Convery . . . with a grenade.'

The reporters had their headline. The court martial was front-page news in Australia. *The Sydney Morning Herald* ran a photo of a straight-backed Private Allen in full military dress and slouch hat being marched from the courtroom by a guard. The paper's usual pro-war attitude was changing. Underneath the photograph of Allen was a story about a US marine lance corporal, Rudolph O. Diener Junior, who had been tried for murder for the killing of an unarmed peasant woman during a raid on a village in 1967. He was found innocent. Diener had been preparing to throw a grenade into a burning hut where he had seen the woman huddling with her two young children when his sergeant stopped him, saying he couldn't kill kids. Diener dragged the mother into a rice paddy and shot her four times in the back. At his trial, Diener claimed his commander, Captain Robert Maynard, had ordered them to kill everyone in the village. Maynard denied this, and was also exonerated. Diener returned to the US, was promoted to sergeant, and given a Meritorious Combat Award and an honourable discharge. Working as a used car salesman, an unrepentant Diener told *The Sydney Morning Herald* reporter Peter Michelmore, 'War is war . . . It's just one of those things. I got paid for doing my job and I did it the best way I could.'

The Sydney Morning Herald went on to report Diener's defence of simply following orders was expected to be used in the upcoming trial of US soldiers charged with killing unarmed civilians at the March 1968 massacre at My Lai. The shocking story and colour photos of the My Lai massacre of up to 504 unarmed civilians – elderly men, and women and children – had broken in the media only a month earlier. It had taken 20 months for photographs taken by US army photographer Ron Haeberle to be published. They first appeared in *Life Magazine* in the US, but Australian newspaper editors considered the pictures too graphic to print.

The only paper in Australia to dare run the My Lai photos was a new anti-war weekly newspaper, *The Sunday Observer*, based in Melbourne. In December 1969 the paper published shocking images showing bloody corpses of women and children piled on top of each other. One photograph showed a terrified elderly woman surrounded by crying children. The caption said that seconds after the photo had been taken they were mown down by machine-gun fire. Their publication had such a huge impact that the fledgling newspaper was charged by the government with obscenity. The charge was eventually dropped, but the publication pushed other mainstream media into following the story, and the revelations surrounding My Lai sparked the Australian media into running a flood of Vietnam War horror stories.

As Peter 'Pedro' Allen's court martial began, Australian public opinion was turning against the war, spurred on by the shift in media coverage. Now the Australian public was hearing the shocking story of a digger turning on his own officer and murdering him. Until now, the Anzac digger had a glowing, almost reverential reputation. He was considered more noble than any other nation's soldiers, an image polished and cultivated since World War One and the landing at Gallipoli. People began to ask whether the image of the fabled Aussie digger was being tarnished by this war.

Daily revelations from the court-martial kept the damaging story in the headlines. The usually stuffy *Sydney Morning Herald* screamed the headline: 'Lieutenant Killed in Cold Blood, Court Told'. In court, Allen's platoon mates were brought in one by one to testify. They said Allen had been drinking with them in the base's bar until they were kicked out at around 9.30pm. Allen bought a dozen beers to the tents where the drinking, smoking and talking continued until just before midnight.

Private Terry Slattery had served with Allen in the 2nd D&E Platoon at the Thua Tich ambush but he only knew Allen by sight. He testified he'd had a few beers with Allen and half a dozen other troops in the tent of Corporal Terry Cunich, Allen's section leader. He said that about 10.30pm Lieutenant Convery had poked his head into the tent and told the men to go to bed. Slattery said he hadn't ever noticed anything unusual about Allen's behaviour. He was asked a set of questions, questions that were put to every witness who had served with Allen: had he ever seen Allen have a fit, faint, suffer nightmares, become moody or go off by himself? The questions were designed to see if alarms about Allen's sanity should have been rung earlier. Slattery answered no to each.

Corporal Cunich added a chilling bit of evidence. He said one of the soldiers drinking in the tent mentioned a Sergeant Cross. One of the others mentioned how unpopular he was, and wondered why he hadn't been 'zapped'. In other words, troops were talking openly of killing their superiors and no one rebuked them for it, or reported it to senior officers. It was accepted as normal talk. Private Kevin Lynch said he was talking with Allen over a few beers on the other side of the tent when they overheard one of the soldiers in the other group talking about killing a sergeant and say it was 'a wonder it hadn't been done'. Lynch said Private John Watson told him it hadn't been done because 'no one could do it and live with it on their conscience for the rest of their lives'.

Private Garry O'Reilly hadn't been drinking that night. He'd gone to bed about midnight in his tent, which was immediately to the left of Cunich's tent. He heard Convery tell the people in Cunich's tent to go to bed. Allen then poked his nose into his tent and asked him for a cigarette. He gave Allen one and then testified that Allen leaned close to him and whispered, 'If you hear an explosion, say nothing.' About 10 to 15 minutes later O'Reilly heard an explosion, then the sound of running feet. They stopped at the tent which Allen shared with three others.

Private Colin Schofield said he'd also heard Convery tell the men in Cunich's tent to go to bed. He heard Convery leave, and then someone yell out 'Spunk bubble!' The court didn't ask what this phrase meant. Maybe they didn't need to. At the time it was a saying referring to the tip of a condom designed to block and trap semen. If you called someone a spunk bubble it implied the person was getting in the way.

Private Cecil Ebsworth, who had also served in the 2nd D&E Platoon with Allen, said that back in August 1969 he'd bumped into Allen walking around the base at night with an Armalite rifle. Ebsworth said Allen told him he was on his way to shoot out the lights in the officers' mess. Ebsworth said, 'Don't be silly,' and invited Allen to have a beer with him. Allen cleared his weapon and a bullet hit the ground.

Ebsworth said Allen told him: 'See? I wasn't joking.' Ebsworth said Allen was angry as he'd been planning on having a beer with mates at a party but it had been stopped by officers.

Lieutenant Ivan Clark was the first person to get to Convery after the explosion. He shone a light into the darkened tent and immediately recognised the smell of an exploded grenade. He switched on the light and saw Convery's body twisted as it lay on a collapsed bed on the left side of the tent. His intestines were hanging out of his torso and blood and tissue was splattered all over the tent above his bed. He knew it was the lieutenant even though he could only see the back of his head. He'd given Convery a haircut that afternoon and he recognised his work. Clark tried to take Convery's pulse but couldn't find one. Corporal John McGrath, another early arrival at the scene, couldn't find a pulse either.

Clark told McGrath to wake Lieutenant John Brien, who was still sleeping in the other bed in the tent. Remarkably, Brien had slept right through the explosion. Clark also told McGrath not to let anyone else into the tent while he raised the Company commander, Captain Graham Dugdale, and brought him back to the tent. He told Lieutenant Peter Cosgrove, who commanded the D&E Platoon at the time, to go over to the tent while he went to organise a parade of all the men. He ordered the men to hand in all their grenades. He recorded that Allen handed in two grenades.

Corporal McGrath searched around the outside of the tent and found the pin from a grenade. Corporal Ernest Hardgrave was ordered by Clark to get all the men out on parade. Private Allen was hard to wake, and several hard shakes failed to shift him. Hardgrave got a bottle of water and tipped it over Allen's head. He said when Allen woke with a start he told him to get out on parade.

Lieutenant John Brien had only arrived in camp that day and had drunk up to 10 cans of beer in the mess before he got to the tent he was sharing with Convery. He said that when Convery returned to the tent around midnight they chatted about old times as they had gone through training together. He said Convery told him he'd had to stop a party down in the troops' tents, and he would probably have to take a corporal's stripes away the next day. Brien went to sleep. The next thing he knew he was being shaken awake and there was a light shining in his face. Just a metre away from him Convery had been blown to bits.

Captain Peter Langman, the second in charge of the Australian Army's Military Police Unit in Vietnam, headed up the investigation. The next morning he interviewed Allen along with all the other troops. Allen claimed he went to bed after Convery broke up the party around 11.30pm and didn't wake up until Corporal Hardgrave poured water over him. Allen said the talk in the tent was how everybody hated Sergeant Cross and that he should be 'ambushed'. He said he had earlier had an argument with Convery over doing a signaler's course.

After Langman interviewed all the other troops in 6 Platoon he called Allen back in at 4.30pm. He told Allen several troops saw him going to bed moments after the explosion.

'Private Allen didn't say anything immediately,' Langman told the court. 'There was a pause of about 10 to 15 seconds then he said, "I did it". I said, "Did what?" He said, "I killed Mr Convery." I asked him where he got the grenade. "Out of my webbing", he said.'

Allen also wrote out a confession. In it he said: 'During the party in Corporal Cunich's tent we were all talking about ambushing a sergeant.' He said Convery came in and told them to go to bed. Then, Allen said:

I then went to my webbing and took out one grenade and then sneaked up to Mr Convery's tent. When I got there he had his light out but he was talking to the new platoon commander from 8RAR. I heard him say that he was going to charge us the next morning and was going to make sure that Corporal Cunich would lose his stripes. I then sat down outside his tent and waited till they were both quiet. I then went round to Mr Convery's side of the tent and put the grenade on so as it couldn't harm the 8RAR lieutenant. As soon as it exploded I ran down to my tent and got into bed where I slept for a short time until Corporal Hardgrave woke me.

The only reason Allen offered for the murder was that Convery had once charged him with drinking. He felt this was hypocritical as the lieutenant had held parties himself and had also joined the men for drinks in the past. Allen said Convery had also ordered him to do a signals course which he didn't want to do. When Allen didn't turn up for the course, Convery charged him again. The charge sheet handed to the court showed Allen lost 14 days' pay and got 28 days' field punishment.

Lieutenant Peter Cosgrove would go on to become one of Australia's most popular and respected Defence chiefs and, in his memoir, written decades after the war, he recounts how he was walking with a group of officers and passed Allen on his field punishment, a pointless exercise of digging a deep hole and then filling it in again. Cosgrove recalls that he was struck by the look of sheer hatred Allen directed at him and the officers. Only a few weeks later, when Allen was court-martialled for Convery's murder, he would remember that look with a shudder. From the evidence given in court, Allen was probably already planning to kill his officer.

'The thought to kill Mr Convery has been with me for some time and last night the talk of ambushing the sergeant and the beers I'd had revived the thought and I carried it out,' Allen wrote in his statement.

During his trial, Allen told the assembled court: 'On the night in question I'd had a fair bit to drink. Before tea I'd had about four or five cans. After tea I went back to the boozer and resumed drinking until it closed. I bought cans and took them down to Corporal Cunich's tent. On the whole I'd say

I had about 15 to 20 cans that night. A lot of the evidence that's been given I've no memory of. I can't remember talking to Private O'Reilly that night at all. I'm very sorry for what happened and if I hadn't been drunk it wouldn't have happened. I've been in trouble before for fighting, and that was through drink. What I've told the doctors, the psychiatrist, has all been the truth. That's all.'

Allen's confession left no room for doubt. He was clearly guilty. But the reason Allen gave for killing his commander was grossly inadequate. The manner in which he dropped a grenade into Convery's tent, carefully placing it in an effort not to harm the other lieutenant in the tent, and then simply returning to his tent – and going to sleep – was simply bizarre. If he'd had a grievance with Convery he only had to hang on a few more days as they were all going home in six days. That night he'd talked with the soldier he knew from the 2nd D&E Platoon, Terry Slattery, about sharing a flat when they got back. Something more had to be involved in this macabre incident. Two psychiatrists examined Allen while he was in custody, but they struggled to find a satisfactory explanation.

The only witness the defence called was army psychiatrist Major Michael Downey. He'd examined Allen four times since his arrest and found him cooperative. Allen told him he'd first met Convery when they both in 1RAR. After that Allen was shifted from one battalion to the next, including the few weeks in the 2nd D&E Platoon with Riddle. He then came under Convery again in 9RAR.

Downey said Allen complained the lieutenant no longer joined his men in conducting sweeps outside the base. Allen was critical of the orders he gave. Allen's respect for him fell and he felt he could do a better job when it came to tracking. Allen told the psychiatrist he'd been involved in six firefights with the enemy in Vietnam. He'd seen one of his mates shot down.

He insisted he couldn't be sure he'd ever killed a VC, but that he may have killed one or two during the Thua Tich ambush. Major Downey said Allen raised no objection to this combat experience, and he had a reputation for being good at his job. The only injuries he ever had were from football and blows to the head during brawls or falls.

Downey said Allen was close to only one or two men in the battalion and sometimes would go off by himself and stare at the ground for hours. 'His prevailing mood was casual and easy-going, but he tended to flare up with minor provocation, especially when drinking. He tended to be shy, avoided responsibility, and was quite critical of those who had responsibility.'

Allen thought of himself as conscientious, but felt the army had turned him into a bludger. He wanted to get out of the army, marry, and work as a bricklayer. He took part in sports including boxing. He had no strong religious beliefs. Downey didn't think Allen had a problem with alcohol although he had started drinking since leaving school at age 15. Allen said he'd smoked marijuana on two or three occasions in Vietnam but gave it up as it made him feel sick.

Downey tested Allen and found he had a surprisingly high IQ of 132. Other tests determined he was not psychiatrically sick. 'The only time Allen appeared upset was when he wondered how his parents and fiancée would react to the news. He expressed surprise that he had no conscience about killing Mr Convery. He did not think about it much, but at one point admitted it was a pretty low thing to do. He said, "No matter how bad a person is, he doesn't deserve to die, not like that anyway. I am positive I wouldn't have done it if I was sober".'

Downey reported, 'Allen said he did not like Convery but didn't hate him. He said he only thought about getting rid of Convery after he had been drinking, and there'd been four or five occasions over the past month when the idea came into his head to get rid of his platoon commander.'

However, Downey did find that Allen's family background could provide more clues into how a quiet, unassuming soldier, said to be good at his job, suddenly turned into a cold-blooded killer. Allen had a fairly chaotic family background with a lot of drinking and violence involving Allen, his father and three brothers. Allen's mother was often ill and he was drawn more towards her than to his father. One of his elder brothers had a conviction for assault and had also been in the army. Allen started drinking at age 15 and came to blows with his father. Allen had temper tantrums up to 10 to 12 years old. His brothers teased him and he would explode with temper and lose control. A teacher described him as a bully at primary school and he was expelled. He moved between three high schools. He had a reputation as a brawler getting into fights with local kids. He was convicted on two occasions for assault as a teenager. Prior to joining the army he couldn't hold down a job for long.

Major Downey concluded Allen suffered from a disordered personality and had neurotic traits developed in childhood. Downey said Allen 'first had sex' when he was just six years old and his family had a history of drinking. 'Allen was suffering from a mental abnormality which was expressed in impulsiveness while drinking, but his ability to know right from wrong was not impaired at the time of the crime.'

Allen told prosecution psychiatrist Lieutenant Colonel Lothar Hoff he killed Convery thinking it was for the good of the blokes as Convery didn't have a clue in the bush. 'He was hanging back, cringing like a dog and gave ridiculous orders.' Allen said he never understood where he was with Convery, as he felt he was inconsistent and a poor disciplinarian.

Then came an indication of how deeply a year of combat in the jungle had affected the young soldier's sanity. Hoff said that when Allen killed Convery he didn't think it was wrong to take another person's life. 'It never entered my head that I was doing wrong. I thought I was doing it for the good of the blokes,' he told Hoff. Later, Allen wished he hadn't killed Convery, but it was a selfish reason. 'If I hadn't done it I would be home by now. It has caused me and everyone a lot of inconvenience.' He had no regret for killing Convery. 'I have no conscience about it.'

Despite this, Hoff agreed with Downey there was no evidence of severe mental illness: 'In my opinion, Private Allen suffers from a mild personality disorder'; that his army records show no sign of mental abnormality and he was an average soldier. 'My final opinion is that Private Allen was not suffering from such abnormality of the mind as to impair his mental responsibility for his acts.' In other words, the army wasn't responsible for the young soldier going mad.

The Judge Advocate, Colonel Kelly, said the case fell short of insanity, and this should not be of concern to the panel in reaching a judgement. It didn't take the court martial panel long to reach its decision. There was never any doubt. The next day Private Peter Denzil Allen was sentenced to hard labour for life.

Back in Australia, Lieutenant Convery's father, Bernard Convery, told reporters he wasn't bitter about Private Allen. He blamed the culture of drinking that was revealed in the trial. 'It was the party that caused the tragedy. If the soldiers had not been drinking heavily and there had not been a hate session it would never have happened.' Mr Convery, who'd been a sergeant in the Korean War, said the NCOs should never have allowed soldiers to talk openly about ambushing sergeants, and should have closed down the party themselves. 'If the NCOs had been doing their job, Robbie wouldn't have had to go down to their tents.'

Allen's father, Athol Allen, told reporters that his son always seemed to have been in trouble. 'He was just a boy. You know what boys are, but he always copped it. You'd think his name was trouble.'

The Sydney Morning Herald editorialised that the trial had exposed a problem with drinking in the lines, and that this seemed to be accepted as perfectly normal by the army. 'These, after all, are troops on active service and Nui Dat is an operational base.' The *Herald* demanded the army hold an inquiry into the administration of the base.

But there were several matters that were not pursued in the court martial. Allen had been desperate to get out of being a forward scout, but was constantly ordered back into the position. The forward scout was the most exposed and dangerous position on a patrol, the first to come into contact with the enemy, and the scout was on constant high alert looking for an enemy ambush or booby trap. Allen's army papers revealed that in April 1969 he formally applied to be transferred out of 4RAR to a D&E Platoon in Saigon or Vung Tau 'because I have been a forward scout since early January and would like a change if at all possible'. The application was denied by his commanding officer, who wrote Allen could be useful to another battalion after 4RAR went home.

When 4RAR went back to Australia in May, Allen was put in the 2nd D&E Platoon with the other men of the battalion who had not finished their 12-month tour. Allen went back to Australia on 16 May for a week's R&R. On 23 May at Sydney airport he vanished for 45 minutes and missed the plane about to take him back to Vietnam. For that absence without leave

(AWL) he was fined $40. Allen didn't get back to Vietnam until 28 May. The very next day he was sent out with the 2nd D&E Platoon and found himself with Riddle in the isolated forward lookout section at the Thua Tich ambush.

A week later he was assigned to the 9th Battalion and was once again put in the dangerous forward scout position. There is no record of him protesting about it, but the court martial did not pursue whether the strain of being a forward scout for close to 11 months, as well as being in the forward section at the Thua Tich ambush, could have had an effect on Allen.

Defence counsel did press the company commander, Captain Graham Dugdale, on how long a soldier should be kept at forward scout. Dugdale said it depended on the person, but the optimum time would be two to three hours a day as it was the most dangerous and tense position a soldier could be in. Dugdale said a commander would remove his forward scout if he thought they were under strain as it would endanger the whole unit. Dugdale said Allen had shown he had the ability to be a forward scout and Corporal Cunich decided to make him a scout. Surprisingly, the defence counsel did not pursue this matter any further, and simply dropped what could have been a viable argument to explain Allen's irrational behaviour. The army might have been embarrassed if it emerged they had pushed a soldier too far and failed to recognise it.

The court martial also did not pursue the matter of the discussion in the tent of murdering Sergeant Cross. Was this accepted talk in the ranks? The focus was on Private Allen, but the assembled senior officers did not try to find out which of the men in the tent had suggested killing a sergeant.

The army had a very real reason to be embarrassed about Private Allen. His personal records suggest he should not have been in the army at all. When Allen first applied to join the army he was just 17. The recruiting officer was definite: 'Absolutely nothing to offer the army and seems the erupting type – Unsuitable'. Allen was rejected. That was 1967. The war was still fairly popular and the army was not struggling for recruits. They didn't need misfits. The recruiting officer described Allen:

> Pansyish, long-haired individual, scared and shy and apathetic and offhand. Gets drunk regularly (age 17!). Last May got booked on two charges of assault and abusive behaviour. Quiet waters run deep when they are drunk . . . Hopeless underachiever, looks like potential trouble to me.

They were prophetic words. Twelve months later Allen applied once again to join the army. By 1968 the Vietnam War was producing hefty casualties and the army was finding it more difficult to get volunteers. Conscription had been stepped up and for the first time in Australian history conscripts were being sent to a foreign war. This time Allen got a more welcoming reception. The recruiting officer noted Allen appeared to have matured over the past year and was now clean cut. 'Nevertheless quiet, colourless and unimpressive. Intelligent underperformer.

Think however he is capable of adjusting to service life even if he is unlikely to be very adaptive – Accept.'

A few months into his training, a 1968 report said he was 'a thin lad, colourless personality. Submissive little man who says he likes action. Apparently coping all right with training. Should give adequate service.' But obviously he wasn't coping. In May 1968 he went AWL from a training base at Kapooka NSW and spent ten days on the run before he was found by military police at Melbourne's Spencer Street Station absolutely drunk. A few months later he was sent to fight in Vietnam.

•

Peter Allen spent just ten and a half years locked up in Risdon Prison near Hobart in Tasmania. It was a civilian jail. The army simply didn't have a facility that could keep a prisoner for years on end. A life sentence usually meant 20 years, and with good behaviour a prisoner could expect to be out in about 13 or 14 years. Allen was released early, and even today nobody can explain why.

In 2010, responding to a question lodged through the Defence Department's media unit, the Department said it could find no papers offering a reason why Allen was released early. The official reply from Defence public affairs officer Elliott Bator states:

> Private P.D. Allen was sentenced by a General Court Martial
> on 15 January 1970. H.M. Prison Risdon, Tasmania, has

indicated that Mr P.D. Allen was paroled on 8 July 1980. It was indicated that the Governor-General granted Mr Allen's release, but no information could be found regarding the reasons for his release.

Defence had no answer to questions about why the Governor-General at the time, Sir Zelman Cowen, would have granted Allen's release. They had no answer as to whether the Defence Department, Defence Minister Jim Killen, or anyone in the Liberal government of the day led by Prime Minister Malcolm Fraser were consulted in the decision to release Allen.

Peter Allen himself doesn't know why he got out in ten and a half years. Responding in 2010 via email from his home, Allen thought he must have been a bit of a political football in the prison system. 'I was a federal prisoner in a state prison. There was a feeling that most people didn't believe I should have been in prison and there would be no public backlash if I was released,' he said in reply to questions for this book.

Allen said that in 1975 he wrote to Labor Prime Minister Gough Whitlam asking for parole since the Vietnam War was over. The request was passed to the then Attorney-General Lionel Murphy. Allen said Murphy told him to 'kick along with it'. It may be that the paperwork moved around for another five years until 1980 when the then Liberal Attorney-General, Peter Durack, finally approved it. Durack, who died in 2008, was a highly respected legal reformer who fought for human rights.

Whatever the reason for his early release, forty years after he murdered Lieutenant Convery, Allen offered some thoughts as to why he did it. He said he was angry at the way the army treated enlisted men, and after almost 12 months in Vietnam he'd become disillusioned with the war and totally changed his mind about whether he should be fighting. The only reason Allen offered for the murder was that after 12 months as a forward scout he had built up a 'blood lust' and life was cheap. 'The cheapness of life and blood lust built up over my time in Vietnam combined to make me do the act,' he said.

'It's something that I wouldn't have done under normal circumstances, like if I'd been in civvie street. I actually thought at the time that I was doing more good than harm, which sounds rather stupid now. My lawyer at the time said I should only have been found guilty of manslaughter, and I still believe that I was railroaded to a certain extent.

'Of course I was suffering the psychological effects of Vietnam. I think we all did.'

Allen said that after his release from jail in 1980 he had problems with alcohol and drug abuse. He was charged with drink driving and later had a nervous breakdown. 'I was diagnosed with post-traumatic stress disorder. I think now I have come to terms with everything, and mentally at least my life is on a fairly even keel.'

Allen couldn't remember much about the Thua Tich ambush. He could only recall being out with the platoon, but the night of the firefight and the morning after with the bodies on the road appeared to have been wiped from his mind. The only thing he had a clear memory of was being on sentry duty behind an APC and seeing a very strange iguana, long and thin with long legs. 'After mentioning this it was recommended I be sent back to Nui Dat as everyone thought I was crazy.'

But he insisted incidents like the dragging of bodies behind APCs and the blowing up of enemy bodies with explosives happened all the time in Vietnam. 'We were always supposed to bury dead bodies. I've seen bodies buried where the re-supply choppers were to land with arms and legs left stuck up out of the ground to shock the chopper pilots. A lot of bad stuff happened there.'

Peter Allen was right about lot of bad stuff happening. This was war, after all. But for every soldier there is a breaking point – and it seems in Vietnam, especially, war had changed. The horror of unnecessary death was too often evident. For Jim Riddle and the soldiers at Thua Tich, 'bad stuff' had definitely happened.

8

THE COVER-UP BEGINS

Within days of the ambush at Thua Tich, the way enemy bodies had been treated began to be covered up. What had been a textbook military operation with many enemy dead and no fatalities on the Australian side quickly transformed into a major embarrassment for the top brass.

It started when the photographs taken by Sergeant Chris Bellis reached the army public relations headquarters in Canberra. Bellis had done his job well, but not in a manner the PR heads could appreciate. Bellis had cut his photographic teeth working for an Adelaide newspaper. As a young cub news photographer he'd chased his fair share of ambulances and been on police raids. He had a good eye for it. When he got his call up papers he dreaded having to slog through the jungles of Vietnam as a grunt, and asked Defence if he could join the army public relations department as a photographer instead.

The army agreed, as long as he signed up for three years. Bellis did so, but it was an awkward fit. An army PR photographer is supposed to take pictures that make the public feel good about military operations. So there were plenty of snaps of happy soldiers playing cards back at base, bold warriors patrolling the jungle paths against a dangerous unseen enemy, commanders pinning medals on brave Anzac chests and politicians bringing joy to the troops by their mere presence. What they didn't do very often was get good photographs of Australian troops in action. It's not that they didn't try, but it was tough getting good action shots in Vietnam. The enemy was usually hidden in the jungle, and firefights in the open were few and far between. What they weren't supposed to do was take photos that might harm the war effort, such as images of dead Australian troops – or pictures of Australian troops doing anything that would disturb the folks back home.

When Bellis's dramatic shots of the action at Thua Tich reached Canberra, army PR officials were initially ecstatic. The image of the 2nd D&E's Len Ellcombe, bravely blasting away at the VC as he surfed an APC on the way to Xuyen Moc, was immediately hailed by his colleagues as the photo of the year. It was released instantly to the media and was published widely in newspapers around Australia.

James Riddle's earliest memories were of German warplanes bombing the street where he lived in Newcastle upon Tyne in northern England. The Germans were trying to hit a nearby tank factory.

Riddle joined the Royal Marines as soon as he was old enough. He was desperate to get away from home and his abusive father, a World War Two hero and major in the army.

Riddle in Vietnam wearing his Royal Marine beret, something the Australian army wouldn't let him do. They also failed to recognise the sergeant stripes, parachute or commando qualifications he earned with the British Marines.

Don Tate in Vietnam.

An unnamed soldier looks back at armoured personnel carriers in front of the battered gate of the abandoned village of Thua Tich. During the night ambush the APCs were in among the trees to the left of the gate. The low grasses allowed an excellent fire zone.

(top) Denis Gibbons's photo of Cavalry Trooper Peter Board in the aftermath of the ambush. The photograph was published by *The Australian* newspaper under the headline 'Digger counts the dead'.

(middle) Privates Don Moss, David Simpson and Ted Colmer of the 2nd D&E Platoon examine enemy weapons captured at the Thua Tich ambush.

(bottom) Ghost Platoon members Private David Simpson (*left*) and Private Richard 'Barney' Bigwood drag an enemy body toward a crater where they will be blown up in a controversial 'engineer's burial'. Private Dennis 'Snow' Manski stands on the right holding something to his face. The soldier with the gun is unidentified.

Lance Corporal Len Ellcombe of the Ghost Platoon rides his APC like a giant metal surfboard as he blazes away with his M-60 machine gun. Holding his feet is Private Brian 'Jock' Rennie. Sergeant Chris Bellis took the dramatic photo during the VC ambush of the convoy on its way to Xuyen Moc.

The district chief of Xuyen Moc, Major Le Van Que (*left*) and Captain Tom Arrowsmith, cavalry commander at the Thua Tich ambush, discuss the operation. Arrowsmith was ordered to take enemy bodies from the ambush to Xuyen Moc for propaganda purposes.

Nguyen Van Sang, the security chief for Xuyen Moc in 1969, said in 2010 that the bodies were never claimed and were buried in unmarked graves outside the town.

One of the photographs glued into the army public relations photo album which was taken by Sergeant Bellis as the APC convoy entered Xuyen Moc. Someone erased part of the original caption that said villagers were looking at bodies being dragged behind an APC, then written 'Not correct' on the right.

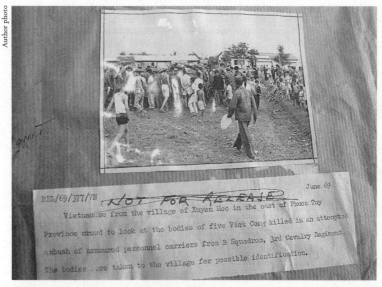

Another of the shots taken by Sergeant Bellis showing villagers crowding around the dead bodies (not in view), marked 'Not for release'. A third photo in the sequence showing bodies on ropes behind an APC did not make it into the album.

(above) Private Peter Denzil Allen, charged with the murder of Lieutenant Robert Convery.

(top right) Private Allen's court martial made the front page of *The Sydney Morning Herald* and played a part in turning public opinion against the war.

(right) This 1966 photo of an American troop carrier dragging the body of dead Viet Cong caused an outcry when it was published in *The Sydney Morning Herald*. The photo, taken by Kyoichi Sawada, won the 1966 World Press Photo of the Year, and shows that towing enemy bodies was not uncommon.

(above) The battered gate to Thua Tich as it
is today. The village was razed to the ground
during the war, before the ambush in 1969. The
village was not rebuilt, but houses line the road.

(left) A Vietnamese war memorial erected
next to the old Thua Tich gate.

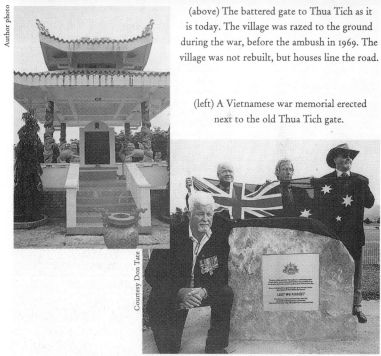

Ghost Platoon members (*from left*) Don Tate, Richard 'Barney' Bigwood,
Kevin Lloyd-Thomas and Ted Colmer at the unveiling of a Vietnam War
memorial which paid tribute to the leadership of Jim Riddle.

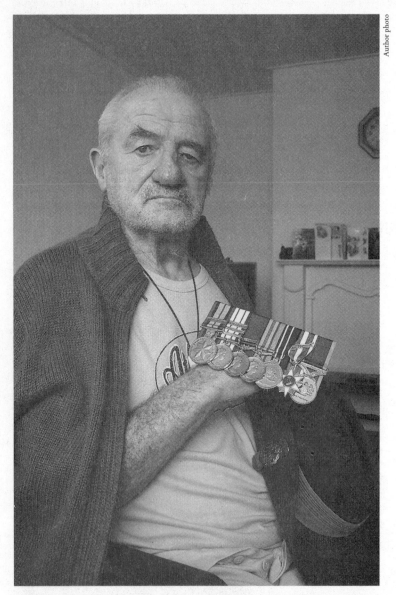

Wheelchair-bound Jim Riddle at his flat in Newcastle upon Tyne proudly shows his medals and an Aussie slouch hat one of his digger mates gave him. Riddle says: 'We all died in that war – some of us are just taking longer to stop breathing.'

But when they looked at the other photos Bellis had taken at the ambush site at Thua Tich they shuddered. His graphic images of Australian diggers walking among the enemy dead were dutifully logged in a central photographic record the PR department kept in their office, a big hand made album of giant sheets of brown butcher's paper measuring about two feet square. Every photo sent back by the Army's photographers was given a number and carefully glued into the album, with its caption glued in underneath. The numbering system wasn't always in sequence. For instance, Bellis's picture of Ellcombe surfing the top of the APC on the way to Xuyen Moc was numbered 353, while the pictures of troops walking among the dead in the aftermath of the earlier action at Thua Tich were numbered higher, in the 360s and 370s.

The album wasn't an official record of the photos taken in Vietnam. It was simply a ready reference for public relations officers to find photos easily rather than having to sift through piles of envelopes and files. The album was also where senior military officers censored pictures, banning them from public release and even destroying some images they didn't want ever getting out to the public. In 1984, 12 years after the last Australian troops left Vietnam, the Defence Department transferred many of its war records and photographs to the Australian War Memorial (AWM) nearby in Canberra. The album went with them. Available in the War Memorial archives today, the album reveals the extent to which Defence PR sought to cover up the gruesome reality of war.

Any picture glued into the album that showed the shattered remains of enemy bodies was outlined in red pen and the words 'Not for Release' scrawled over the caption. Bellis's shocking picture of diggers dragging enemy bodies by the heels towards the burial pit at Thua Tich was deemed not fit for the public to see and was marked in this way. So were his dramatic close-up pictures of a dead Vietnamese soldier lying on the road, Australian diggers milling around looking on in the background. This kind of suppression happened often. Photographs of other firefights taken by Bellis which showed enemy bodies on the ground had actually been ripped out of the album, the space where it had been glued marked 'Censored'.

But the photos were not lost to history. Every army PR photograph taken in Vietnam was sent back to Canberra by the photographer in its own separate brown envelope. It contained a print of the image stapled to the envelope along with a brief description of where and when it was taken. Inside the envelope was the negative and two copies of the caption from the photographer.

The decision to censor photos or mark them 'Not for Release' seem to have come from the very top of the Army PR hierarchy. In 1969 the head of the Defence photographic section was Major Ross McKenzie. He reported to the deputy director of the Defence Public Affairs unit, Lieutenant Colonel Lance Logan. It's undestood that both have since died, but according to people who worked as PR officers at the time, most decisions to censor photographs came from them.

However, there was one occasion when film footage sent back by one of the photographers caused the chief of the defence force himself, General Sir Thomas Daly, to hit the roof. It was dramatic action captured of a patrol that had run into some armed Viet Cong. The footage showed troops chasing several VC up a road, shooting as they ran. The diggers killed two of them and dragged the bodies back closer to their APCs to search them for documents. One of the dead was a woman, and as she was dragged her loose pants came off on the ground, leaving her naked from the waist down. The photographer kept on filming as a soldier laughed and stuck the muzzle of his rifle into her vagina. The photographer left the footage on the film he sent back to Canberra, thinking that it would give the lads in the photographic section a laugh before they cut if off the reel.

But they didn't. As one former PR officer told it, Major McKenzie saw only the first half of the footage and was so excited that he called in the top brass, including General Daly, to view the film. He explained it was very rare, dramatic footage as it was out in the open and that the photographer had risked his life to get it: it was possible the fleeing VC were leading them all into a trap. But as the film played to the end and revealed the digger's callous act, General Daly rose from his chair in a fury and ordered the entire film be destroyed. Then he ordered the photographer be pulled out of Vietnam in disgrace and the soldier who committed the act reprimanded. If the footage had found its way to the press it would have been disastrous for the army and destroyed their efforts to maintain public approval for the war.

Former members of the army public affairs team stress that theirs was a public relations operation, not a news agency. Their task was to boost army morale and present the best possible public image of what the army was doing in Vietnam. 'Of course there were dead bodies, that was what the troops were there for – to kill the enemy,' said one former officer who did not want to be named. 'But as a PR machine, it wasn't our job to lay out these gruesome sights in front of the punters in their morning paper as they ate their cornflakes.'

It's strange, then, that two pictures among the photographs Bellis sent back to Canberra which didn't show any dead bodies at all were clearly marked 'Not for Release' in the album. They had been taken at the town of Xuyen Moc, after the action at Thua Tich and the second firefight.

Photo number 376 shows a group of Vietnamese children and one man looking shocked and horrified as they stare at something just off to the left and below where Bellis took the photo. He was sitting on top of Arrowsmith's APC, so what they were looking at was on the ground behind the vehicle. One little boy is using his hand to cover his mouth and nose. Two young girls look absolutely horrified at what they see off camera. What is more significant about this is that someone in Canberra was desperate to destroy evidence of what the children were looking at. The caption glued into the album, which would have been sent by Bellis, has been partly obliterated by someone scratching over it thoroughly with a pen. Half a dozen words have been deliberately obscured. A small arrow points to two words handwritten beside the caption: 'Not Correct'.

It isn't clear whether the censorship of the words happened while the album was in the army public affairs unit, or after it was handed over to the Australian War Memorial archives in 1984. But War Memorial archivist Joanne Smedley says the tampering must have happened many years ago as it's against War Memorial policy to deface any original document held in their archives. 'We have no idea where or when or by whom the album caption for Number 376 was partially scratched out,' she says.

All of the photos originally marked 'Not for Release', as well those marked 'Censored', were eventually released to the public in 1997 on the Australian War Memorial's website. Ms Smedley said the 'Not for Release' markings weren't given any extra consideration about whether or not to post them on the website, as the entire photo series had already been 'access examined and cleared'.

The caption supplied by the Australian War Memorial for photo 376 says:

Xuyen Moc – Villagers in eastern Phuoc Tuy province recoil at the sight of the bodies (not in view) of dead Viet Cong killed when they attempted to ambush armoured personnel carriers (APCs) of 2 Troop, B Squadron, 3rd Cavalry Regiment in an area north of the village.

But whoever tried to wipe Bellis's original caption from the record forgot about the duplicate caption kept in the envelope that he'd sent back to Canberra. That caption is still there in the envelope four decades on. The difference is slight, yet significant. It reads:

> Villagers of Xuyen Moc in eastern Phuoc Tuy Province recoil at the sight of Viet Cong bodies being dragged along behind an armoured personnel carrier of 2 Troop, B Squadron, 3rd Cavalry Regiment. The enemy were killed when they attempted to ambush the Australians in an area north of the village.

The words the Defence censor had obliterated in the album were: 'bodies being dragged along behind an armoured personnel carrier'. It was the very start of attempts by the army to eliminate any record of the event.

The next photo in the Bellis series stuck into the album was numbered 377. Taken from about 20 metres away, it shows a large crowd of more than 100 Vietnamese villagers gathered around something in their midst that can't be seen by the camera. Off to the left are four Australian cavalrymen, recognisable by their distinctive black berets. The caption reads:

> Xuyen Moc – Villagers in eastern Phuoc Tuy Province crowd to look at the bodies (not in view) of five dead Viet Cong killed in an attempted ambush of armoured personnel carriers from 2 Troop, B Squadron, 3rd Cavalry Regiment, in an area

north of the village. The bodies were taken to the village for possible identification.

It's not clear why the caption states five bodies were displayed at Xuyen Moc. Perhaps two more were added later, or Bellis got the number wrong.

This seemingly innocuous photo in the album was also marked in red pen 'Not for Release'. The caption on the War Memorial website is unchanged from Bellis's original. Why would the army public relations top brass have ordered this photo be banned from the public? It didn't show any gruesome bodies. It didn't mention dragging bodies behind an APC.

The answer is that there is one photo missing from the sequence. Bellis took another photograph in between numbers 376 and 377 – one that was considered to be so damaging it was destroyed by the top brass. It didn't even make it to the album.

Photo 376, the image of village children recoiling in horror, was taken by Bellis as the APC he was riding on rolled into the market square of Xuyen Moc, the bodies being dragged by ropes behind. As the APC came to a stop, Bellis jumped off. From about ten metres away, he took a photo of the bodies, then moved further away and took photo 377. By this time the villagers had completely enclosed the scene and Bellis's photo showed only their backs, the bodies hidden from sight.

The story of the missing photo doesn't end there. Bellis had copies of all the photos that he took in Vietnam, as well as the contact sheets. He'd kept them for 41 years since the war.

From his home in a remote part of Australia, Bellis told me, 'I vividly recall Captain Tom Arrowsmith saying to me, "Don't take any pictures of the bodies" . . . So I did.' Like so many press photographers, Bellis hated being told by others what photograph to take and what not to take. And understandably so – it's an insult to their professionalism. When a press photographer is told *not* to take a picture, they will invariably take it anyway, even if they never use it.

'Of course the bodies were dragged into Xuyen Moc,' Bellis said. 'That is shown by the look on the people's faces in photo number 376.' And after some searching among his photographic records, Bellis found the photo he'd taken between 376 and 377. 'The image shows three bodies behind an APC with a hootchie [a canvas sheet used as shelter] hanging around the back of it and a mob of people hanging around looking on. It's a picture I took from the rear probably about 20 to 30 feet away. You can clearly see the three bodies.'

Crucially, Bellis revealed that he didn't have the negative, which means he must have sent the picture and the negative to Canberra in an envelope as he did for other photographs he took that day. This photograph was not filed in the album. The only possible conclusion is that it had been destroyed by someone in army public relations or elsewhere in the army hierarchy in Canberra – a conclusion that is bolstered by the attempted scratching out of Bellis's damning caption which stated bodies were dragged behind an APC.

•

Bellis wouldn't have known it at the time, but the strong reaction in Canberra to his photo of bodies being towed behind an Australian APC was due to a similar photo published three years earlier. On 26 February 1966, *The Sydney Morning Herald* ran a photo on page three of an American APC towing the dead body of a Viet Cong on a rope behind it, an American soldier sitting triumphantly on the vehicle's turret above the gruesome scene.

The picture had an immediate impact on the public. Several disgusted people wrote protest letters to the editor of the *Herald.* One said the photo didn't 'ring true'and must be a fake. 'It looks like a typical anti-USA propaganda horror photo . . . I don't believe it,' penned F.E. McElhone of Sydney. Frank Sawyer of Collaroy Plateau said he hoped bodies of Australian soldiers would be treated better if they were captured by the enemy. 'What could be the purpose of this callous method of removing a body?' he asked. 'Was it done (horrible thought) in order to terrorise a village sympathetic to the Viet Cong?'

How right he was. Three years later the Australian cavalry unit did exactly the same for just that purpose, albeit at the request of the local South Vietnamese army officer.

Allan Anderson of Port Macquarie wrote to the Minister for the Army, Malcolm Fraser, to express his disgust. Anderson's letter and Fraser's reply were revealed in a confidential file opened only in 2011 at the National Archives. The file was called 'Allegations concerning atrocities in Vietnam'. The exchange of letters from 1966 was significant considering what happened to the photo taken three years later by Bellis.

Anderson sent his letter to both Fraser and the *Herald* editor. 'All Australian troops should be warned that if they behave in such a barbaric manner they should be punished for all the world to see,' Anderson wrote. He said war was a dirty business, but dragging the body of an enemy killed in action was an unnecessary step too far and that, 'Any nation that allows such behaviour to go unpunished is branded uncivilised, barbaric and not fit to be a member of associations of honourable nations.'

The letter struck a chord with Fraser. It came at a critical moment for the Australian government as in less than a week's time they were planning to announce they would treble the number of Australian troops in Vietnam, including for the first time young men who had been conscripted. It was a huge step for Australia. Throughout two world wars and the Korean War, Australia had never sent conscripts to fight overseas. Fraser would have known this momentous and controversial announcement was going to be made within a matter of days. The government was desperate to tamp down any anti-war sentiment that could be built on such horrific photographs coming out of Vietnam.

Under his Minister for the Army letterhead, Fraser immediately wrote back to Anderson saying he agreed with him. 'I do not think any decent person would quarrel with your description of the photograph . . . I am pleased to recall that the photograph was not linked in any way with the activities of Australian troops in Vietnam. Indeed, I think it is a fair thing to say that the dragging of a dead enemy behind a vehicle would be repugnant to the very fine men – both Australian and American – in Vietnam.'

Fraser concluded the letter saying he suspected the photo was a fake and had been distributed as communist propaganda. 'Like you, I very much suspect the origin of the photograph. It has not been unknown for the communist authorities in Hanoi to manufacture false photographs for their own purposes.'

Publishing the offending photo caused such an uproar and cries of fakery that the editor of the *Herald* took the rare move a few days later to explain its origin. In a note on the letters page, the editor explained the image of an American APC towing a dead Viet Cong by ropes was supplied by the American newsagency United Press International. 'If newspapers refused to publish such pictures they would be denying their readers information just as surely as if they refused to publish unfavourable dispatches,' the editor said.

Three years later when Bellis's photo of the three dead Viet Cong being towed by an Australian APC landed in Canberra, Fraser had been promoted to Minister for Defence. If Bellis's image, or even word about the incident, had reached the public sphere, Fraser would have been made to look a total hypocrite because of his 1966 letter. It is not known whether

Fraser ever saw the photograph, but what seems likely is that the army brass buried the photo and covered up the incident.

Other former members of the army public relations team from that era, including several who were close colleagues of Bellis, all confirmed that the army brass in Canberra routinely ordered the destruction of photographs which would have damaged the army's reputation. One former colleague and friend of Bellis – who did not want to be named – said that several years ago Bellis had shown him photographs he'd kept from the war. The friend confirmed Bellis had kept many photographs that were not included in the Australian War Memorial collection, but he couldn't be certain he saw the photo showing enemy bodies towed behind the APC at Xuyen Moc.

When I initially spoke to Bellis he recalled he had more photos taken on the way to Xuyen Moc after the herringbone manoeuvre in the bush. 'I have three pictures of a group of females all in black pyjamas; four of them and a little girl,' he said. 'They have their hands on their heads. It's taken from behind the turret of the APC with a 50 calibre machine gun pointing at them.' Bellis said the talk among the Australians in the APC at the time was along the lines of, 'More fuckin' VC. Are we going to blow them away?' He said, 'We suspected they may have been part of the same mob [from the ambush] and we were wondering if we were going to shoot them, too.

They were out in a rice paddy and we had stopped to check them out.' He didn't say whether the soldiers in the column had fired on the villagers in the field, or whether he'd taken pictures of any bodies in the field.

I told Bellis I would fly across the country to come and talk to him about the photos, and we set a time and date for a few days' time. Six hours later, Bellis rang to call off my visit. He was distressed and nervous. He now had second thoughts. Bellis said he didn't need the hassle in his life of all this being raised again.

'I've only thought about the bloody war three or four times in the past 40 years. Since I talked to you it has brought it all up again, and I don't want to be part of it.'

Finally, after a week of my efforts to change his mind, Bellis wished me luck with the book but said that he no longer wanted to talk to me about the photographs.

'You have inspired me to do what I should have done a long time ago,' he said. 'I have burned the lot.'

•

The account given by Bellis was backed up in a separate interview I did with Allan Stanton, the driver of Captain Arrowsmith's APC which Bellis was sitting on when he took photo 376. Stanton had written in his 2009 memoir *Before I Forget* that enemy bodies killed at Thua Tich had been blown up after the ambush.

In his book Stanton said the bodies were hung by their ankles from the back of an APC to be taken into Xuyen Moc. 'That is accurate,' he told me. 'The bodies weren't dragged back all the way. They were tied up to the back of the chariot, and they came loose as we approached Xuyen Moc. Unfortunately their heads were battered and parts of the skulls were missing.'

Stanton also confirmed the lead APCs shot into the rice paddies after they emerged from the jungle. 'As we came into open ground we could see the houses of the village about a kilometre ahead. A group of civilians were standing in a paddock and the lead APCs fired one or two bursts from the 30 cals, but they saw they were civilians and stopped.' He insisted no civilians were hit by rounds fired. 'We stopped to check, and we could see no one was wounded or hit, so we moved on. It is total bullshit to suggest someone was killed or run over. It didn't happen.'

Stanton's account helps to explain Bellis's photograph of the terrified peasants in the field, standing with their hands on their heads. It is also possible that if somebody had been hit and collapsed into a rice paddy they might not have been seen. Stanton felt Arrowsmith was unfairly 'shafted' for the blowing up of the bodies at Thua Tich. 'We had orders to dispose of the bodies and we were in a position where there was a large force of enemy somewhere around us. We had to move quickly.' He showed Arrowsmith the passage about it in his manuscript before his memoir was published. 'He didn't have a problem with it. He said we all knew it happened; the army knew about it.'

'Look, a lot worse things happened in that war than blowing up bodies at Thua Tich. We had to go out and pick up SAS blokes in the bush and some of the things we saw there were really bad, hair-curling stuff. But that sort of thing will never make it to the public.'

Tom Arrowsmith declined to make any comment. His army mates said he is reluctant to talk about the whole Thua Tich matter, even with them. They believe it damaged his military career. He spends much of his time travelling in a campervan around remote parts of Australia with his wife.

•

In 1976, a few years after the Vietnam War was over, one of the army engineers who'd placed the explosives under the bodies at Thua Tich rang a radio station and told them his conscience had been weighing heavily on him. On air, the engineer said that he'd taken part in an atrocity, blowing up enemy bodies, then told the announcer that several enemy bodies were tied to the back of an APC and dragged to Xuyen Moc.

When pressed by the media for answers, the army ordered an inquiry. The task was given to Major Gordon Pound. He'd been an artillery captain for six months in the Vietnam War, then nine months with the Australian Civil Affairs Unit, a specialist group which built infrastructure and carried out medical and welfare projects for Vietnamese civilians as part of the 'winning hearts and minds' campaign. He'd been based for a time at Xuyen Moc, so he knew the area and what went on there.

Major Pound found no evidence of any wrongdoing. According to Defence documents obtained under Freedom of Information legislation, the army said Major Pound's investigation found 'there was insufficient evidence upon which to proceed'. But Defence could not produce Major Pound's actual report. They said it would have been included in army records from that era that were sent to the National Archives. In their documents, Defence had blacked out the name of the engineer who had raised the original claim on the radio. Some of the 2nd D&E Platoon veterans say they know who it was, but when they contacted him many years later he denied being the one. In fact, he denied ever being in the army.

Six months of searching in the National Archives by archivists failed to find the 1976 report by Major Pound, and their frequent requests to the army for help proved fruitless. The Pound Report seems to have completely disappeared from public records.

In another document obtained under the Freedom of Information act, the Australian War Memorial's chief military historian, Ashley Ekins, said in a 2008 email to Army historian Bill Houston about the atrocity allegations, that War Memorial researchers had been unable to find any evidence in the records to support the claims and that 'contradictory evidence from other soldiers makes it impossible either to verify or disprove these claims'.

Ekins declined interview requests about the matter for this book, as well as questions as to whether he has personally sighted the Pound report.

Veterans of the 2nd D&E Platoon believe the Pound report was little more than a whitewash. They say Pound did not speak to any of the soldiers who were there. They believe he merely looked at the army's operational records of the day. It was hardly surprising the major found nothing in those official records saying they had blown up enemy bodies and dragged them across the countryside behind an APC.

One thing is certain: Pound's report allowed army chiefs to insist there was no evidence anything untoward had happened.

•

Jim Riddle and several other members of the 2nd D&E Platoon said the ambush at Thua Tich was highly unusual because it was outside the range of artillery support. It was the extraordinary accuracy of artillery that saved Australian troops during the battle of Long Tan in 1966. Since then it had been standard practice to mount operations only with the possibility of that kind of support.

In the years after the war, the army dismissed concerns expressed by platoon members that they'd been ordered to take part in a highly risky, dangerous mission. They argued the APCs had mortars, and this was adequate to mount the ambush. However, retired Brigadier Vince Williams, a former artillery officer and Macquarie University lecturer, said there was no situation in Vietnam where regular troops fought without artillery cover. 'Having troops operate without indirect fire support is bizarre and dangerous,' Williams stated. He was making his comment about troops in Afghanistan complaining about a soldier being killed in an action where they had no mortars and no artillery coverage.[1]

Little has changed in war.

9

THE WAR THAT NEVER ENDS

Don Tate's problem is that he doesn't remember a thing about the Thua Tich ambush. It's been driven from his mind.

Some of his 2nd D&E Platoon mates say he was with Arrowsmith at the old shellmarked gate. Others suggest he must have been with the men of the platoon north of the gate, positioned there with the nine APCs which were not involved in the action, but came down in the early morning. Riddle says he remembers Tate risking his neck to deliver ammunition to the forward section in the heat of battle. 'Silly bugger threw it and clocked me on the head,' he says. No one else remembers that. Tate just doesn't know where he was.

Tate's enemies among the Vietnam veterans, and there are many, claim he wasn't at the ambush at all. But then, they certainly weren't there either, so their claims can't be relied upon. But as Tate became a leading figure in the fight to win recognition for the 2nd D&E Platoon, his memory gap became a cudgel used to bash his reputation.

Tate's fight began decades ago when he discovered the army's official record keepers were denying that the entire 2nd D&E Platoon ever existed. The army said there was no trace of such a platoon. There wasn't a single mention of them in the files. And if the platoon never existed, then it followed that the atrocities that Tate and some others were claiming occurred could never have happened.

Tate reveals the dilemma as he sits in a corner of his living room in a working-class town on the coast south of Sydney. As he fought a long and bitter battle to get official recognition of the platoon he turned the room into a campaign office. A big bull of a man with a white goatee who never backs away from a fight, Tate struggles with a hip that was badly wounded during the war. He insists he does remember the drive into Xuyen Moc on the APCs. There's a sequence of images in his mind of a woman being killed in the paddy fields. It runs over and over, like a silent movie on an endless loop. But the rest is blank.

The platoon was broken up almost immediately after the Thua Tich action. Tate says they got a few days' leave and went into Vung Tau to raise hell with grog and Vietnamese women who were available for a few bucks. Troops who'd been jungle fighters strongly resented the 'pogo bastards' – servicemen who rarely left the safety of headquarters or the rear echelons of the supply base. He remembers Riddle plonking the large pile of cash he'd taken from a dead VC on the bar and telling the bar girls to keep the beers coming until it was all gone.

'The pogos watched us in horror as we were a filthy stinking mob of blokes, but we didn't give a stuff,' he recalls. We'd been in the bush risking our necks while they sat back in safety making up stories of how they'd been in the horror of war. Bullshit. We'd seen it all, and we had blood on our hands. We would be stuck with the fucking nightmares. We drank and got stuck into the women as though we were trying to wipe ourselves clean.'

A camaraderie had grown among the men of the platoon. They had lived through intense fighting together and they had survived. They were pariahs among the officers and men of Nui Dat as word had got around about the treatment of the bodies. As they drank themselves stupid on the liberated cash of the enemy, some swore eternal mateship to each other. Tate solemnly shook Riddle's hand and thanked him for looking out for him and the unit. Tate says Riddle became quite emotional. He confided that this compliment was worth more than a medal to him and that he'd always have a special spot in his memory for Tate and the men of the 2nd D&E Platoon.

When they eventually got back to Nui Dat the platoon was split up and sent to different units. Riddle, Tate and most of the platoon members were posted to the 9th Battalion, but scattered across the various companies and platoons. Few were kept together. For Tate, it was the fourth unit he'd been allocated to in the seven months he'd been in Vietnam. This constant movement was a disadvantage for soldiers in war. The new arrival in a unit always struggles to fit in. An outsider, he doesn't know the intimate details of how a close unit of fighting men anticipate each other's moves in action, how they work together, who to trust with your life, how the NCO and officer operate under fire.

He found out a few weeks later. The company that Tate was now a member of was ordered to advance up a gap in the hills of the Long Khanh mountain range. The day before they'd encountered a squad of VC in a creek and after a brief firefight two VC were left dead. But several were thought to have got away and escaped up the hill. Tate's company had been ordered to follow them in the hope it would lead to a VC stronghold, which they would then attack. When he heard the news, Tate exchanged a glance with a machine gunner he'd befriended. They knew they were being ordered to move into a trap.

As Tate described the action in his 2008 memoir *The War Within,* the heavy storm clouds that had gathered overhead suddenly broke, thunder and lightning crashed, and rain thrashed down. The men couldn't see a thing in the thick jungle ahead and still their young lieutenant ordered the section to advance. US bombers had hit the area for days, and the ground ahead was littered with the debris of smashed trees and craters.

Tate had been made scout, which meant he was usually out in front of all the others. With six months' experience under his belt Tate had got over the youthful need for heroics, the belief that you are invulnerable. He knew death, and what a body hit by machine-gun fire looked like. He wasn't keen on becoming one himself. He promised himself that when he came under fire he would take it steady, judging what was needed to be done, and doing it as safely as he could. No more than that. No charging ahead, leaping over ramparts. Keep it simple.

One section was out in front of Tate's as they moved up the hill. He was happy about that. Another scout in Tate's section, Private Ray Kermode, a conscript who had been in Vietnam nine months, volunteered to take the lead as Tate had been out front the day before. It was a fateful decision, and one that would haunt Tate all his life.

The storm broke with all its fury as they moved up the hill and the rain pelted down. It was tough going following a narrow trail around boulders, over tree roots and fallen logs. The track became a muddy quagmire and the men slipped and slid as they climbed. They failed to see any sign of the enemy, although Tate later thought they should have picked up telltale signs of VC preparations for an ambush, such as tree branches tied together and fire-paths cleared through the undergrowth. 'It wouldn't have happened in 4RAR or under Jim Riddle, that's for sure,' Tate says.

Suddenly the thumbs down signal came down the line from the men ahead. Kermode had heard sounds ahead that weren't jungle noises: metal clanging on metal. The section froze. Hearts beat faster and bodies tightened as they strained to hear anything that could indicate where the enemy was. The platoon sergeant came sliding down the trail and told them the first section was ordered to go ahead to investigate. He then scrambled back up the trail. Tate looked at his mate the machine gunner. They both knew the men ahead were moving into an ambush. They could see it, why couldn't the sergeant?

But surprisingly, there was no sound of gunfire, and within minutes they were ordered to continue up the hill track. Tate had a bad feeling. Were they being allowed to advance further into the killing ground before the trap was sprung, just like the strategy against the VC at Thua Tich?

'Suddenly, the whole universe exploded,' Tate wrote in his memoir.

Lightning and thunder crashed around my ears, and at the same time the enemy machine guns opened up. Their fire was so ferocious, so cacophonous, the noise of one all but blotted out the other. The foliage was torn to shreds and the rain lashed us like a flailing cat-o'-nine tails like we were being punished for our past sins.

Tate and his section dived for cover, eyes and ears scanning the jungle for something to shoot at. They worked their packs off their backs to reduce the target they made. Heavy firing was coming from up ahead. The first section ten metres ahead of them was copping it hard. Tate could see the lieutenant and sergeant ahead of him at the rear of the section. The lieutenant yelled at the sergeant to get the second section up to give his first section covering fire with their machine gun.

Tate and the two men manning the gun struggled up the hill, almost crawling over the top of the lieutenant as they headed upwards into the maelstrom of fire up ahead. One of the gunners cheekily asked the officer whether he was coming up with them. It was met with a scowl, and the lieutenant shouted at them to move.

The three crawled up the incline, trying to keep the muzzles of their guns out of the mud. Tate was in front and looked through the teeming rain. No one was making a move to follow them up towards the roar of the fighting ahead. What would he have to do when he reached the lip of the ridge above? Would he have to run across open ground to cover? Or would he dig in and try to pick off the enemy ensconced in hiding places in the jungle?

He crawled up the last bit of track and, through some bush, slowly peeked over the lip of the rise. It was a disaster. He could see the last couple of men in the first section lying wounded on the muddy bush track. There was very little return fire coming from the Aussies. *Bugger*, he thought. It meant that as soon as he and the machine gunners broke cover they would become targets for all the VC hiding in bunkers and the jungle. The thick foliage on either side of the track meant there was little chance of a flanking movement. The only way forward was straight ahead.

It was strange, but at that exact moment Tate felt a cloak of invincibility descend over him. He felt he was destined not to be shot, just as he hadn't been shot in tight spots he'd been in earlier. It was insane, but these things happen in combat. If they didn't, no soldier with an ounce of sanity would ever run straight into the path of enemy guns poised to tear him to shreds.

The three diggers braced themselves. Tate had a hand grenade in one hand and his M-16 in the other. The machine gunners were ready with their heavy weapon. They looked at each other and nodded. Tate yelled 'Let's go!' and as one they leapt up and ran right into the firestorm.

The VC had placed their bunkers in a classic buffalo-horn formation – a straight line in the centre with curved wings on each end to encircle anything that came into the killing zone. Once he was over the lip, Tate discovered the ground ahead opened up into a relatively flat area. Fire-paths had been cleared for the VC machine guns and bullets poured in from all angles, along with rocket-propelled grenades. Flashes from behind the bunkers meant there was a second dug-in flank of VC firing mortars into the killing ground. Bullets and shrapnel zipped across the open space, shredding plant and human in its path. This was a big enemy force, well protected and in control. Tate knew they were up shit creek without a paddle; without even a bloody canoe.

He reckoned there was only one thing to do to keep his head on and stay alive and that was to get up and run like buggery straight at the bastards. With his gun and his grenade, he sprinted up the track into the open ground as fast as he could. He veered to the left and hurled the grenade towards the bunker in front of him, opened fire with his gun on automatic and then threw himself into the mud. He saw bullets from the bunkers follow the two machine gunners, who had veered to the right once they hit the open ground. Everything seemed to be happening in slow motion. Tate got to his feet again and fired his M-16 from the hip in the general direction of the bunkers. He knew he probably wouldn't hit anything, but so long as he was moving he would divide the VC fire.

After a few paces he dived into the mud again. He looked to the right over his shoulder, just in time to see the ammunition carrier hit in the shoulder, blood and bone spraying into the air. Tate watched in horror as the digger tried to lift the ammunition belt off his chest as he fell. The rounds seemed to explode into flames, setting his hands ablaze. Tate couldn't tear his eyes away from the horrific scene. He saw him fall to the ground, screaming. The soldier carrying the machine gun continued on, firing the gun in short bursts as he headed towards the cover at the edge of the jungle.

Tate got up and ran for a large tree that seemed to be directly in front of the bunker on the left, firing as he ran. But his luck was running out. As he dived to the ground at the foot of the tree a bullet thudded into him. He wasn't sure where – it was somewhere down below his chest. He knew immediately it was a bad one, but he was still breathing. Crazily, his first thought was that it was bad enough to get him home out of this madness. That is, if he lived. Then the pain took over. He looked down and saw his pants near his right hip were covered in blood, and it was spreading down his thigh. *Jesus, it hurts*, he thought. Explosions continued around him as grenades went off. The ground shook and he bounced into the air with it.

The tree seemed to be providing some cover. Tate quickly rolled down the top of his pants and was shocked at what he saw through the blood. A hole had appeared in his hip the size of cricket ball, exposing muscle and bone. Steam rose from the gaping hole in his body as rain fell into it. Bullets continued to whip over his head as he tried to wriggle his way further down into the mud, holding his hand over his wound. He could hear the machine gunner call out for more ammunition and his mate screaming out that he couldn't help, holding up his ruined fingers to prove it. *This is it*, Tate thought. *The end of the road*. He felt dizzy, his eyes closing on the shocking scene like a curtain on a bad stage show. Finally he fell into the mercy of unconsciousness.

The next thing Tate knew was that he was back down the trail, lying next to a pile of wounded men. The scene was awful: guts hanging out of some, one with a huge piece of shrapnel sticking out of his head, others screaming that they were blind. Ray Kermode lay nearby, his life ebbing away. One soldier rolled in agony as he desperately searched his groin and the ground around him for the testicles he thought had been shot off. One had to be gagged because he was screaming so loudly – even though he didn't appear to be wounded. It wasn't until a regimental reunion 20 years later that Tate learned he'd been pulled out by the unit's medics. They'd risked their lives to drag him out of the firing line and down the hill to safety.

The sergeant now appeared to be in charge of the platoon as the lieutenant who'd ordered them into the trap had been hit by shrapnel in the foot. The sergeant was organising a desperate rearguard fight with the remainder of the platoon as they waited for an American medevac chopper to fly in despite the risk of being hit by ground fire. Displaying incredible bravery, the chopper pilot hovered above the jungle canopy while, one by one, the worst of the wounded were winched up on a litter.

Tate was the second soldier loaded into the chopper. He watched in fascination as the litter carried him up through the jungle trees, right up into the arms of a massive black American GI who reached out and pulled him into the chopper as though he weighed no more than a bag of oranges. Ignoring the bullets that whizzed around them, the Yanks winched four more men up, until the winch jammed when the last man was only metres below. The pilot set off with him hanging below, spinning in the downdraft and the driving rain.

Tate sighed with relief and slipped into the darkness. His time in the madness of the Vietnam War was over. This wound would take him home. What he didn't know, however, was that his war would go on and on for the rest of his life.

•

The bullet had smashed Tate up pretty badly. His whole hip had to be reconstructed in a series of operations and he would spend the next two years in hospital. He was just 20 years old. The unfairness of it all hit him hard, and he was terrified of the life that lay ahead of him. Tate's hip struggled to heal and, month after month, he was kept in plaster. His mind would never mend.

It started on the long, painful trip home. While he'd flown to war in a gleaming Qantas jet with lovely hostesses serving drinks, he flew home on a stretcher that was one of many stacked three and four high in the back of a screamingly loud, crowded Hercules transport plane, hooked up to a urine bag and a drip. He'd spent 212 days at war. When he'd left, a band on the tarmac had played 'Waltzing Matilda'. Senior officers had saluted them goodbye. But when he arrived home the plane landed in the middle of the night at a secluded section of Brisbane airport. There was no one to welcome them . . . no bands, no fanfare, no salutes and no officers. Just a line of ambulances to whisk them away.

Through the window of the ambulance Tate spotted his mum and dad, who'd been waiting for him at the airport. Tears ran down his mother's face. She'd waved him goodbye as a 19-year-old, and the army had brought him back a broken man at 20. Tate's parents weren't allowed to speak to him at the airport, so they followed the ambulance all the way to hospital. When they got there they still weren't allowed to see him. They were told to come back in the morning.

Tate quickly discovered a frustrating civil quirk. He'd been at war for almost a year, killing and maiming the enemy, making life and death decisions for his mates. But back home he still wasn't legally an adult. The voting age was 21. In some parts of Australia he still wasn't old enough to drink alcohol. The voting age wouldn't change to 18 until 1973, under the Whitlam Labor government. During the 1970s the drinking age was lowered to 18 only because of the absurdity of young men returning from war being denied a drink in a pub. For Tate, the absurd reality was that even though he was old enough to have a bullet smash his body, when the hospital needed a decision regarding his medical treatment they had to ask his father for permission. At one point a doctor wanted to amputate his leg. The hospital wrote to his father giving all the reasons why it would be better for his son to lose his leg. A telegram came back with just one word: 'No'. The doctors worked a bit harder and saved the leg.

Lying in hospital, Tate had time to think – far too much time. Over and over the questions haunted him. Why was he alive but others were dead, like Ray Kermode, the scout who had taken his place? If there'd been only a slight change in the bullet's flight it could have hit him in the chest and killed him. What led that bullet to take that particular path and not another?

The questions tormented Tate as his body struggled to repair itself. His anger spilled over at times and he lashed out at those around him. He was a mess. At night the nightmares flooded in. He felt an enormous distance from everyone around him, particularly soldiers who hadn't experienced the same kind of ordeal. He'd faced an enemy who could easily have turned out to be a woman or a young boy. He felt no one else could understand what he'd been through; no one could appreciate what he was going through now. He felt trapped, still in the powerful grip of the evil that had been let loose in that war, something 'dark and malevolent' that held him like a vice and wouldn't let him go.

•

After a year in hospital with plaster up to his waist, two old mates from the 4th Battalion came to visit him. Tate was pleased to see them and they talked of the good times they'd had in Vung Tau and the jokes they'd played on each other. The talk moved on to what had happened after the two had left Tate behind in Vietnam. When Tate told them he'd been in the 2nd D&E Platoon which had pulled off the ambush at Thua Tich, the soldiers' first reaction was to say that there had never been a second D&E Platoon. They insisted there was only ever one D&E Platoon at Headquarters, and that Tate must mean that unit.

The discussion left Tate frustrated, confused and angry. He might not remember what role he'd played at Thua Thich, but he knew the platoon had been there. He had been part of the unit for almost six weeks before it was broken up. He remembered the convoy to Xuyen Moc and the bodies being tied up, then dragged, behind the APCs. He had nightmares of a peasant woman being shot on the way there. He knew the people who'd been in the platoon, such as Riddle. Why did they insist the unit never existed?

Not one to let anything rest, Tate wrote to the Central Army Records Office (CARO) and asked for any documentation they had of his time in the 2nd D&E Platoon. He received a rather curt answer that no such platoon ever existed. CARO said the records showed there was only one D&E Platoon based at the Australian Task Force Headquarters at Nui Dat.

The answer left Tate flabbergasted. But he had other things on his mind at the time, like learning to walk again and trying to get his head in order. Some six months later he was walking on crutches and allowed out of hospital for the first time to go into the city of Brisbane. It just happened to be the day of a moratorium march, a large anti-war demonstration, and the streets were packed with thousands of people carrying placards against the Vietnam War.

Tate was 21 now, so he could legally drink in a pub. He settled himself on a bar stool with his crutches leaning on the counter beside him and watched the assortment of long-haired hippies, schoolkids, uni students, middle-class women, unionists, a few men in suits and a couple of well known politicians marching past in rows of ten to twelve. The younger protesters yelled out, 'One, two, three, four, we don't want your fucking war' and 'Out of Vietnam now'. Tate's anger and frustration grew. He thought of the blokes still fighting in Vietnam and his mates who'd perished there. 'They'd died for nothing if Australia pulled out now. The war might be fucked up, but it was wrong for these people who'd never seen a shot fired to rubbish their sacrifice.

Then he heard some protesters chant, 'Ho, Ho, Ho Chi Minh' and 'One side right, one side wrong, victory to the Viet Cong'. He spotted a couple of uni students walking around with buckets collecting money for the Viet Cong. That was the last straw for Tate. He snapped. He picked a crowd of men about his own age, screamed, 'You gutless bastards!' and hobbled out into the mass after them, pushing, shoving and swinging punches at any of them he could reach, his crutches dangling off his arms.

'You fucking cowards!' he yelled as he thrashed into them. A few pushed back, but none wanted to take on this screaming madman on crutches. Cops saw the fracas and waded in, pulling Tate out of the crowd. When Tate told them he'd just come back from Vietnam with a bullet in his hip, the cops were sympathetic. 'Give them one for me, mate,' said one. They allowed Tate to wade in again and only pulled him out when it got too much for him.

As the crowd finished their march and listened to the speakers, Tate worked his way to the front. He spoke to one of the main organisers, left-wing Labor Senator George Georges, and asked for permission to address the crowd as a Vietnam veteran. It was an unusual request. Not many veterans were speaking out at that time, and Tate had made quite a spectacle attacking the protestors. But Georges was a battler for civil rights and believed Tate had a right to speak. Tate took to the stage and hobbled to the microphone on his crutches.

He wasn't there to win friends, and he let the anti-war demonstrators have it with both barrels. 'None of you have a clue what you're talking about,' he blasted them. 'I was there. I have fought for my country. The Americans are supporting the South Vietnamese fight the communists and we are right to be there supporting them. If we don't stop them in Vietnam they will advance right on towards us in Australia. Fight them there or we'll have to fight them here . . .'

The argument was straight from the conservative government textbook on why Australia was fighting in Vietnam. Years later, Tate came to believe the whole war had been a mistake, but at that moment all he could think of was his mates being killed and wounded and he regarded these protesters as people who'd never risked their lives yet were pouring abuse on them.

In America some veterans had started to join the protesters, some even tossing their medals onto the steps of President Nixon's White House. But not in Australia. Diggers returning from the war generally kept their mouths shut, resenting opinions expressed by anyone who hadn't been there. It would take most of them years to express their opinions publicly. Attitudes to the war were changing in 1970 – news of the massacre at My Lai was stirring passions in the Australian heartland and the shocking photo of a young girl screaming as she fled the napalming of her village, her clothes burned off her body, brought home the horror of what was going on.

So when Tate spoke in Brisbane it wasn't what the crowd wanted to hear. The crowd booed, howled him down as a 'Yankee lackey' and jeered him as he hobbled away from the microphone. Tate was shocked at the hatred he'd seen in their faces. *But why?* he thought. *I'd gone to war for the right reasons, hadn't I? If they don't like the war they should attack the bloody politicians who sent us there, not the poor buggers who had to do the fighting.*

That day Tate returned to the hospital angrier and more confused than ever. But further bad news was waiting for him. Doctors told him they'd discovered major problems with his hip. It had been quietly rotting away deep inside the joint and down the thigh bone. The bullet had done more damage than they'd realised. He'd need another six months in traction and plaster.

But even then the wound wasn't much better. Surgeons had dug around inside his hip so many times that the wound now gaped open the size of half a soccer ball. Seeping pus and dead flesh had to be regularly cleaned out. Tate was in absolute despair. The doctors said there'd have to be one more operation, a major one. Tate feared it would never end. He began to think it might have been better if the bullet had hit him a bit higher – then the nightmare would have stopped there.

When Tate awoke from the operation he was horrified to discover he was covered in plaster from his chest right down to his toes. As the months rolled by and the last troops were pulled out of Vietnam as the Americans declared victory and left the South Vietnamese to their fate, Tate was driven to the point of insanity. His body was encased for almost an entire year. He raged against the treatment from bullying matrons and disdainful army nurses. They all had army ranks higher than him. The only thing that kept him going was the love of an extraordinarily tolerant woman called Carole who cared for him and helped nurse him through his terrible time. She put up with all his foul temper tantrums, his rants against the unfairness of his condition, and his frustration with the military medical system.

As soon as he had one leg free from plaster and was able to hobble around once again, he went AWL. Finally up on crutches, he casually hobbled past the nurses' station saying he was on his way to the toilet. He kept right on going, out the front door of the military hospital and into a taxi. He had to lie across the back seat because of the plaster. He gave the cabbie Carole's address. But when the cab driver heard on the radio that the military police were looking for him and had set up road blocks, Tate had to tell him what was going on. The sympathetic cabbie took Tate to Carole's house via the back streets and then helped him up to the front door. Carole was shocked to see him, and shocked even further once she had him inside to hear military police pounding on her front door demanding to know if Private Tate was in the house. She ignored them, leaving the military police waiting outside all night while she comforted the young soldier.

In the morning Carole opened the front door and Tate stumbled out with a sheepish grin, straight into the arms of a couple of bear-like military police. The red caps weren't too thrilled about their all-night vigil while this private was getting his jollies inside, and they weren't too gentle. Back in the hospital, Tate got a severe reprimand from his superior officers and doctors. He was given the ridiculous sentence of being confined to barracks for two weeks and lost his beer ration. Tate had memories of his night with Carole to console him.

Some months later he was allowed out with Carole. Still in plaster from the top of his chest to the bottom of his right leg, she managed to get him to the beach where they walked out on a pier. The itching from months in plaster was driving Tate round the bend. He smelled the salt air of the ocean, looked down into the clear blue water below and, without a second's thought, jumped in. He later explained in his memoir he wasn't thinking of suicide. All he could think of was the maddening itchiness and his desperation to break free of the plaster. The relief of the cool salt water on his skin was magic and he had a brief second of bliss. Then he hit the sand about two metres below the surface and realised what a stupid thing he'd done. With his one good leg he managed to push himself to the surface and grab a breath of air before he sank under the water again, the weight of the plaster dragging him down. *Oh Christ, this is it*, he thought. *What a bloody stupid way to go, and Carole up there watching me.*

Tate pushed up with his one working leg and again broke the surface. He heard Carole on the pier screaming his name and pleading for help. Tate decided this wasn't the way he wanted to die after what he'd already been through. He pushed off again and again, hopping his way back towards the beach. Carole rushed into the water and helped him out. People watching cheered.

There was one good result of his crazy act. The body cast was ruined. When the doctors replaced it they made a smaller one which only covered him from the stomach to the knee. Tate thought it was heaven and worth the abuse he copped from the medicos.

Eventually his hip healed enough to remove the plaster and Tate walked out of the hospital, leaving behind army doctors and the whole military life. At last he was free. The Vietnam War was over as far as Tate was concerned. The Australian government thought so too, and had withdrawn all troops by the end of 1972. It wouldn't be long before North Vietnamese tanks crashed through the gates of the South Vietnamese president's palace for total victory.

But the war hadn't finished with Don Tate. Not by a long shot.

10

HOMECOMINGS

Don Tate decided to celebrate his first day of freedom from both the plaster and the army by taking his girlfriend Carole out for a romantic evening at one of the swankiest restaurants in Brisbane. For the first time in years Tate was happy and looking forward to the future, as any young man should.

Walking hand in hand along the river boardwalk after dinner, he anticipated the best was yet to come for the night. Suddenly a car nearby backfired. Without thinking, Tate immediately dived into the rain-filled gutter, his head digging down into the filth as far as he could. The sudden bang had thrown him instantly back into the jungles of Vietnam. His survival instinct had kicked in.

Tate looked up, highly embarrassed. Passers-by thought he was just another drunk in the gutter. They walked past shaking their heads. Carole looked on, shocked. She helped him to his feet and he sat down on a bench nearby, shaking uncontrollably as adrenaline raced through his body. His new suit was soaked. He realised what he'd done, and felt so foolish. He looked in shame at Carole. To her credit she said nothing, guessing what had just happened. But Tate was worried about how long Carole, or any woman for that matter, would stick with a wreck of a man like him.

Tate's war ground on. Many nights he found himself waking in a sweat on the floor beside the bed, his body shaking. In his nightmares he dived for cover as shadows in black pyjamas came at him out of the dark. His waking hours were worse. Anger and rage were constantly seething just beneath the surface. Resentments against people and authorities for perceived wrongs grew and festered. Suspicion of others and their motives mounted. Never one to shirk a fight, now Tate went looking for them. In one pub brawl he was glassed in the throat and ended up needing 31 stitches. His soldiering didn't necessarily mean he'd win every fight.

For years Tate avoided veterans' groups. He didn't march on Anzac Day, nor join the main veterans' organisation, the Returned and Services League (RSL). He didn't want to join men who sat around drinking and talking of war. Most of all, he couldn't stand the notion of World War Two veterans telling him that his wasn't a real war, that he'd only been sent for 12 months. They, on the other hand, had to serve until the bitter end, victory or defeat. They hadn't walked away when their time was up. Tate wanted to get as far away from all that as he could. He got menial jobs, drifting from one to the next. He was a powder keg, at times exploding into violence. Each job tended to end in a fist fight.

But Carole saw he had ability, and pushed him to finish his Higher School Certificate. He passed and got into university, eventually qualifying to be a teacher. But Tate felt he was discriminated against as a Vietnam veteran, and he struggled for a long time to get a teaching job. He wrote to George Negus, a prominent TV journalist who had been Tate's teacher when he was at high school. Negus raised the issue publicly on his program and grilled education bureaucrats. Suddenly Tate was offered a job teaching English, however he didn't fit in easily with his predominantly leftish, anti-war teaching colleagues. For 13 years he stuck at it and found a revelation in the power of words. He loved Shakespeare and started to master his own skills in expressing himself.

For 18 years Tate's terrible memories of the war had hounded him. No matter how much he tried to ignore them, horrific images continued to haunt him. He decided to write it down. He added some thoughts about the Vietnam War, and in 1987 he posted it to *The Sydney Morning Herald* from the town on the New South Wales south coast where he and Carole now lived. It was dynamite. The paper passed Tate's account to one of its top reporters, Michael Cordell. He did his best to check it out, but ran into brick walls. Cordell wrote an article for the paper on Vietnam veterans and interspersed it with quotes from Tate's letter.

It was published as the major feature on 25 April: Anzac Day.[1] The date had special relevance that year – for the first time, Vietnam veterans were invited to lead the Anzac parade. It was a gesture by the RSL to try and make up for the lack of respect shown for Vietnam veterans since the last troops left Vietnam. The paper's feature, headlined 'Coming Home', focused on Vietnam veterans struggling to come to terms with the war which had now been ended for 15 years. It highlighted Tate's words, which spat out from the page like machine-gun bullets.

In a blistering tirade, Tate told how he'd volunteered to go to Vietnam filled with youthful comic-book visions of war and the heroic Anzac legend that had been forged in Tobruk, Gallipoli, the Somme and Kokoda. He'd believed his tour of duty would be a patriotic and honourable deed, a noble and splendid fight against the dark forces of oppressive communism. He'd believed he would be standing shoulder to shoulder with digger mates who would stand by him, through thick and thin.

'I was 19 years old. I knew nothing,' Tate had written.

I don't know when the patriotism, and the pride, first began to die. But it did. Perhaps it was the art of learning to blow children to smithereens in ambushes. They may have been Viet Cong. They may not have been. Maybe, as was often the case, they had been forced to carry weapons and supplies for the Viet Cong. What it boiled down to was that they were in the wrong place at the right time for us. Dark shapes on obscure little tracks in a vast Asian jungle.

Atrocity or justifiable act? If we let them pass, the weapons they carried could conceivably be used against us. It was after curfew. Press the Claymore buttons. Splatter little lives all over the jungle. Battalion figures needed a boost anyway. Worry about it later . . . when the nightmares started.

Tate dropped a bombshell. He said there was one memory in particular that caused him pain and nightmares. He remembered an incident in which civilians were killed without cause or reason. The *Herald* published Tate's claim that Australian troops fired on a woman fleeing up a path, killing her. He said when they caught up to the body, they found a baby strapped to her front. Tate claimed the Australians ran over the bodies in the APC to obliterate trace of the atrocity.

'I always recall that as one of the most horrific things I saw,' Tate had written. 'There was no need for it. The woman was walking along the track minding her own business. There were no weapons or supplies on these people. This was just clear-cut murder.'

It was an enormous allegation. The *Herald* said they had not been able to substantiate the claim and the Defence Department emphatically denied it ever happened. It was a statement that started a bitter battle among veterans that would last for more than two decades.

Perhaps realising the animosity the claim would stir up, Sir William Keys, the national president of the RSL, told the *Herald* it was best to let the allegation go by. Keys, a distinguished World War Two and Korean War veteran, said it was extremely difficult in war to tell friend from foe, and sometimes unfortunate and unavoidable incidents happened.

'I don't think an investigation would be at all helpful,' Keys told the *Herald*. 'It would be time-wasting, costly and counterproductive . . . At the end, if anything was clearly established what good would it do anybody?'

The repercussion for Tate was quick and it was ugly. The next morning his phone rang. Tate's eight-year-old son was quick off the mark and answered it before his mum or dad could pick it up. The caller was a man who didn't give his name, but said in a threatening voice: 'Tell your father if anything more is said about Vietnam his wife and kids will be killed,' and hung up.

The boy was terrified and ran to tell his dad. Tate was understandably furious. An anonymous death threat for speaking out was bad enough but, worse, the caller didn't have the guts to speak to him personally and had dropped his cowardly death threat on his son. Tate called the police – and then the *Herald* and the local newspaper *The Illawarra Mercury*.

It was big news for the local paper. Headlining the story 'Viet Vet Reprisal Threat', reporter Irene O'Brien wrote that Tate had received death threats after he'd alleged Australian troops had committed atrocities during the Vietnam War. 'The thing is, I could not identify any of the people involved in the incident which took place during 1969,' Tate told the *Mercury*.

> At the time you did not know what day it was or where you were. The platoon I was in was thrown together and I didn't know the bloke next to me, let alone the people involved . . . It was only one Australian incident among a lot of strange things that happened. I did nothing at the time because I was just a 19-year-old foot slogger.

After the *Mercury* story, Tate found himself thrown back into a vicious war, but this time it was against his fellow Vietnam veterans. George Negus invited Tate onto his television program *Today* to tell his story of the incident. Tate wasn't prepared when he found himself facing Normie Rowe, the pop star conscripted to fight in Vietnam. Rowe had served in the cavalry and became a crew commander with the rank of corporal in an APC. He'd even been in the Xuyen Moc region at the time of the Thua Tich ambush, but wasn't present at the actual fighting. Since the war he'd become an outspoken advocate for the welfare of Vietnam veterans. His singing career had moved into musicals and at the time he was singing the role of Jean Valjean in *Les Misérables*. Tate was up against a very popular bloke.

Tate admits he was 'torn limb from limb' by the questioning, and by Rowe's outrage at the allegations which, he angrily decried, dishonoured veterans.[2] Tate couldn't back his allegations up with any corroborating facts. It was a disaster for Tate. He'd wanted to blow the whistle, alert the public to what happens in the madness of war. Instead he was branded a liar and had become a pariah in the veteran community.

Five years later, Tate's teaching career came to an abrupt end. One night, while chaperoning his school softball team to a competition in Sydney, he was hit over the head with a steel bar. He'd tackled a man who was hanging suspiciously around the girls' motel. The man was dressed all in black, which gave Tate the shivers and sent him into a battlefield flashback. Tate launched himself at the man. But his hip gave way, and he came off second best when he fell, giving the man in black the chance to belt him over the head with the bar before running off.

Doctors stitched him up, but discovered he'd got a bit of brain damage from the blow. The flashbacks began to worsen and Tate was retired from teaching on medical grounds. He was back where he'd started. It was devastating.

Not one to stay knocked down, Tate threw himself into writing. In 1997, on the 25th anniversary of the withdrawal of Australian troops from Vietnam, *The Sydney Morning Herald* ran a feature article written by Tate titled 'Courage After Fire', a bitter reflection of the impact of the war on those who'd served.[3] Tate told of how he'd recently heard another army mate had taken his life by blowing his head off. A few weeks before that he'd learned a veteran had hanged himself in his family's garage. 'It's been happening for years,' said Tate. He said around 275 Vietnam veterans had committed suicide since they came home from the war. 'No one really knows why,' Tate wrote.

> Perhaps they've been told just once too often to 'get on with your life' or to 'put it behind you'. Such platitudes cut the veteran deep. Repressed sadness can't be repressed forever. The sadness does damage. The demon is born from years of isolation, and from outright rejection by all except their fellow soldiers.

He wrote he'd sometimes felt like taking that route himself. He said that if he explained why he didn't, it might help dissuade another veteran from taking his own life. Tate wrote vividly of the fear and confusion of fighting against an enemy that you rarely saw. He wrote graphically of being wounded. He said that on the day Neil Armstrong walked on the moon he was told by doctors he might lose his leg. He spoke angrily of mates being killed, officers getting medals while privates got none, and how the army treated its wounded like second-class soldiers; no longer of use, forgotten and discarded. He also wrote painfully of returning to a homeland where he felt he didn't belong, that a world had passed him by as he lost the best years of his youth in hospitals, traction and plaster casts. He wrote about the struggle of searching for a job physically disabled and mentally scarred; of the flashbacks, the fights, the rage; of the alienation from family, friends and workmates; and of battling uncaring bureaucracies.

Tate explained the only way he could cope was to insist to himself that he had served his country and had done his duty when he was called.

> I give this message to every digger left standing – mate, put the bottle, or that rifle, or those drugs away. Stand tall because you laid your life on the line for your country. Be bloody proud of it, because there's no greater thing a man can do.

●

Tate's story of rejection and alienation resonates with many of the veterans of the Ghost Platoon. Don Moss never had another fight in Vietnam as intense as the action he was involved in at the forward lookout post with Jim Riddle at Thua Tich. He was a good soldier and saw out his 12-month tour, even planning to do a second tour.

But when he got back to Australia, the army told him he'd be training new recruits and conscripts. Moss suddenly cracked. Two weeks after his return to the Singleton army base near Sydney he simply walked out and never went back. Going AWL was totally out of character for Moss. He'd joined up at the age of 24 after his younger brother Ronald had been conscripted. Ron had fought with distinction at the Battle of Long Tan.

'I'd had enough,' Moss reflects, decades later. 'I was prepared to go back to Vietnam myself, but not to send others.'

Moss hitchhiked his way up to Brisbane where he married his childhood sweetheart. Six months later a distant family member discovered he was AWL and reported him to the military police. Days before he was due to face a court martial he took off once again.

'I was finished with the army,' Moss says. 'I don't speak real well, and I didn't want to stand up in front of those new kids telling them what to do. I could tell them how to fire a gun, but how could I explain to them what it was really like, what do you do when you have women and children in your sights?'

This time, Moss wasn't caught. When Whitlam's Labor government was elected in 1972, Moss was given a discharge and received all his back pay. 'Funny thing was that I found my brother had done the same thing. After his first tour, where he'd fought at Long Tan, he decided to join the regular army and went back for a second tour. But when he came home on R&R he just ran away. When Whitlam was elected he ended up getting the same discharge.'

But the war didn't let Moss just walk away scot-free. He drank heavily and smoked incessantly. He was extremely suspicious of others, had a short temper and couldn't keep a job as he had trouble with anyone in a position of authority. He had little self-motivation, didn't socialise and moved around a lot. He worked in the timber industry and often thought how easy it would be to kill himself. He had continual family troubles because of his rages and belligerence. He developed bowel cancer – his doctors said it was due to stress. Nightmares came frequently, especially around Anzac Day.

In his 50s Moss was diagnosed with depression and sent to a psychiatric unit named after Keith Payne VC, who'd won his Victoria Cross in Vietnam. It specialises in veterans suffering from post-traumatic stress disorders. In group therapy discussions with other veterans, Moss finally opened up to others about his experience at the Thua Tich ambush. Moss won't reveal what he told them – he fears it will stir it all up again – but he found many things in common with the other veterans at the hospital. For the first time he didn't feel quite so alone.

However, anger and resentment were never far off. Moss was from a small country town in northern New South Wales, and when an honour roll of local people who'd served in war was put up in the town hall they omitted Don Moss and his brother Ron – the only two from the town who had fought in Vietnam. When Don protested, the council put their names on a separate plaque. 'For a long time they didn't care about us,' Moss recalls. 'But once all their World War Two blokes died, they asked us to come and lead the town's Anzac Day march. I said "No". Stuff them,' Moss says, still angry at the treatment.

Bob Secrett was a close mate of Jim Riddle's. He'd joined up at 19 and had already served five months in Vietnam when he was sent home with malaria. He was in camp in Sydney about to be sent back to Vietnam when he teamed up with a tough newcomer with an odd accent – Jim Riddle. 'He was real gung ho,' Secrett says. 'We hit the bars hard in Sydney before we left. I wanted to be beside him in Vietnam because he knew how to get us out of a tight spot – far more than all those national service officers with no war experience who didn't want to listen to a seasoned professional soldier because he was a bit rough around the edges.'

After the war, Secrett hit the grog hard. 'I felt numb towards every other human being. I had no time or respect for anybody. I was so disheartened. I felt I had no purpose. I was an alcoholic and aggressive. I managed to give up the grog after 20 years and that helped me get my life in some sort of order. There is no doubt it was due to war. I was trying to drown memories of what I did.'

•

Don Tate didn't mention the 2nd D&E Platoon in his 1997 article for *The Sydney Morning Herald.* Nor did he mention the allegation of atrocities he'd originally raised in the *Herald* ten years earlier. That was a battle for another day. But in his desperation, Tate finally decided to seek some solace among his fellow veterans. Ever since the war he'd avoided veteran groups such as the RSL or the Vietnam Veterans Association of Australia. He regarded them as being made up mostly of bludgers who hadn't done much in the war. He believed they were just trying to get the most out of army pensions. He felt many of them were blaming all their personal failings and problems on their experiences in Vietnam – real or exaggerated.

So it was with a sense of deep suspicion and a chip firmly perched on his shoulder that he walked into a meeting of Vietnam veterans that had just been established near his home. When the organiser asked Tate what unit he'd been in, Tate told him he'd finished up in the 9th Battalion where he was wounded. The organisers went away and looked up the battalion's official record, but there was no sign of Tate's name. There'd been a few cases of men falsely claiming to be ex-soldiers, and veterans despised them. So it was little wonder they turned angrily on Tate, and told him in no uncertain terms to get out, accusing him of being a fake. One of the veterans recognised Tate's name from the 1987 article about the killing of women and children, and told him he was a liar and an imposter.

Tate's blood was boiling. He hadn't expected a warm welcome, but perhaps at least some sort of understanding and recognition of what he'd been through from fellow servicemen. He knew the 2nd D&E Platoon wasn't in the official records, but to find that his name had also been left out of the records of the 9th Battalion, even though he'd been wounded fighting with them, was the last straw. In a rage, he told the organisers where they could go. Chests were thrust out, words got hotter, accusations grew and suddenly punches were thrown. Other veterans interceded and Tate was escorted out of the meeting.

After that, Tate was shut out of the veterans' loop altogether. Anything he did from then on would be on his own. He began to write down his story. He could write well, and all his pent-up pain and anger poured into the manuscript. Then, as the new millenium was about to dawn in late 1999, a man approached Tate in the street. He said his name was Kevin Lloyd-Thomas, and he remembered Tate from the 2nd D&E Platoon. Tate didn't remember him but, over a beer, Lloyd-Thomas told Tate he'd also discovered that the platoon wasn't recorded in the official records, and that no other veteran believed it had existed. Days later, another 2nd D&E soldier, Dennis 'Snow' Manski, rang Tate and told him the same thing. The Ghost Platoon circle was slowly widening.

Tate wrote down all he knew about the unit, and in 2003 posted it on a website he'd started. If Tate was expecting instant fireworks, he was disappointed. It wasn't until two years later that an email finally came in. It was from Jim Riddle. He was back in England, living in his old home town, Newcastle upon Tyne. Riddle wrote that he'd thought Tate was dead. He'd heard Tate was badly wounded, then nothing until his son found the website. Riddle supplied his phone number in England and Tate called him. Tate was shocked when Riddle told him he was struggling to survive because he had no pension. Somehow Riddle had fallen through the cracks in both the British and Australian veteran entitlements system. Riddle wanted to come back to Australia, but he had no way of paying for the journey.

Tate swung into action. He contacted the Department of Veterans' Affairs and found Riddle was entitled to a significant pension because of his war service with the Australian army.

Riddle had served an amazing total of 734 days in Vietnam – far more than most soldiers. He'd started just before Christmas 1968 and finished on 9 March 1972 – making him one of the very last Australian infantrymen to leave Vietnam. During that time Riddle had served in the 4th, 9th and 8th battalions. The records show that, when each battalion returned to Australia, Riddle was placed back in the pool of soldiers awaiting re-assignment in the 1st Australian Reinforcement Unit. The records didn't mention Riddle's service in the 2nd D&E Platoon, but did show that he'd served at Headquarters, 1st Australian Task Force, between 14 May and 16 June, 1969, which covered the period that the 2nd D&E was active. The records showed the same for almost every member of the platoon, without mentioning the unit by name.

What the official records didn't show was that by Riddle's own admission he'd spent most of his last 12 months in Vietnam as drunk as he could get. He drank to get drunk, which is about as bad as a drunk can be. 'I got into a lot of trouble,' Riddle recounts years later. 'There was a bit of me that I didn't like, and I drank to try and forget it.

'The last 12 months I was in Vietnam didn't have that same esprit de corps. I never did get those stripes. I'd done a corporal's course and qualified, but there were too many drunken fights. I was in trouble too often. I was on the last ship to leave Vietnam and I realised I had wasted my time. I had gained nothing, I had gone nowhere. The whole war had gone nowhere. Then we came back to a lot of bad vibes.

I felt we had been fighting a lost cause that wasn't worth fighting in the first place. All those dead and wounded – for what? We'd been fighting for a stupid American adventure. Everybody knows that if you side with the Yanks you end up in debt – a bill to be paid in blood and money.'

Once Riddle had returned to Australia the army was keen to be rid of the troublesome soldier. With no fighting to be done he was superfluous, an irritant. At Lavarack Barracks in Townsville he was once more charged with being drunk in the lines. The commander called Riddle in and offered him a discharge. Riddle had nowhere to go, and said no thanks. They made him undergo a psych test to see if he could be forced out. Riddle says he passed and one of the doctors told him he'd scored high enough to have been an officer.

'Maybe if they'd done that at the beginning it would have gone differently,' he recalls. 'But they wanted me out. They saw me as a waste of their time, a nutcase. The troops called me Old Shellshock. They knew what I'd been through. But the army said leave now or they would throw me out. I figured they had run out of paper to keep charging me. So I left.

'I was a wreck. I couldn't get through the day without drinking. Heavily. I tried suicide several times. I drove a car into a pole and put my head through the windscreen. When I came to, someone asked me if I was all right. I said, "Sure, I just decided to park here." I should have got a medical discharge, but they didn't give me one and I got no assistance. I was abandoned by the army. All I got from them was a visit to a dentist to fix my teeth which had been smashed up by a ricocheting bullet.'

Out in civvy street in Queensland, Riddle managed to get a licence to operate heavy machinery and bulldozers. For a while he worked with the railways. But the boozing and the fighting meant he couldn't keep a job for long. Word got round, and he found it increasingly difficult to find anybody prepared to take him on. Fed up, he decided to go back to the UK. But when he tried to book a flight he found the Australian passport he'd been given in London when he joined the Australian army had expired. He sent it off to be renewed. But when it came back it wasn't an Australian passport – it was a British one. He was told he'd have to go back to the UK on the British passport, then go to the Australian High Commission where they would sort out a new Australian passport for him.

Riddle was peeved. He felt that the country he'd risked his life for was now disowning him. When he arrived back in the UK, he called the Australian High Commission and they told him to bring in his passport to process. However, before he could do that he was offered a job in Libya as a supervisor for an oil operation. It was the sort of rugged, no-nonsense operation that Riddle liked. There was no grog on site, and Riddle was forced to dry out. When it was over he grabbed the chance to do a similar job in Saudi Arabia. The rough and ready work seemed to suit him. So did the absence of alcohol.

After a year, he returned to England. It wasn't a great homecoming; the simmering tensions between him and his father spilled over. Riddle's mother had died while he was serving in Vietnam, and Riddle hadn't been able to return for the funeral. His father was livid. He accused Riddle of killing his mother by going to fight in Vietnam. Riddle's fury rose as his father's accusations rained down on him – that his mother had died of a broken heart, that he had neglected her and hadn't even come home when she was dying.

All Riddle's years of anger and resentment flooded into his fists, and he punched his father as hard as he could. The old man rocked backwards and fell on a glass coffee table, smashing it to pieces. From the floor he yelled at his son, 'Go ahead then, kill me!' Riddle stood over his father, struggling to control himself. Finally, without a word, he turned his back and walked out the door.

Riddle stayed at his cousin's house, where he met a divorced woman who had a young son. After a while they married, and had a son together. Riddle admits his drinking and rage destroyed any chance the marriage had of working. 'It was bad for her as she had this drunken post-traumatic stress mad bastard on her hands. I made life very difficult for her. I knew I was destroying her life.'

Seven years later they separated. He'd wanted to take her and the two boys to Australia, but he discovered he'd missed the deadline for applying for the new Australian passport. Despite his war record fighting for Australia, he was denied Australian citizenship by an unbending bureaucracy. The bureaucrats told him that his first Australian passport had been valid only while he was serving in Vietnam. Now he would have to apply like any other migrant and he'd have to pass health checks. By now he was suffering from the lasting effects of drink and bad living and was in his 60s, so the likelihood of passing those tests wasn't high. Riddle was trapped in a nightmare of red tape. The British government refused him an army pension as he had left the Royal Marines before he'd qualified for one. The Australian government refused him a pension because they had ruled he wasn't a citizen.

Riddle was running out of options. Then one day his son googled his father's name and Vietnam on the internet. Up came Don Tate's website about the 2nd D&E Platoon. In 2005 Riddle sent an email to Tate, their first contact in 36 years. In many ways that first contact was a lifesaver for both men. Not only did they and others find a unity of purpose in fighting to force the army to admit the 2nd D&E Platoon had existed, but it was also a long, hard campaign that gave them a common enemy in the obstinate army officials they met at every turn. What they didn't expect was the open hostility from other veterans.

It took more than a year of letter-writing and the lobbying of journalists and politicians by Tate and other veterans to get the government to take note of Riddle's plight. Radio talkback host Howard Sattler pushed it hard. On 26 February 2006 Liberal MP Alby Schultz, a bit of a maverick among stuffy conservatives, berated his own government for the treatment of Riddle. 'I find it reprehensible that we grant illegal immigrants citizenship and yet Mr James Riddle, a person who has fought for this country, has not been treated appropriately,' Schultz told parliament.

Finally, Riddle was granted Australian citizenship and awarded a proper veteran's pension. In late 2006 he finally got his wish to return to Australia. But he was alone. His wife would not come with him, and his sons had their own lives to lead. Word got around Riddle was coming back, and the Vietnam veteran community pitched in to offer Riddle accommodation. When Riddle finally touched down in Perth, officials from the Department of Veterans' Affairs met him at the airport. They reimbursed him the price of his plane ticket and handed him his veteran's pension entitlements. He was welcomed by his old army mates and feted at reunions around the country. He decided to settle in Brisbane and found a hostel for single men.

With Riddle back in Australia, Tate wanted to press on with his mission: to get army authorities to admit the Ghost Platoon had existed. He also wanted them to acknowledge that atrocities had occurred. But the former members of the platoon were deeply divided over whether to keep going. Half a dozen had since died. Many didn't want to have anything to do with Vietnam reunions, let alone campaigns for recognition, and some could not be located, perhaps preferring to forget the war. A few told Riddle that, while they were glad to have a beer with him, they didn't want to talk about their time in the 2nd D&E Platoon. They didn't want any part of the furore raised by Tate's accusations.

11

SOLDIERS TURN SLEUTHS

Since Jim Riddle had been the de facto commander of the 2nd D&E Platoon, Don Tate hoped that his presence in the campaign would embarrass the military authorities into finally doing the right thing and acknowledging the platoon had existed.

But he knew that first they'd have to come up with some sort of evidence. So far the army hadn't listened to the veterans – all former privates – who'd claimed to have been in the unit. It was clear they needed to uncover something solid, some skerrick of proof, such as a logbook entry or a mention in a commander's diary to back up their claims.

Several ex-members of the platoon stepped forward to join Tate in the detective work needed on the military archives.

Ted Colmer, who had been on the M-60 machine gun with Riddle at the forward post at Thua Tich, had worked for the Australian Federal Police after the war. He would focus his investigative skills on digging up any evidence buried in the dusty files of the Australian War Memorial and the National Archives in Canberra. Allan Roach embarked on the difficult task of identifying all 39 members of the platoon. Others set about tracking down the key army officers who were involved in forming the platoon.

They faced a huge uphill battle. Official war historians at the Australian War Memorial had already concluded there was never such a unit as the 2nd D&E Platoon: there was no record of it being established and it wasn't named in any document they could find in their vast archives. It was a position they would stick to all the way through the heated battle the veterans were embarking on. At times the fight would get personal and ugly, but the historians stuck to their guns, insisting to the Department of Defence, the government and the platoon's veterans that it could never have existed.

For the veterans, the most obvious place to start their own work was to seek confirmation from the officers who, according to the platoon's ex-members, actually formed the men into the platoon – the officer in charge of the Australian Task Force, Brigadier Sandy Pearson; the officer in charge of the Headquarters troops, Major George Pratt; and the officer Pratt put in charge of the platoon, Lieutenant Barry Parkin.

Tate feared their campaign for recognition could die in the starting blocks unless it got some heat under it. 'We had to be as aggressive as we could,' he says. 'We would come out with our guns blazing – the reason the platoon was wiped from the records was because of the atrocities committed at Thua Tich.' But they needed some sort of evidence to suggest a conspiracy.

The veterans' research had uncovered a mysterious anomaly in the personnel records of the 39 men who had served in the 2nd D&E Platoon held in the Central Army Records Office. A list of the soldiers left behind when the 4th Battalion returned to Australia on 14 May 1969 showed that 22 of them had been posted to the 6th Battalion, even though not one of the soldiers ever set foot in that unit. In reality they were all at Headquarters in the 2nd D&E Platoon. Adding to the mystery, another list appeared in the Routine Orders dated 17 July 1969 – a full month after the 2nd D&E was disbanded. It said the soldiers' records for that period were to be amended from them being in the 6th Battalion to them being in the Headquarters 1st Australian Task Force (HQ 1ATF), which was the Nui Dat base.

Tate's argument that the army deliberately buried the existence of the platoon because they didn't want the public to find out about the blowing up of the bodies after the ambush or the bodies that were towed behind the APCs into Xuyen Moc certainly stirred up media interest. The ABC and local newspapers ran stories about it.

Tate had been campaigning since 2000 to set up a Vietnam Veterans memorial at a sportsground in his New South Wales south-coast town. After battling council regulations and struggling for funding, the Department of Veterans' Affairs donated $4000 and the project finally came to fruition with the planting of 230 trees. In 2007, with Riddle back in Australia, Tate and other veterans got a plaque placed on a small stone monument which said it was erected by local veterans of the Vietnam War. The memorial was marked with the Army's rising sun crest and the words Lest We Forget.

The plaque states it was unveiled by James B. Riddle, Platoon Commander 'discrete infantry platoon' HQ 1ATF, South Vietnam May–June 1969. However, Riddle hadn't been able to make it down from Brisbane to do the unveiling as he was unwell. Tate was hugely disappointed as he'd hoped the unveiling would focus publicity on Riddle and boost the campaign to get the platoon recognised. At least the story made the local paper with a photograph of the local mayor and MPs, along with Tate, Colmer and Lloyd-Thomas, as well as 'Barney' Bigwood, who had been photographed at Thua Tich dragging enemy bodies along the road.

However, the publicity and allegations of atrocities made many of the veterans uncomfortable. Some pulled out of the campaign, and others would only help if they could stay anonymous. But Tate was convinced that no matter how hot the reaction to the allegations became, it was the only way to force the authorities into action.

'The story of the atrocities tarnished the whole image of the noble Anzac,' Tate says. 'Some of the veterans of the platoon said to let sleeping dogs lie. But for me, it was the truth of what happened. I saw it as a reason the officials were denying the unit had existed – no 2nd D&E Platoon, no atrocity.'

One of those who felt any mention of wrongdoing should be avoided was former platoon section leader Kevin Lloyd-Thomas. In a 2007 email to platoon campaigners including Tate, Riddle and Colmer, as well as the head military historian at the Australian War Memorial, Ashley Ekins, Lloyd-Thomas argued they should all take the heat and emotion out of the campaign; that accusations of war crimes – even if they were true – would create a whole other range of problems.

Despite the divisions on how to go about their campaign, they finally got a breakthrough through dogged research. The Australian War Memorial had insisted they were unable to contact the officers the veterans had named as forming the platoon. However the veterans managed to find them without too many problems. George Pratt, long retired from the army and living in rural New South Wales, sent Tate an email on 27 February 2007 saying one of his tasks when he was a major and the officer in charge of the Headquarters Company at Nui Dat in 1969 was to reinvigorate the D&E Platoon. He confirmed he had formed the 2nd D&E Platoon.

Barry Parkin, the lieutenant who was put in charge of the 2nd D&E Platoon, also confirmed in writing to Tate that Major Pratt had called him in and told him a second D&E platoon was to be formed from soldiers of 4RAR who had yet to serve out the full period of their 12-month duty. Parkin said Pratt's intention was that the new platoon would carry out independent duties with the squadron of APCs and act as a ready reaction force. The platoon was to undergo watermanship training as it could be patrolling rivers in the area.

Parkin said that, at the time, he was also helping the departure of 4RAR at Vung Tau. After that he had some R&R leave. By the time he returned to Headquarters at Nui Dat in mid-June the platoon was already being disbanded; he had spent virtually no time with the platoon. No officer was told to replace him. Parkin said he was later briefed on the 'significant actions' carried out by the platoon at Thua Tich.

'This unit of soldiers was always referred to as the 2nd D&E Platoon,' Parkin wrote.

The veterans had their evidence – written statements from the officer who formed the platoon as well as the officer who was put in charge of it. Armed with this fresh proof, Tate approached his local member of parliament to see if the government could now be pressed on the issue. His local MP, Jennie George, came from the opposite end of the political spectrum from Tate. While he was an arch-conservative who detested unions and lefties, she was a former head of Australia's union movement and a committed left-winger. She is said to have been a communist in her younger years, although she denies it. However, she makes no apologies for her sympathies for the underdog, and her life-long battle to improve workers' conditions.

Like Tate, George had been a teacher. But while he hated the education system, she became the first female head of the militant NSW Teachers Federation. She rose in the tough world of union politics to become the first woman president of the Australian Council of Trade Unions, a post she held for four years before being elected to parliament as Labor MP for the working-class south-coast seat of Throsby. They may have come from opposite ends of politics but, like Tate, George was a battler and a fighter. She knew what it was to be socially alienated. She was born to Russian parents in a refugee camp in Italy after World War Two. When the family migrated to Australia she spent her first years in tough migrant housing. It was a struggle for her to get into university and qualify as a teacher.

It was to become a strange alliance – the angry Vietnam veteran and the union leader turned politician. Jennie George was impressed with the evidence Tate and the veterans had gathered and she agreed to take the issue to the Liberal government. On 31 March 2007 she wrote to federal politician Bruce Billson, the Veterans' Affairs Minister under conservative Prime Minister John Howard, asking him to look into the matter. Billson passed it on to his department for an answer. The case was now inside the grind of the federal government's bureaucratic machinery – a place where problem questions often die a slow, dust-gathering death.

The Australian War Memorial (AWM), a government statutory authority under the Department of Veterans' Affairs, employs military historians paid from the public payroll. The AWM is undoubtedly one of the great military museums of the world and its exhibitions attract more than 800,000 visitors a year. Its purpose is to 'commemorate the sacrifice of those Australians who have died in war'. Its mission is to 'assist Australians to remember, interpret and understand the Australian experience of war and its enduring impact on Australian society'. Its enormous archives contain most of the records of the Australian war experience and an impressive historic archive of documents, photographs and interviews. Ashley Ekins, the AWM's head military historian, is a South Australian academic who specialises in World War One and the Vietnam War. It was inevitable the matter of the 2nd D&E Platoon would land on his desk. It was, perhaps, a day he'd come to wish had never happened.

While they waited for a response from the government the veterans didn't stop digging. Don Tate's son-in-law, Adam Rainford, a documentary film maker, dug around in the AWM archives hunting for anything which might identify the platoon in the Nui Dat daily orders. Parkin had mentioned in his letter to Tate that the platoon had undergone watermanship training. Rainford focused his search to try and find those orders. Finally, buried in an innocuous section of the archives, he discovered *The Engineer's Narrative*, a commander's diary recording the routine daily comings and goings of engineers at the Nui Dat Headquarters.

On 12 May 1969, the engineers' commanding officer, Major R. Rowe, noted a long list of troop movements, personnel reassignments and mine-clearing operations. But Rainford's heart leapt when he read Major Rowe's first note for the day:

A small group of instructors and boat operators from 1 Troop carried out watermanship training for the new ATF D&E Platoon in an area near the Song Cao May bridge. The Squadron also provided Mark 1 assault boats and motors.

The veterans were ecstatic. It was irrefutable evidence that there was another D&E Platoon on the base. Nobody had found it before because it was in the engineers' commander's diary, not the infantry's. It was the first small, but highly significant, piece of official evidence. The veterans were confident nobody could now deny that their platoon had existed.

Six weeks after Jennie George had written to Minister Billson putting forward the veterans' case, the Australian War Memorial invited a representative group of the platoon to come to Canberra to discuss the issue. On 18 May 2007, Don Tate, Ted Colmer and Kevin Lloyd-Thomas made the three-hour drive from Sydney to Canberra where they were met by Ashley Ekins as well as the AWM director, retired Major General Steve Gower. Gower is a Vietnam veteran who'd been an artillery forward observer, and the platoon men hoped he'd be sympathetic. Tate wanted other veterans to attend, including Jim Riddle, but he maintains the AWM wanted to keep the meeting small.

Tate says Ekins began by handing them two pages which listed all the records the AWM researchers had examined. Ekins told them that despite this extensive search, the AWM had found no trace of any so-called 2nd D&E Platoon. He told them it could not be a properly constituted platoon as it had no officer assigned to it. He dismissed the statements of the officers Pratt and Parkin as memories, not documentary evidence. But Ekins did say he would accept that a unit which called itself the 2nd D&E Platoon had existed for a short period.

The veterans weren't surprised by the intransigence of the AWM historians. They'd been warned by other veterans that the officials didn't like having their opinions challenged. Australian War Memorial historians see themselves as highly respected custodians of the official military history, and would resist former privates telling them they were wrong.

The focus of the meeting was the existence of the platoon and not allegations relating to the treatment of enemy bodies. But Tate recalls Gower, the AWM director, telling them during the meeting that Tom Arrowsmith had told the AWM that all enemy bodies at Thua Tich had been wrapped in tarpaulins and stacked on the side of the APCs before being transported elsewhere for a proper burial.

The veterans didn't challenge this at the time. They wanted to keep the focus on the platoon's name. The AWM seemed dug-in, and weren't going to be shifted no matter what was hurled at them. But the veterans had something hidden up their sleeve. Tate said Ekins and Gower were 'stunned' when he handed them a copy of the engineer's diary that Adam Rainford had discovered in the AWM's very own records. But still they refused to retreat. The meeting itself was cordial enough, but almost immediately afterwards relations between the platoon veterans and the War Memorial soured dramatically.

Just hours after the meeting, Gower issued a memo describing what had been discussed at the meeting and distributed it as an email to various members of the wider veteran community, including the platoon members he had just spoken with. Gower said the determination of the AWM was that it was 'not possible to refer to the unit as the 2nd D&E Platoon as no official evidence of such a platoon exists in the 1ATF [1st Australian Task Force] establishment table, rolls or order of battle.' The memo said Ekins would, however, mention that the operation at Thua Tich was carried out by a 'group that called themselves unofficially the 2nd D&E Platoon'. Gower said they had decided the group was a sub-unit under the command of Headquarters Company, 1st Australian Task Force at Nui Dat. He said it would be identified as a 'discrete group' in the official history of the Vietnam War, which was being written by Ashley Ekins.

As if that wasn't enough of a dismissal, Gower added something which infuriated the veterans. He said the infantrymen had served with D&E Platoon 'possibly as a single rifle section under command of a junior NCO'. He concluded by saying that he thought the meeting had been 'most worthwhile' and thanked those who had attended it. He couldn't have been aware he'd just started a war with the veterans of the platoon.

When the veterans got home and saw Gower's email they were absolutely furious. That night, Tate fired back. Tate replied to Gower that as a former senior officer he must feel sick to be witnessing 'a disgraceful cover-up'. In a blistering email that also went to Ekins and the veterans, Tate said he'd been warned the AWM would brush them aside, treat them condescendingly and even contemptuously. He slammed Gower and Ekins for describing the 39 men as serving in a 'single rifle section under a junior NCO'.

'It diminishes the platoon and everyone in it – making it sound like a bunch of useless yobbos,' Tate fired back. He said a military historian should be aware of the Australian army structure: that a platoon is around 35 men, led by a lieutenant and a sergeant, which is divided into three sections each led by a junior NCO, usually a corporal.

Tate also took exception to the description of the unit as being a section under a 'junior NCO'.

He had a name – Corporal James Riddle – and our deep respect for him and his leadership. He was far from junior as he had served with the British commandos in Borneo and Malaya before joining the Australian army. Riddle performed extraordinarily and this must be recognised.

Jim Riddle wasn't in Australia to hear all this. After a year of being honoured by his mates among the Vietnam veterans, he'd fallen on hard times. He'd hit the drink in a big way, and was a difficult man to be around. He was severely depressed at the bitter wrangling that had sprung from other veterans over the existence of the platoon. Some of his fellow members had just walked away, not wanting anything more to do with it. The whole row stirred up too much anxiety and unpleasantness at a time when they were finding the war demons hard enough to deal with.

Riddle got into a brawl with a fellow veteran at a hostel and went down, hitting his head on some brickwork. He insists he was king hit, and he was in a bad way. He had a stroke shortly afterwards. He had no family in Australia, so he was flown back to England where his sons and their wives could look after him. With his Australian army pension he could pay for a small but clean ground-floor flat in the outer suburbs of Newcastle upon Tyne. Tate was keeping Riddle informed of what was going on back in Australia, but since his stroke Riddle had trouble using his fingers to type email responses.

Ted Colmer wrote off an even more furious email to Gower. He accused the AWM of conspiring to pervert the course of natural justice and withholding vital evidence. Colmer said his research had uncovered a plot by the top levels of the army to deceive the government about the true level of military manpower in Vietnam. Colmer had done significant detective work establishing through battle orders that there had to be two separate D&E Platoons operating in the province in late May 1969. The original D&E platoon, under Second Lieutenant Raymond Woolan, was engaged in operations more than ten kilometres away from Thua Tich.

Logbooks kept at Nui Dat headquarters recorded that the Thua Tich ambush was carried out by '2 Tp 3 Cav & D&E'. It did not specify which D&E unit and, as there was no official registry of a 2nd D&E Platoon, according to these records it must have been the original D&E unit under Lieutenant Woolan.

Lieutenant Woolan was awarded the Military Cross for his leadership and bravery during an ambush by his D&E Platoon conducted on the night of 27 May 1969 – two days before the Thua Tich ambush. Part of the reason for the anger among the Ghost Platoon was they felt Woolan's platoon had been given the credit for their successful ambush at Thua Tich.

In 1998 the Mention in Dispatches awarded to Captain Arrowsmith for his leadership at the Thua Tich operation was upgraded to a Medal of Gallantry. It was done in the End-of-War List, a government reappraisal of medals awarded during the Vietnam War, which had ended 35 years earlier. It followed a vigorous campaign by Vietnam veterans which argued that many deserving soldiers had missed out on medals during the war, or had received lesser medals than they deserved. The army's decision during the war to recommend medals was largely based on rank and many veterans believed there was a quota system for the sharing of medals around the various battalions and divisions of the army. The veterans asserted medals should have been awarded regardless of rank. A total of 78 new medals were awarded in the 1998 list.

While Colmer and Tate were battling the AWM, Jennie George was pressing Veterans' Affairs Minister Bruce Billson for an answer on whether Jim Riddle could be recognised with a medal for his leadership at Thua Tich. A document obtained under the Freedom of Information Act shows the Defence Department drafted a response for Billson saying that, in any conflict, there were people who deserved recognition or decorations who did not receive them, but the Army warned that to do so now would set an 'unsustainable precedent'. The army piled on the excuses. It argued many years had gone by and it would be difficult to confirm the claims, and so requests such as Riddle's would have to be declined. It concluded a line had been drawn under the Vietnam War with the End-of-War List, and no further awards would be considered.

The Ghost Platoon veterans' protests had run into a brick wall. Billson wrote to Tate and the platoon veterans in August 2007 following the line set by the AWM. He told the men that he had been advised by the director of the Australian War Memorial that staff members there had undertaken a thorough search of all the pertinent records and files in the institution's collections, but that no documentary evidence had been found that showed the creation or existence of a second D&E platoon. He said that commanders and other soldiers who were serving at the time were also called upon for information in the matter and that 'none have any recollection . . .' Then he said, 'I hasten to add that this is not in any way to deny the existence of a group that may have called themselves by that name.'

Billson said he realised this would not satisfy their demand that the group be formally named but that 'there is simply not the documentary evidence to justify this'. Billson went on to say the official historians had acknowledged there was 'conflicting evidence' on the issue of the treatment of the enemy dead after the ambush at Thua Tich and that 'the issue may never be resolved satisfactorily'. He said questions remained over the disposal of the enemy bodies but there was no evidence to support the 'conspiracy theories' advanced over the matter. Then he said:

> I do accept that the above does not meet your requests of me but there is one final point I would want to make. I regret very much that all of you have suffered so much and for so long about this matter. Let me assure you that your service and integrity is in no way being called into question, and there is no doubt that all of the men performed in an outstanding fashion on the night of 29–30 May, 1969.

It was a huge setback for the veterans. They seemed destined to remain the Ghost Platoon forever. But they weren't about to give up.

In November came another significant breakthrough. Tate received a handwritten letter from retired Major General Sandy

Pearson setting out his thoughts on the platoon. Pearson wrote that there was a full-time D&E Platoon whose duties were to protect Headquarters as well as other duties as directed. He said it was normal that there were times when there were extra soldiers in HQ waiting for reposting to other battalions. He wrote that in May 1969 there was a group of additional men who came to be referred to 'informally as the 2nd D&E Platoon'. He said:

> The group who were unofficially termed the '2nd D&E Platoon' did conduct themselves with distinction when used with a Cavalry Troop (the modern term would be 'assault troops') in the Xuyen Moc area in late May 1969. This was, to their credit, a most successful operation under the Cavalry commander Captain Arrowsmith.

Pearson signed off, saying both Veterans' Affairs and the Australian War Memorial were aware he was sending this letter. He did not say that the platoon had been formally established, but he did describe them as assault troops – something which boosted the flagging morale of the platoon veterans.

A week later, Labor won the federal election and Kevin Rudd became prime minister. Jennie George was now a government MP. Former army officer and lawyer Dr Mike Kelly was a star new recruit for Labor and he won the key seat of Eden-Monaro from the Liberals. He was rewarded with a newly created post of Parliamentary Secretary for Defence Support.

An imposing man who sported an impressive moustache, Kelly had a PhD and had served as a qualified army lawyer in East Timor, Somalia and Bosnia. He prosecuted a brutal war lord in Somalia who was eventually executed. After the Iraq War, Kelly had inspected Allied detention facilities such as the infamous Abu Ghraib Prison, reporting his findings to the then Howard government. He was part of the legal team that successfully prosecuted Saddam Hussein, which ended in his execution. He left the army as a colonel in charge of Army Legal Services before he turned politician. Kelly was not a man to be trifled with, and he knew his way around the military bureaucracy.

Meanwhile, some of the platoon veterans had fallen out over the way the meeting with the Australian War Memorial was handled. They didn't want to be part of the abuse that was flying around the internet, and they pulled out of the campaign. It had always been an uneasy alliance. The veterans were suffering the symptoms of post-traumatic stress disorder – extreme suspicion, anxiety, rage, paranoia and resentment of authority. But a small core pressed on. A few weeks after the federal election they approached Jennie George with the new evidence they'd gathered over the previous 12 months. They hoped a new Labor government, a party which had opposed the Vietnam War, might be more receptive. George passed all the information on to Mike Kelly with a plea to re-examine the case for recognising the 2nd D&E Platoon.

As a new minister, Kelly had to proceed cautiously. He was aware of the furore in the veteran community stirred up by accusations the platoon veterans had made against the Australian War Memorial. He wasn't going to go down that route. Kelly decided to keep his investigation inside the army. He asked the army's respected military history unit to look into it.

It landed with a thud on the desk of Lieutenant Colonel Bill Houston, the senior member of the Australian Army History Unit. It's a small world among military historians in Canberra, and one of the first things Houston did was to ask Ashley Ekins for his opinion. In an email to Houston obtained under the Freedom of Information Act, Ekins repeated his previous stand that there was no documented evidence the unit had existed. Ekins said sections of the established D&E Platoon were used as 'assault troopers' with tanks and APCs on mobile strike force operations. These were under the command of a cavalry or tank commander, usually a captain, which was standard operating procedure.

Ekins said he had received a note from Colonel David Chinn who was senior operations officer at headquarters at the time. Chinn had specifically denied the formation of a 2nd D&E Platoon, and he'd added that infantry of the existing D&E Platoon were employed on operations with armour in May and June 1969. Chinn died in December 2007.

Houston asked about the veterans' claims of treatment of the enemy dead. Ekins replied they had been unable to find any evidence in operational records to support the claim and that 'contradictory evidence from other soldiers makes it impossible either to verify or disprove the claims'. Following a further query from Houston, another AWM historian, Craig Tibbitts, searched the AWM records to see if there was any diary kept by the Headquarters Company (the command unit which included the D&E platoon) which recorded the activities of a second D&E platoon. Such a diary should also show exactly where the 39 leftover men from the 4th Battalion had been assigned and what they did.

After a week of searching, Tibbits told Houston no such record could be found. In an email to Houston obtained under Freedom of Information, Tibbitts concluded there were four possibilities:

1. The Headquarters Company wrongly assumed the Task Force commander's diary would cover their activities.
2. They were told they didn't need to maintain their own diary.
3. They never bothered to create their own diary and nobody ever told them to do it.
4. They did create their own diaries, but for whatever reason they did not survive or did not pass into archival custody.

'We can only guess which of the above was correct at this stage,' Tibbitts told Houston. But the historian's conclusion was significant: for the first time the War Memorial admitted it was possible that records which would prove the existence of the 2nd D&E Platoon might not have survived the war or might not have been included in the archives. But the War Memorial had kept that to themselves. Neither Ekins nor Gower mentioned to platoon members or to the public that another AWM historian had said this. Of course, the words 'did not survive or did not pass into archival custody' includes the possibility that that the records relating to the 2nd D&E Platoon could have been destroyed or withheld before documents relating to the war were transferred to the archives.

Next, Houston went to the Central Army Records Office (CARO). They insisted there was no 'cover-up', and that they held no information to support claims the unit was a separate entity from the established D&E Platoon. They suggested the group might have been 'colloquially' referred to as the 2nd D&E. They also said claims that the platoon was without an officer were 'fanciful' as they were led on operations by Cavalry Captain Arrowsmith. It noted Riddle was a temporary corporal at the time, not a private. They concluded: 'CARO has no records pertaining to the "serious allegations" relating to the "disposal of enemy bodies".'

Houston wrote to platoon veteran Ted Colmer asking for any papers he had that might help. Houston told Colmer he had confirmed the platoon did exist, but that it had never been intended to be more than a group put together to be used as assault troops. He said:

Clearly the platoon performed well in this role but I am convinced from what I have found that 'Ad Hoc D&E

Platoon' would be a more appropriate title. I have found nothing to suggest any intention to officially raise a second D&E platoon in Headquarters company.

The veterans weren't downhearted at this. On the contrary, it was great news. Houston had at least confirmed that their unit was a special unit used as assault troops. It was better than being ghosts. They felt they were inching towards proper recognition.

A few days later, on 23 March 2008, Don Tate wrote to Jennie George and Mike Kelly saying Houston's email was a significant admission the unit had existed. Tate argued there was now no reason for the government not to recognise the platoon. 'Mr Kelly, this platoon killed a large number of enemy in a very short time,' Tate wrote.

But the fact that there were contentious issues surrounding the disposal of bodies was so contrary to policy at the time (and against the Geneva Convention) that there is no doubt that the authorities took the pragmatic approach – disband the platoon, disperse its members across other units, then falsify the individual records of the men involved.

Never one to be subtle, Tate bluntly warned he would go to the press with stories of a war crimes cover-up unless the government recognised the platoon. He also wanted the bravery of the men of the platoon recognised, in particular that of its commander, acting corporal James Riddle. Tate suggested Riddle be awarded a gallantry medal similar to the one given to Captain Arrowsmith for the same action.

That really stirred things up. Kelly demanded answers. Documents obtained under the Freedom of Information Act show that just four days later, on 27 March, one of the army top brass, Major General David Morrison, wrote to Kelly saying the previous response from Billson had suffered from gaps in the records archived at the Australian War Memorial. He said the platoon veterans had promoted their case in the media and he warned they 'could seek media coverage if the response is not to their liking'. He noted the veteran community had mixed views of the group, which was a bit of an understatement.

Morrison said the Directorate of Operations and International Law had looked into the allegations of atrocities committed at Thua Tich. It had replied that the inquiry by Major Pound in 1976 had found no evidence of wrongdoing. Morrison said the incident had happened almost 40 years before and any further investigation would encounter many difficulties including reliable documentary evidence and appropriate witnesses.

Kelly's subsequent letter to Jennie George, written on army advice, said documents had made it clear there were two distinct D&E platoons operating at the same time. He said the researchers had found there were gaps in the official record-keeping at the time. But he repeated the historians' conclusion that no evidence had been found to support the claim that one of the units was officially named the 2nd D&E Platoon. Kelly said researchers had not been able to contact Tom Arrowsmith to ask how many infantry were attached to his cavalry unit. Lieutenant Parkin had not been formally recorded as the officer in charge of the unit, and there were no formal records to shed light on the command arrangements within the platoon. Kelly pointed out that it was not unusual in either of the two world wars to have a junior NCO in temporary charge of a platoon, and records showed that at the time Riddle was being paid as a corporal.

But that wasn't the end of it. With the 39th anniversary of the Thua Tich ambush on 29 May 2008 fast approaching, Kelly went back to the army and asked them specifically if he could formalise the existence of the 2nd D&E Platoon. Further paperwork obtained under the Freedom of Information Act suggests Major General Morrison was stunned by Kelly's suggestion. Morrison was an army-machine insider. He'd worked his way up the ranks as a logistics and training specialist to the high post of Deputy Chief of the Army. He wrote to Kelly strongly recommending (in bold type) that the minister 'not approve' formalising the platoon. Morrison warned the minister ominously that before he did anything that changed the official records, he should get legal advice. 'Setting such a precedent in amending archives is unprecedented and attracts high risk,' the general thundered.

At the foot of the page Morrison noted that he had consulted Ashley Ekins before writing the memo. In lines that could have been lifted straight from the great British TV series *Yes Minister*, the general fired off this final warning to the minister: '. . . Allowing the archives to be amended to reflect personal recollection or preference risks opening the floodgates to anybody who wants to change or caveat records. Such an initiative would seem to have the potential to undermine the concept of archival records.'

In other words, whatever is written in the army records, right or wrong, should stand as the official and correct record of what happened, regardless of what those who were actually there have to say.

12

A GHOST PLATOON NO MORE

On 29 May 2008, 39 years to the day after the fateful ambush at Thua Tich, a small group of the Ghost Platoon veterans were invited to Canberra to meet Mike Kelly and Jennie George.

They were the platoon's prime agitators for recognition: Ted Colmer, Richard Bigwood, Kevin Lloyd-Thomas and Don Tate. A supporter, retired Brigadier Neil Weekes, joined them for moral support. He'd been a lieutenant in Vietnam himself and, while he'd had nothing to do with the platoon, he'd heard of their struggle for recognition and was upset at the way the issue was dividing the veteran community. He was a member of the Prime Minister's Advisory Council on Ex-Service Matters and wanted to use his influence to calm everyone down should things get heated as they had in the past with the Australian War Memorial.

The four veterans didn't know for sure what Kelly was about to tell them. They'd almost been this close before, only to be rejected. They were ready for disappointment. At least Kelly was prepared to tell them his decision to their faces, rather than send a cold ministerial letter.

The room where they were to meet was innocuous enough, a small, quiet meeting space in Parliament House. There was no fanfare, no one in uniform. Kelly greeted them with respect and thanked them for their service in the war. Jennie George had a big smile on her face. Their hopes rose. This looked good. She wouldn't be there if Kelly was going to give them bad news. After fighting for so long, could it be they were about to hear the words they needed?

Finally Kelly told them of his decision. On that afternoon over tea and biscuits, the new Labor government did something no government had done before: despite protestations from the army and official military historians it formally recognised that a military unit had existed in a war. Kelly ruled the evidence uncovered was sufficient to formally recognise that a unit called the 2nd D&E Platoon had fought in the Vietnam War, and that they had fought with distinction and honour. He also did something no one in the army hierarchy had been prepared to do for almost 40 years – he publicly acknowledged the bravery of the temporary corporal who led the platoon in battle, Acting Corporal James Riddle.

It was an unprecedented moment in military history. For the first time ever, a small group of men – all former army privates left damaged by war – took on the formidable might of the immovable military bureaucracy and, against the odds, fought through to an incredible victory. Through dogged determination, they had beaten a small army of stubborn historians, generals, archivists, army technocrats and 39 years of denials. On the way they'd had abuse heaped on them from fellow war veterans; even death threats. Men traumatised by war had become even more traumatised in their fight for recognition during peacetime. The army and taxpayer-funded historians had erected a massive fortification against their claims, yet the veterans managed to dig deep under the foundations to uncover enough snippets of evidence to bring it tumbling down.

The announcement released to the public by Kelly read:

THE HON. DR MIKE KELLY MP
Parliamentary Secretary for Defence Support

COMBAT HISTORY OF THE 2ND D&E PLATOON
IN THE VIETNAM WAR

The Parliamentary Secretary for Defence Support, the Hon. Dr Mike Kelly AM MP, and Ms Jennie George MP met today with veterans of the 2nd D&E Platoon who served in the Vietnam War as part of the Australian Task Force (ATF), to discuss the acknowledgement of the Platoon and its history in that conflict.

For many years now the surviving members of the platoon have been battling to have their record and role in the Vietnam War officially recognised.

Kelly said, 'I am pleased to announce that I have been able to bring this long struggle to a conclusion by confirming that the Rudd Labor Government and the Defence Department have been able to determine that the platoon did indeed exist and engaged in a series of important actions in Vietnam as part of the Australian Task Force.

'I would like to pay particular tribute to the courage and dedication of the men of the 2nd D&E Platoon. They were a team that was effectively born in battle, not having been formally raised and trained as a sub-unit in Australia before deploying to Vietnam, but being assembled in country in response to the particular security requirements of the ATF. They were able to come together as an effective fighting force thanks to the professionalism of the soldiers and in particular the Non-Commissioned Officer who led them, Corporal James Bertram Riddle,' he said.

The action for which the 2nd D&E Platoon should particularly be noted for was the successful ambush they executed together with 2 Troop, B Squadron, 3rd Cavalry Regiment, in May 1969 at Thua Tich. This was a ferocious battle that involved the engaged troops taking on a much larger enemy force beyond artillery support and through many heroic individual and collective efforts were able to soundly defeat the enemy without loss. Their success was a tribute to their professionalism and the outstanding leadership and courage of Corporal Riddle whose personal actions ensured the survival of many members of the platoon who would otherwise surely have been killed.

'I am delighted to advise these proud veterans that their role in the war will be forever enshrined and acknowledged in the official history of the Vietnam War which is soon to be published. I was privileged to have been able to meet with them personally and thank them for their service to the country and the Australian Army. They served and performed in the finest traditions of the Australian Defence Force and they will have an honoured place in its history. As part of my responsibility for education and training in the ADF I intend to see that our future generations of army leaders will have the opportunity to not only be aware of this legacy but to have the opportunity to learn from it,' Dr Kelly said.

They were a ghost platoon no longer. At long last, they had been formally recognised by the Australian government. The unit also had a unique place in Australian military history: the only platoon to be recognised by a government but not by its army or official military historians.

However, Kelly's announcement didn't mean that all ghosts had been laid to rest. The men who had fought so hard for the recognition at first felt shock and disbelief at the announcement. Later, they reflected it was strange that they felt no immediate sense of triumph, no soaring elation. It had been such a long and bitter struggle that they were simply exhausted. For the government to finally acknowledge they had existed meant it was only catching up to what the men of the ghost platoon had known for the past 39 years.

'It was a pyrrhic victory,' says Tate. 'The harassment from other veterans didn't suddenly end with the announcement. In fact, many came out on veteran internet sites condemning the government decision. "Bullshit" was one word they used. They claimed the government did it just to try to make the issue go away. They still wouldn't accept that the platoon had existed. There were a lot of personal attacks on me and others who had fought to get the platoon recognised. It had been a horrendous experience for us as we had to raise issues in public that we as army men would prefer not to have raised. If they had just conceded our unit had existed from the beginning, none of the stuff about bodies being blown up would have been raised in public.

'Defence only had itself to blame for all that coming out. They had tried to deny the facts and denied the unit existed. The saga proved the army does lie, it does corrupt its history, and it will do anything to protect its reputation and power.'

The Australian War Memorial immediately made it clear the government announcement would not change their position. Ashley Ekins told *The Canberra Times* the government's recognition of the 2nd D&E Platoon did not change the stand taken by the Australian War Memorial. 'They were not a "phantom" platoon,' Ekins told the paper. 'They were an ad hoc squad put together with armour. They were just one of many ad hoc groups.'

After the announcement, Tate would not let the matter rest. He emailed a long list of questions to Gower and Ekins. He demanded to know whether they had been party to a deliberate corruption of the history of the war to protect the reputation of certain officers. He asked whether the AWM would now admit the truth had been hidden for almost 40 years. It got uglier. Gower emailed Tate declaring there was no conspiracy, no official line, no protection of people, no hiding of records and no cover-up of the truth. Gower told Tate he'd had enough of his tirades and that it was sad to see veterans abuse each other.

Tate didn't have time to add the government announcement to his memoirs before they were published in 2008. *The War Within* proved to be a gritty and racy tale of Tate's life growing up on the wrong side of the tracks, his experiences in the army, and his struggle after the war to come to terms with his wounds – both physical and mental. It got excellent reviews. *The Daily Telegraph* said it 'scaled new heights in war writing'. *The Herald Sun* said it was a 'brutal insight into soldiers at war'.

The release of the book prompted quite a deal of publicity about the Ghost Platoon saga. On 8 July 2008, Lisa Whitehead from ABC TV's *7.30 Report* did a strong story on the platoon's long struggle for recognition. She said Tate and 38 others fought in a 'maverick' unit called the 2nd D&E Platoon for six weeks in some of the toughest fighting of the war. 'Roll books originally held by central army records which could have proved the platoon's operational status had disappeared,' she reported.

Richard 'Barney' Bigwood told the ABC reporter that the Australian War Memorial claimed the bodies of enemy dead were wrapped in green tarpaulins and properly buried. 'But that wasn't true,' Bigwood told the ABC. 'They had an engineer's burial – they were dragged into a bomb crater with plastic explosives and blown up.' Bigwood said he was ordered by an officer to tie three of the bodies up to the back door of an APC. 'There were two males and one female. It was a very emotional moment because one of the bodies I turned over had no face.'

Tate suggested the unit had been thrown together without officers or sergeants because, as privates, they were expendable. They were all regular army privates – no conscripts among them – and they would not be missed by the army if killed, nor would it cause a stink for the politicians back in Australia. 'We'd been set quite an ambitious and dangerous task. I think it was quite in all likelihood we could have lost an officer and we could have lost a sergeant and that would have been hard for the brass to explain. However, losing privates would have been no loss.'

Kevin Lloyd-Thomas, a platoon section leader, said that when Minister Mike Kelly finally recognised the unit had existed he was relieved. 'Finally, finally, we found somebody who's going to say, "Yeah guys, you've proved it to us. That's it, we quit. You win."' Tate added: 'This has been the most acrimonious battle. There's been veteran against veteran, mate against mate. There are men who, right from day one, have said, "That's complete rubbish, it never would have happened." We said it did happen because we were in it.'

Despite Colmer's leading role in the campaign for recognition, he wasn't available to be interviewed about the government's announcement.

On 31 July, ABC Radio's *AM* program reported members of the Ghost Platoon had been met with cynicism for decades after the war because many people had been found to have exaggerated or fabricated their war records. But that suspicion had ended with the government's declaration. Tate told *AM*: 'This has been a full on battle for the past two years . . . There's been a cover-up going on here for 39 years and it's taken us 39 years to crack through the bureaucratic walls of the Australian War Memorial and the Australian Defence Force.'

But the surge of publicity and the success of Tate's memoir provided yet more ammunition for his enemies in the veteran community. They slammed Tate as a publicity monger. He was accused of doing it all only to increase sales for his book. Ironically, Tate would make little profit from his book – any income derived from the book was taken off his war pension. Hiding behind code names like Spartakus, Shadow and Fergus, anonymous veterans posted abusive messages on a website called Australian Veteran Matters. Despite the government's declaration and the documents that had been unearthed, Fergus used the website to insist to the veteran community that there never was such a unit, and those who made the claim were wrong.

It wasn't a sophisticated debate. Using language from the playground, Fergus called Tate 'a huge snuffling dumb and dangerous boar pig rolling around in excrement of its own making.' Spartakus said Tate was a coward, arrogant and self-centred.

Among other critics was Normie Rowe, the pop singer who'd served in the cavalry and later clashed with Tate on television over his allegation of atrocities. Rowe still doesn't believe the 2nd D&E Platoon existed despite the government's announcement. 'Mike Kelly was railroaded by those blokes,' Rowe says from his Queensland home. 'There was no controversy about what happened. We cavalry blokes are all in contact and if it did happen we would have to know. I'm not talking about blowing up bodies. Tate has been claiming the APCs ran down and killed a woman and a baby – that is not true. We would know if it was.'

Rowe is still furious that Tate made the allegations of atrocities just before the 1987 Welcome Home parade for Vietnam veterans. 'It was terrible timing for us. We had worked hard for that parade, and it was a big turning point for Vietnam veterans to be accepted as much as World War Two veterans. We were trying to bring order back into the life of Vietnam veterans. We saw a lot of healing after the parade, but then this bastard was prepared to say this sort of thing just to get a book published.

'We don't need to be told how atrocious war is,' Rowe says. 'Nobody is saying it was all sweetness and light. War is ugly and terrible things do happen. The pain is always close to the surface for those who lost people close to them. Those who lost mates in war never forget. Death is all so arbitrary. You can be talking to them one second and the next they have got a bullet through their head and are dead. That pressure never lets up, seven days a week for the whole tour of duty.

'It was so detrimental to claim that mates did things that were not correct. It hurts us all. Why did he do it? Tate did get wounded and have a rough time, but he is now trying to take down others.' Rowe says that, like many veterans, he tried to help Riddle get back to Australia when he heard about his plight. He says Riddle didn't follow the right bureaucratic procedures, but like many veterans, didn't do forms well.

But there was worse to come for Tate than being attacked by a former pop star and anonymous abusers on a web site. A few decided a more direct expression of disagreement was required. Death threats against him and his family continued to come – one or two a year. Occasionally someone decided to throw a punch or two. Eventually Tate ended up in court after a fight with a fellow Vietnam veteran. The judge heard the fight was a culmination of a decade-long row, of trading nasty insults and accusations of faked war wounds. The other veteran, a former sailor, admitted he'd taunted Tate until Tate had let fly with a punch. The magistrate found Tate guilty of assault but took into account his war service and community work, and placed him on a good behaviour bond. He didn't record a conviction.

The two key advocates for recognition, Tate and Colmer, had always had an uneasy alliance. When their falling out came, it was spectacular. It wasn't long after the happy scenes with Mike Kelly at Parliament House. During the long battle with military bureaucrats and official historians they'd both raised the matter of atrocities as a lever to push for recognition, arguing the platoon had been edited out of the history books because of them. But now that they had won recognition, Colmer wanted to drop public airing of anything to do with the allegations.

It came to the crunch when Tate announced that he was taking the matter of the alleged atrocities to the Australian Federal Police for investigation as war crimes. The police response was that such things were outside their jurisdiction as 'no crimes were committed against the Commonwealth', but Tate's move sparked an ugly war of words with Colmer who accused Tate of denigrating the platoon.

The row rapidly degenerated into a nasty public spat carried out over the internet in the full view of the wider veteran community. It sank further to physical threats and some of it ended up in court. Tate was furious and wrote to everyone he could think of saying he believed his life was in danger. He also told politicians their lives might also be in danger.

Colmer agreed to an interview with me and gave quite a detailed account of how he remembered the ambush and other events relating to the platoon. But a few weeks later he wrote to me withdrawing everything he'd said and stressing he wanted nothing to do with this book.

Colmer said he'd enjoyed the talk and wished the book well, but said I had raised issues such as the treatment of enemy bodies that were 'fallacious'. He insisted there were no dark secrets, no cover-ups, no dirty tactics, no firing on of civilians on the way to Xuyen Moc.

Colmer explained that he suffered from chronic post-traumatic stress disorder and that he wanted nothing more to do with any controversial issues to do with the Vietnam War as it would cause him unnecessary angst and bring the defence department into unwarranted disrepute. He said it would also dishonour his peers.

Earlier, Colmer had insisted Richard 'Barney' Bigwood also be at our first meeting. During our interview Bigwood also gave me a vivid account of the ambush. He hadn't been involved in the shooting that night because he was with the other APCs north of the Thua Tich gate, but he had a clear memory of what happened the next morning. However, like Colmer, Bigwood contacted me several weeks after the interview to withdraw everything he had said. Bigwood was concerned about going further into the events of the 29th and 30th of May 1969 and wanted no more to do with it. He wanted back all the papers he'd given me for this book, and withdrew permission to use them in any form. I did so, and haven't used anything Bigwood told me during our interview.

The Ghost Platoon may have been formally recognised and its achievement in its short life praised from the highest level of government. But the men of the platoon had themselves become ghosts – men haunted by war, their lives taken over by overpowering demons of suspicion and anxiety.

13

SPOILING FOR A FIGHT

While the men of the Ghost Platoon and thousands of others were fighting in Vietnam, the politicians who sent them there were having a different sort of battle back home. It was, of course, a battle that wouldn't leave them with any physical or mental damage. In fact, they did quite well out of it.

Weeks before the men of the 2nd D&E Platoon were engaged in the fateful ambush at Thua Tich, Minister for the Army Phillip Lynch was being ushered around the Australian bases by the top brass. Lynch was 29 when the Menzies government sent the first Australian troops to Vietnam in 1963. He was young enough to have joined the army himself, but Lynch – a strong supporter of the war at the time – thought he could best serve his country by going into politics. He joined the

Liberal Party and by 1969 the ambitious conservative Catholic was in charge of the army. Aged just 35, he was younger than most of the senior officers who accompanied him on his tour of Phuoc Tuy province.

At this stage of the war Australian Prime Minister John Gorton was slowly scaling back the involvement of Australian troops in Vietnam. Gorton became prime minister in January 1968 after Harold Holt literally disappeared into the surf off the coast of Victoria. Gorton was a bit of a maverick inside the conservative Liberal Party. He was born the son of working-class immigrant parents and, like his school classmate Errol Flynn, was a larrikin who loved drink and women.

When World War Two broke out Gorton immediately joined the RAAF. He was 29, the same age as Lynch when troops were first sent to Vietnam. Gorton had an action-packed war and was lucky to survive. His face was badly scarred when his fighter plane crashed, a wartime disfigurement that seemed to endear him even more to the ladies. As prime minister, Gorton was at times erratic, something that worried the American allies, particularly as he refused to adhere to the script drafted by foreign affairs officials who were close to the Americans.

It seems to be a universal truth since the world wars that those politicians who've never seen a shot fired in anger are those most keen on sending young men and women to war. Anyone who has seen the horror of war firsthand is generally far more reluctant to commit others to the horrors of battle.

Gorton was never a strong supporter of the Vietnam War. His very first act as prime minister was to freeze the number of Australian troops deployed to Vietnam. Eleven months after taking office, and after too many pre-Christmas tipples with the press gallery, he invited attractive 19-year-old journalist Geraldine Willesee – the daughter of a Labor senator – to join him for a drink at the US Embassy Christmas party. Willesee jumped at the chance as any good reporter would.

At 1am the pair was seen huddled on a couch at a far end of the embassy's reception room talking quietly. Americans and Australians who witnessed them together immediately assumed the topic of discussion was of an amorous nature. On the contrary, Gorton was discussing high matters of state; top secret stuff at that. Their discussion had got around to the Vietnam War. Gorton was angry with the Americans – that very day the US had broken off bombing North Vietnam, a huge development, and hadn't bothered to consult with their Australian ally about it. Gorton confided to the young reporter that he really wanted to pull all the Australian troops out of Vietnam immediately, but his party wouldn't let him.

It was a sensational scoop for the young reporter: a prime minister wanted to end the war but his party was stopping him. If it had become public it would have caused a massive schism in the conservative government. It would have most likely ended with Australia pulling out of the war or Gorton being forced to resign. But the next day, as Willesee typed up her exclusive story, her editor at Australian United Press, Ken Braddick, ripped the page from her typewriter and tore it up, telling her that her discussion with the PM had been 'off the record'. Her story was buried and she lost her job.

Meanwhile, at Christmas, 1968, the 8500 soldiers fighting and dying in Vietnam, their families waiting back home and the Australian public remained unaware that their prime minister secretly believed the troops should be brought home immediately. Gorton's thoughts on the war meant Canberra was immobilised. A ceiling remained on troop numbers, and the interest from Canberra in prosecuting the war diminished at all levels.

By early 1969 Australian commanders in the field were bewildered and disheartened as their daily dispatches about the state of the campaign disappeared into the black hole of Canberra without comment or reaction. Many military officers felt Australia's continuing role in the fighting was pointless, that the war was unwinnable. Much of this was filtering down to junior officers and the troops themselves. A malaise had set in. Despite this, young Australian men were still being sent into the jungle every day to kill and be killed.

In May 1969, as the army top brass flew Lynch around Vietnam in military helicopters and he posed for cameras in hulking Centurion tanks, the war was rapidly losing support among the Australian public. An opinion poll in June revealed 55 per cent of people now wanted the troops to come home – the first time a poll found a majority was against the war.

The last 12 months had been the bloodiest of the war, which had now been going as long as World War Two. The death toll of Australian troops had risen to several hundred without any apparent progress in the fight against the communists, and anti-war demonstrations were steadily building at home. Morale among American troops was low, too, and in the US pressure was growing even among conservative political heavyweights to find a way to get out of the war.

It was natural, then, for war correspondents to ask the visiting army minister whether there was an Australian policy to break off contacts with the enemy in order to keep casualties down. Lynch indignantly denied such a notion, spluttering that such a suggestion was against all the proud traditions of the Australian army. He warmed to his fighting talk.

'Our people are spoiling for a fight,' he thundered. 'They don't evade the enemy. They seek him out. In fact, this is one of the most frustrating things, because the enemy keeps moving on.'[1]

The army must have been thrilled to tell reporters the very next day that a cavalry squadron had successfully ambushed and killed six Viet Cong. It seemed to back up the minister – Aussie diggers were indeed spoiling for a fight. But the news had a nasty twist. At the foot of the triumphant *Daily Telegraph* story headlined 'Australians Kill Reds in Ambush' were three poignant paragraphs stating that Private Barry George, 21, unmarried of Rylestone, NSW, was killed and that another

21-year-old soldier was wounded in a separate action in Long Khanh province.[2]

It can't be known whether Lynch's frustration that the enemy wouldn't stand still long enough to be killed had anything to do with Headquarters' decision a short time later to deploy the hastily formed ragtag 2nd D&E platoon to Thua Tich to ambush an enemy column expected there. However, it was certainly in line with the positive headlines that Lynch and the army top brass were seeking for use back home.

Lynch was probably still smarting from being made to look a complete fool shortly after he received his ministerial post the year before, when he had vigorously defended the army in a scandal involving allegations of an atrocity committed by Australian troops. American journalist Martin Russ had written in his Vietnam memoir, *Happy Hunting Ground*, that Australian soldiers had water-tortured a Vietnamese female civilian. The technique involved placing a towel over the victim's face and pouring water over it, giving the victim the impression they are about to drown. Lynch appeared on television to declare he could not find 'one scintilla of evidence for the charge'. The next day Australian journalist John Sorrell wrote a detailed account confirming the story along with photos of the woman prisoner. He reported he was outside the tent in Nui Dat when it happened.[3]

Prime Minister Gorton made the situation even worse when he breezily told parliament the woman had been well enough to pose for photos after her 'so-called torture'.

'A bit wet, perhaps,' interjected a Labor MP.

'Yes, a little wet, I agree,' said Gorton.

Gorton's flippant remark and Lynch's apparent lie inflamed the anti-war movement and became a rallying call for protesters. It also marked a turning point for Australian journalists covering the action. From that point on they hunted for stories of Australian atrocities; editors were prepared to run them, and the growing anti-war public consumed them voraciously to confirm their view that the Vietnam War was cruel and barbaric, and that Australia should get out.

Lynch continued to insist the army had investigated the allegations and found the press stories were wrong – that there was no water torture. However, files of the Gorton government cabinet meeting minutes which were released after 30 years in the National Archives reveal the extent of concern the story was causing. One file shows that the government received advice that the interrogation procedure contravened 'the letter of the law' in regard to the Geneva Convention. But there was a problem – a confidential army report prepared for the government said this was one of the 'standard interrogation techniques' taught at the intelligence centre and was in use by the Australian armed forces. After receiving this piece of bad news, Cabinet decided not to open an inquiry into the incident. Instead, they decided to make a public statement stressing the woman was a Viet Cong spy who had endangered the lives of Australians.[4]

But the truth has a way of coming out. In 2010 one of the soldiers present at the water-torture interrogation finally spoke up and revealed the enormous efforts the army had gone to cover up what really happened. Former SAS sergeant Peter Barham told journalist Toni McRae, a veteran reporter and star of the Queensland regional paper *Fraser Coast Chronicle*, that he had been the interpreter in the tent while the water torture was carried out.

'These two soldier cowboys bound her wrists behind her back, placed a wet towel across her face and as she breathed in the towel went in and they poured water down her,' Barham said.

> They weren't that good at it, but it went on for at least half an hour. I felt sick, but couldn't leave the tent because I was the interpreter and had to relay what she said during her torture. She was distressed and this was after the soldiers asked me to tell her in Vietnamese that they would pull her nails out, stick objects up her orifices and do to her just about anything else very painful that you could imagine.[5]

Barham said they'd lied to army investigators about the water torture. Perhaps the army heard what they wanted to hear, and went to great lengths to keep the three soldiers silent. They posted Barham to a secret SAS base in Perth where he was out of reach of pesky reporters and promoted him to sergeant in the hope it would keep him quiet. Forty years later Barham revealed the anguish and guilt he felt then – and continued to feel. 'I have kept this bottled up for too long,' Barham told McRae.

> I used to swear that Vietnam vets asking for compensation, let alone recognition of their war service, were just wankers. This I said while I was rolling around in the gutters in my own vomit with no money in my pockets and nowhere to live. Then one day I realised I was one of them.
>
> War stuffs up young men and they go on to stuff up others' lives, as I did. It's all about hurt, hurt, hurt and you change after war. You become angry and violent, and in my case you try to drink yourself to oblivion.

While soldiers like Barham would be traumatised for life and forced to live a lie, the minister for the army, Phillip Lynch, went on to bigger and better things. He rose to become deputy leader of the Liberal Party and was one of the prime plotters who helped bring down the Whitlam government in 1975. He was rewarded with the senior post of Treasurer in Malcolm Fraser's government. In 1981 he was made a Knight of the Order of St Michael and St George. He quit politics in 1982 due to ill health and died two years later, never changing his opinion about his leading role in the Vietnam War.

Lynch's successor as Army minister was Andrew Peacock, a dashing, wealthy man from Melbourne's high society. Peacock was 24 and president of the Young Liberals when Menzies first sent troops to Vietnam. He was a strong supporter of the action but, like Lynch and other pro-war activists, he decided he would best serve his country in parliament. When Menzies retired in 1966 the war was in full swing and Peacock entered parliament by inheriting Menzies's blue-ribbon seat. By late 1969 Peacock had succeeded Lynch as Minister for the Army. Just 30 years old, Peacock was younger than most senior NCOs and army officers above the rank of captain.

Peacock found himself in an embarrassing position in August 1970 when evidence emerged that the army, in its desperation to fill its ranks, had sent a young conscript to Vietnam even though he was close to being blind. Twenty-three-year-old Private Stanley Gordon Larsson of Adelaide was killed when he stepped on a mine. Larsson had been found to have deficient eyesight by two separate medical boards. Larsson was unable to see further than four feet in front of him without his thick glasses, but army medical officers reversed each board decision, forcing Larsson into active service.

Peacock insisted proper procedures had been followed. The Larsson family's local Labor MP, Norman Foster – a wharfie and veteran of the famous Rats of Tobruk – challenged Peacock to put on glasses which restricted him to seeing only four feet in front of him, then decide whether the youngster had been fit to be sent to war.[6]

During the Vietnam War Malcolm Fraser was Minister for Defence, effectively in charge of Lynch and Peacock. Fraser was also responsible for the despised conscription program – the first of its kind in Australian history. Fraser went on to lead the government and become an elder statesman for his party but it wasn't until 2010, when he wrote his memoir, that he revealed he believed the war had been a mistake. He said he'd never believed in the domino theory; that the war had been doomed to failure from the start. He claimed that it wasn't until 1995 that he discovered that the US had been intimately involved in the 1963 overthrow of Vietnam's puppet President Ngo Dinh Diem – something that just about everybody else knew in the 1960s. Even though he was at the leading edge of Australia's involvement in the war he claimed he was 'mystified and concerned' about the way war policy was made.[7]

Fraser went on to tell *The Herald Sun* that Australia should not repeat the mistakes of Vietnam and refrain from blindly following the Americans blindly into war. He felt that the war in Afghanistan could not be won.[8]

Sir Robert Menzies, who enthusiastically sent Australian troops to both the Korean and Vietnam wars, did not enlist for World War One when he was a young man. When the Great War broke out in 1914, Menzies was 20 and a very successful law student at the University of Melbourne. Before the war he was already in the part-time university militia unit, the Melbourne University Rifles. He seemed to like the military life, quickly rising to the rank of lieutenant in the university militia. But as the war years dragged on and his contemporaries joined the Australian armed forces in their thousands, Menzies sat resolutely at his desk, going on to win university prizes. Despite being a strong advocate for conscription for overseas service and a patriotic supporter of the Empire, Menzies never explained why he sat out the war while he urged others to do their patriotic duty and enlist. Labor stalwart Eddie Ward once noted dryly that Menzies had 'a brilliant military career that was cut short by the outbreak of war'.

John Howard was president of the Young Liberals between 1962 and 1964 and he was also a strong supporter of the Vietnam War. Even though he was 26 when Menzies sent the first combat troops to Vietnam, like Menzies, Lynch and Peacock, Howard decided he could best serve his country inside Parliament House. Howard rose to become the second-longest serving prime minister after his idol Menzies. Shortly before he visited Vietnam on a trade mission in 2006, Howard was asked whether he thought the Vietnam War was a mistake. 'I supported our involvement at the time and I don't intend to recant that,' he told reporters.[9]

Howard's close friend and ally in the Iraq War, US President George W. Bush, was also a strong supporter of the Vietnam War. Bush managed to avoid the actual fighting by enrolling in the Texas Air National Guard, but he loved being photographed as the 'war-fighting president' in full combat pilot gear on aircraft carriers. Bush's vice-president, Dick Cheney, who pushed for the invasion of Iraq and Afghanistan, managed to get five draft deferments during the Vietnam War. 'I had other priorities in the '60s than military service,' Cheney told *The Washington Post* in 1989.[10]

Malcolm Fraser wasn't the only Vietnam War hawk to change their minds many years later. The chief architect of the war was the then US Secretary of Defence, Robert McNamara, who had pushed the vigorous prosecution of the war from the start. In his 1995 memoir, *In Retrospect: The Tragedy and Lessons of Vietnam*, McNamara said he and his senior colleagues were 'wrong, terribly wrong' to pursue the war as they did. He said they were mistaken in seeing it as a communist war of aggression. In reality it was a civil war. 'We just didn't understand that,' he said in an interview at the time.

McNamara acknowledged he failed to force the military to produce a rigorous justification for its strategy and tactics, and admitted he kept the war going long after he realised it was futile, lacking the courage to admit they'd been wrong. He admitted the reason the US gave for commencing the bombing of North Vietnam and sending thousands of combat troops into South Vietnam in 1965 was based on a lie.

The Gulf of Tonkin Incident, as it became known, was an alleged torpedo attack by North Vietnamese gunboats on the warship *USS Maddox*. At the time, the US claimed their ship was in international waters but it emerged it was well inside North Vietnamese waters, spying on the coast. No missiles struck the *Maddox* but sonar operators thought they had seen multiple streaks coming at the ship. McNamara said the situation on board was confused and the ship's officers weren't sure there really had been any torpedo attacks. It turned out to be a misreading of the sonar and McNamara failed to tell President Johnson of the doubts of the ship's captain. Years later, it emerged US spy agencies had suppressed the doubts and errors in the initial accounts of the attack. McNamara had only passed on information that supported the notion there had been an attack by North Vietnam.

'It was confusion, and events afterwards showed that our judgement that we had been attacked that day was wrong. It didn't happen,' McNamara said later. But at the time, the incident was pounced on, the US military launching 'retaliatory' bombing raids on North Vietnam the next day. The war they began that day would result in the deaths of millions of people. The official death tolls, presented below, are based on the figures kept by authorities on both sides, but in reality no one knows for certain how many Vietnamese died since so many of the bodies were never recovered or identified.

South Vietnamese civilians:	2 million
North Vietnamese Army and Viet Cong:	1.1 million
South Vietnamese Army:	260,000
North Vietnamese civilians:	65,000
United States:	58,267
South Korea:	5,099
Australia:	521
Thailand:	351
New Zealand:	55
Philippines:	7

But these numbers do not reveal the true extent of the losses from the war. They don't include the countless millions more who were left with a life of pain and suffering from wounds and the ongoing generational effects of Agent Orange and other defoliants. It doesn't reveal the constant mental torment that overshadowed so many veterans' lives, condemning many to see out their days as living ghosts. As time wears on, some of the politicians who sat in their offices and pushed for the war, sending thousands to their deaths, seem happy to clear their conscience as they approach the end of their lives. But it's worth noting that they only come forward with their newsworthy confessions when they have a memoir to push.

But the truth is that, while America dropped the first bombs in North Vietnam, Australia played its own role in encouraging and intensifying the unjustified war. Research by Michael Sexton, who later became Solicitor-General in New South Wales, revealed that Menzies and his foreign minister, Paul Hasluck, exerted pressure to escalate the action. They had decided to send Australian forces to fight in South Vietnam long before the US made their own decision. In 1964, Australia's diplomats in Washington urged the Americans to increase the bombing of North Vietnam. In February 1965 the US State Department said it was under 'some pressure' from the Australian government to make a request for troops. Australia's push to scale up the war was made without any regard to the wishes of South Vietnam. Menzies' aim was to lock the Americans into the ANZUS treaty in case of any trouble in the future with Indonesia. The first American combat troops landed in Vietnam in March 1965 and on 29 April 1965, Menzies announced in parliament that an Australian battalion would be joining them. But behind the scenes, Menzies had actually pressured South Vietnam to issue the invitation for Australian troops.[11]

Throughout the war, the lies and half-truths just kept on coming, and the men in power walked away healthy, wealthy and scot-free. They were promoted, feted and honoured. From then on, the Australian military culture became steadily woven into the very fabric of nationhood. More than any other prime minister, John Howard poured money into bolstering the Anzac legend and the militarisation of Australian history. His term as the nation's leader saw huge growth in pilgrimages to Gallipoli, the Somme and Kokoda by young and old alike. He increased funding to war memorials, especially the National Australian War Memorial, which expanded rapidly. A sound and light spectacular of a helicopter landing and with audio of real radio transmissions greets visitors to the Vietnam War exhibition. More and more war memorials have appeared on the wide Anzac Parade leading up to the AWM in a direct line from Parliament House on the other side of Lake Burley Griffin. There are ten, one each for the Navy, Army and Air Force, the First World War, the Korean War, the Vietnam War, nurses, the Rats of Tobruk and two for New Zealand. Future sites are marked for the Boer War and peacekeepers.

'The Anzac legend has helped define who we are as Australians,' Howard declared in 2005 as he left for Turkey to attend the lavish 90th anniversary of the landings at Gallipoli. Howard said the original Anzacs, and those who followed them in serving their country in times of conflict, represented the values Australia holds dear: 'determination, courage, compassion and resourcefulness'.

Since the boom days under Howard, the Australian War Memorial suffered a shortfall in funding and the custodians of the Anzac legend there saw nothing wrong in encouraging corporate sponsors to climb on board if they handed over cash. More than 87 corporate sponsors now have their name associated with exhibits at the memorial, including two of the world's biggest arms manufacturers, BAE Systems and Boeing. There are also an alcohol conglomerate, several banks and a large media corporation. The AWM finally called a halt to the sponsorships when it was revealed that a power company would sponsor the performance of a bugler who plays the 'Last Post' every day outside the AWM.

The real experience of war is very much absent at the child-friendly displays at the memorial and it has come markedly closer to glorifying war. There is no display at the Vietnam exhibit showing the war was unjustified and based on a sham. There is little mention of the lasting effects of the war on Vietnam veterans' physical and mental health. A video at the exhibit lambasts journalists for 'sensationalising' the war, in particular for making allegations of atrocities committed by

Australian soldiers such as the water-torture incident. 'For some [war correspondents], truth became the first casualty in the search for sensational headlines,' instructs the War Memorial video. 'Australians at home were often given a false impression of what Australian service men and women were doing in Vietnam, because they saw only stories relating to Americans in action.'

The massacre at My Lai, it goes on, was one example. 'Although the My Lai massacre fuelled the anti-war movement, it was completely unrelated to operations being conducted by Australians in Vietnam.' And 'like My Lai', the video goes on to explain, the allegation of water torture of a female prisoner by Australian interrogators was 'an extreme example of sensational press reporting of the Vietnam War'. In a chastising female voice, the AWM video explains that both incidents were thoroughly investigated by the military and involved 'much misreporting of the truth'. 'Public opinion, however, was swayed by these stories and contributed to the growth of the anti-war movement,' it concludes.

Strangely, the War Memorial doesn't seem to consider that it was cold, hard documentary evidence – photographs of dozens of murdered innocent women and children – that turned people against the war. The AWM regards the massacre at My Lai and the water torture of a female prisoner by Australians as mere irritations in its depiction of the Vietnam War as noble, exciting and praiseworthy. So ingrained is the military in Australia's concept of its own culture that its efforts to present war as a positive highlight in Australia's past continue at the very highest level on both sides of politics. In March 2011, Labor Prime Minister Julia Gillard told the United States Congress they had a 'true friend Down Under'. She reminded them of 60 years of Australian fighting alongside Americans in various conflicts, and offered even closer military ties.

But the vast majority of Americans have no idea that 521 Australians were killed in Vietnam in the hope of keeping that alliance going. Most don't even know that Australian soldiers were there. In the hope of educating Americans about Australia's willingness to stand by their ally in war, Prime Minister Gillard bequeathed $3.3 million towards the construction of a special Australian exhibit which will be part of a Vietnam War education centre to be built near the Vietnam War Memorial in Washington.

It's not only the veterans who are still paying for the war. Taxpayers are forking out, too.

14

NO ONE IS EVER CURED

The men of the Ghost Platoon weren't the only ones who would be forever haunted by the war. The mental trauma of the Vietnam War was to play a long and agonising role in the lives of many of those who served.

In the months after the ambush at Thua Tich, the army and the Gorton government was undoubtedly relieved no word had leaked to the press about the treatment of the enemy bodies. But in the months ahead there were even more ominous headlines emanating from Vietnam. By the end of the year the platoon's Private Peter 'Pedro' Allen was on the front pages with the trial for his murder of Lieutenant Convery. A few months later a corporal was found guilty of negligence after accidentally killing a 21-year-old digger at Vung Tau while adjusting his machine gun. Then, on Christmas Day 1970,

Private Paul Ramon Ferriday, after a day of heavy drinking at the Nui Dat base, retrieved his automatic rifle from his tent, got down on one knee, took aim at the sergeants' mess and fired three shots, killing Sergeants Allan Brian Moss, 22, and Wallace James Galvin, 32. He also wounded Sergeant Frederick Edwin Bowtell, 38.

Witnesses said that Ferriday, 21, a regular soldier with an air dispatch unit, had talked about how he wanted to kill a warrant officer he claimed had harassed him. During his court martial Ferriday said he hadn't intended to kill anyone; he just shot into the mess. The only reason he could offer was that for a while he'd 'lost his head'. He didn't even know the men he'd killed. He was found guilty of murder and sentenced to life in jail but an appeal found Ferriday was insane at the time of the shooting. His conviction was reduced to manslaughter and his sentence was cut to 10 years.

The case was eerily similar to that of Private Allen 12 months earlier. No reason was given for the killing, just a vague resentment against an NCO. Ironically, Ferriday's sentence for killing two sergeants and wounding another ended up being about the same as Allen's for killing one officer.

Ferriday's state of mind was significant. Psychiatrists told his court martial that he suffered from a paranoid personality. Lieutenant Colonel Maddison, psychiatric consultant to Eastern Command and Professor of Psychiatry in the University of Sydney at the time, said the recognisable features of this disorder were a pervading tendency to distrust and suspicion of others, an extreme sensitivity and a readiness to see hurtful double meanings which were unrecognised by others. These led to isolation and the avoidance of close relationships. Maddison said Ferriday's principal techniques for mastering his anxiety, insecurity, frustration and resentment were withdrawal, isolation and projection. He'd blame others and his circumstances rather than himself.

Alarm bells should have been ringing among army psychiatrists that a pattern was forming. The actions of some soldiers coming home should also have caused concern in the defence hierarchy. Unfortunately no one was taking any notice.

Trooper George William Franklin, 23, spent 358 days in Vietnam over two tours with the elite 3rd squadron Special Air Service. He was a highly trained soldier, a member of the most respected and highly trained unit of the Australian army. It's extremely hard to get into the unit and anyone who looks like they can't take the pressure is rejected. The SAS reconnoitre deep behind enemy lines, tracking enemy and, if necessary, killing them. They have a fearsome reputation. When there's an impossible job, these are the men the army commanders turn to. The SAS work in deep secrecy, often undercover, often on 'black operations' that are off the books. A lot of what they did in Vietnam is still top secret. They are virtually untouchable.

Franklin was one of their best, home for a bit of R&R before he went back to Vietnam with a deserved promotion. In March 1970 he went to a dance at a club in Lithgow looking for a bit of fun. He met up with Beverley Alma Philips, a 30-year-old mother of three young children who had separated from her husband. The kids were at home with a babysitter. She took a shine to the dashing young soldier, and they went back to her place. In the morning her children found her dead body on her bedroom floor. Police saw that, from the bruises around her neck, whoever killed her strangled her with their bare hands. Police quickly picked up Franklin who admitted to being with her. He told police they'd had sex and then she'd said something about him having a wife and children. He didn't remember what happened next. 'It was a nightmare,' Franklin said.

He couldn't tell the court why he'd killed the young mum. He just didn't know. He had no motive. He didn't even remember doing it. He'd blacked out.

Justice Rae Else-Mitchell, a highly respected judge and keen historian, said from his bench at the Central Criminal Court that the army had to accept some of the blame for the murder of Mrs Philips. They had trained Franklin to kill, and then let him loose among civilians. 'There seems little doubt that the army, to which you are so devoted, must take more than a small responsibility for the grievous wrong you did to your victim,' the judge said. The top brass must have been aghast when *The Sydney Morning Herald* carried the judge's comments on its front page:

On the evidence given it seems not only that your term in Vietnam was partly responsible for your having succumbed quickly to violence, but that the way in which you killed your victim with your own hands was one which you were encouraged to learn in the course of your training.

Such knowledge and the capacity to inflict sudden violent death may be among the necessities of jungle warfare. However, the cities and towns of this State are not the jungle and although you have shown yourself to be an eager and disciplined soldier, you have not shown yourself to possess the measure of self-control and self-discipline essential to life in an ordered civilian community.[1]

The jury found Franklin not guilty of murder but guilty of manslaughter. Sentencing him to 12 years' jail with three years before parole, the judge added he believed it would be 'inappropriate' for the Army to give Franklin a dishonourable discharge as it was also accountable for what happened.

These tragic incidents do not suggest that large numbers of Vietnam veterans were going on murderous rampages. It's also true that some murders are committed for no apparent motive or reason by people who have no experience of war or the military. But something terrible was happening to a large proportion of servicemen returning from the Vietnam War. At first it wasn't noticed by the general public. It happened behind closed doors. Wives and children were the first to feel the brunt. Their husbands and fathers had brought the demons of war back home with them.

The afflicted returned veteran ran their home with stern authority: questioning everything their loved ones did, abusing their family as nothing they did was ever good enough. There was little love, little intimacy. These were highly damaged men. They displayed extreme mood swings, irrational tantrums at small or imagined slights, uncontrollable bouts of rage, retreats into brooding silence, incessant suspicion, resentment and paranoia, a hatred of authority, morbid feelings of worthlessness and self-pitying behaviour.

At night came the nightmares – sweating profusely, crying out, wrestling with unseen enemies, waking with a desperate determination to survive – even if that meant attacking the one sleeping closest to them. For many, the nightmares were the same night after night. Wives and children lived in fear and the ones who stayed often became the victims of domestic abuse. Relatives and friends stayed away. Alcohol and drugs were a common refuge.

Their feelings of alienation from society hit them almost immediately on their return. They came back to a widespread public attitude that they shouldn't have been fighting in the first place. There was no honour in that war, no big welcome parades. Many were flown back in the middle of the night, quietly discharged and told to go home. The army didn't need them anymore. The wounded, especially those who were psychologically damaged, were dumped into a civilian world which didn't understand their plight, and the defence system made little attempt to help them.

Veterans of the other wars looked down on them. Men who'd fought the Nazis and the Japanese in World War Two told Vietnam vets that they hadn't been in the real thing. Vietnam wasn't a fight to the finish like theirs had been. They were sneered at, told they'd fought village boys and women in black pyjamas, not a real uniformed enemy army that was confronted standing tall in the field of battle. And of course the most bitter comment of all was that the soldiers sent to Vietnam had lost.

For decades there wasn't a name for what was going on with these men. For a long time no one identified it as a collective phenomenon. They were just regarded as Vietnam vet crazies, and pity the poor women and children who had to live with them. The vets themselves resented any suggestion they were different. They felt that only other Vietnam veterans could understand what they were going through.

A joke went around among Vietnam veterans and those who knew them: Q: How many Vietnam veterans does it take to change a light bulb? A: How the fuck would you know? You weren't there!

But the reality is that their condition had always existed – for as long as men had fought other men in battle. Warriors of the ancient world suffered from it. Homer recorded Achilles acting on it in *The Iliad*. Shakespeare gives a dose of it to his characters in *Macbeth* and *Henry IV*. In the US Civil War it was labelled 'soldiers' heart'. In the Great War it was called 'shell shock' and World War Two changed that to 'battle fatigue'.

Clinical figures were hard to come by as no one was collecting them. But just about every family knew a veteran from the world wars who suffered in some way. Jim Riddle certainly experienced it from his father. Police and medical workers spoke quietly of the shocking extent of suicides among world-war veterans. Many of these deaths weren't entered in the records as suicides – to do so would bring shame on the families and the insurance companies wouldn't pay up. Instead they were listed as farm or work accidents. The extent of the lasting impact of war remained hidden.

It wasn't until the 1980s that researchers sought to estimate just how bad the long-term effect of those wars really was. Going over medical records from World War Two, British researchers estimated more than 20 per cent of people officially listed as wounded were actually victims of battle fatigue. Some American researchers put it as high as 30 per cent. They looked at medical records from World War One and found the same level for what was then called shell shock.

In 1980 the American Psychiatric Association's *Diagnostic and Statistics Manual of Mental Disorders* gave the condition an official new psychiatric designation – post-traumatic stress disorder (PTSD). For the first time the symptoms shown by the generations of men returned from war were recognised as a specific mental illness. It was, the psychiatrists said, a normal reaction to stressful situations. Soldiers weren't the only ones afflicted. Anyone who had been exposed to extremely stressful situations could be afflicted, including victims of rape or violence, life-threatening events, bullying and physical or mental abuse.

People react differently and show different intensities of the symptoms that go with PTSD. Many people could go through the same experience and not suffer PTSD at all. Some might not react until decades later. Depression, anxiety disorders, social phobia, and alcohol and drug abuse are common afflictions associated with PTSD.

According to the Clinical Research Unit for Anxiety and Depression at Sydney's St Vincent's Hospital, victims can have some or all of the following symptoms:

- Recurring memories of the traumatic event which you can't shake
- Recurring nightmares of the trauma
- A nagging feeling the traumatic event was happening again with hallucinations and flashbacks
- Simple events which trigger an overreaction in the belief it is happening again
- Nervousness, anxiety and panic attacks triggered by memories of an event
- Withdrawal from people or conversations which might bring up memories of the trauma
- Avoiding places or objects which could remind of the trauma
- Memory loss of the traumatic event, or even days surrounding the event.
- Lack of motivation, listlessness, losing interest in people and activities you used to care about
- Feeling emotionally estranged, separated or cut off from others

- Unable to feel emotions, especially love, tenderness and sexual passion
- Difficulty sleeping
- Outbursts of anger or rage
- Poor concentration and failing to complete tasks
- Overly vigilant and alert
- Constantly feeling edgy and easily startled
- Lack of confidence in everyday situations
- Difficulty keeping a job
- Distrust of authority and suspicious of strangers
- Obsession with supposed enemies

Finally, mental health experts had a label for the suffering of the war veterans. But something strange was emerging from the data. The number of veterans from the Vietnam War coming forward with these problems seemed to be far higher – and was on the increase – than veterans from previous wars. A 1990 study of US Vietnam veterans found 30.6 per cent had experienced PTSD at some time. In 1992 a report from the Australian National Audit Office presented to parliament said 25 per cent of Vietnam veterans were on a disability pension for either medical or psychological reasons. A 1996 study of Australian Vietnam veterans seeking help found two-thirds could have PTSD. One explanation was that now there was a name for the condition, veterans were more willing to seek help. It was an illness with a cause, not an inherent disorder.

Medicos were now able to categorise their patients – but the extent of the problem was very real. An Australian Department of Veterans' Affairs study looking at Vietnam veterans' health between 1980 and 1995 showed that up to 45 per cent of veterans suffered mental disorders, and they had a higher rate of suicide. A third of Vietnam veterans had problems related to excessive drinking. A further study estimated 56 per cent of Vietnam veterans exhibited some of the symptoms of PTSD. Then, in the mid-1990s, the number of veterans who successfully claimed compensation for PTSD soared to 3000 a year. Treatment was costing up to $348 million a year.[2]

The Department of Veterans' Affairs has 20,000 Vietnam veterans recorded as receiving benefits after being diagnosed with PTSD. A further 2500 Vietnam veterans outside this classification are receiving treatment for PTSD. At the same time, 4600 veterans from World War Two and the Korean War are PTSD pensioners.

There's an explanation for why Vietnam veterans were more afflicted with mental problems caused by war than veterans of previous wars. It's an explanation that would surprise World War Two veterans who disparaged the conflict fought in Vietnam as not a real war. An Australian Senate committee looking into the health of Vietnam veterans was told by Brigadier William Rodgers, a former director of the Australian Army Medical Services, that the stress levels faced by the average soldier in Vietnam were 200 times higher than those faced by the average soldier in World War Two.

In Vietnam, soldiers usually did a 12-month tour of duty compared to the World War Two soldiers who was in for the duration. But those 12 months were nearly all in the combat zone under the constant threat of attack. In the world wars, soldiers faced long periods in the rear zone with an average of just 60 days in actual battle. In Vietnam, soldiers were deemed to spend 300 days or more in combat zones where an enemy hidden in the jungle could attack at any time. They fought in small units, sections or platoons, while world-war soldiers generally fought in far larger units.

Australian soldiers in Vietnam had to be constantly hyper-alert on jungle patrols, concentrating on looking for booby traps and signs of hidden enemy shooters. Mines could go off anywhere, anytime – there was no front line. In fact, as many as 50 per cent of Australian casualties in Vietnam were caused by mines. In the world wars the enemy was clearly delineated. There was a front line and an enemy in uniform. In Vietnam there was no front line and the enemy could be anyone around them.

After World War Two a US study found only 20 per cent of American soldiers actually fired at an enemy soldier. In Vietnam this rose to 90 per cent.[3] Unlike the world wars, Vietnam was a war in which the enemy was indistinguishable from civilians. The enemy, virtually invisible in the jungle and their hidden bunkers, placed an enormous psychological strain on the soldier. The average age of the World War Two soldier was 26. In Vietnam the average age of an Australian private was just 20, largely due to conscription and the recruiting of 19 year olds.

There was another big difference in the experience of Vietnam veterans. They didn't have the full support of the people back home. Their mission was unclear and questionable. Australia wasn't threatened by invasion. Families back home didn't need to be defended against an attacking force. Local people didn't see them as liberators from a foreign invader. They lost the war. They weren't welcomed home as heroes. On the contrary, they were shunned. All this added to the likelihood of succumbing to mental illness and PTSD.

Members of the 2nd D&E Platoon had one more significant reason for psychological strain. They all had one thing in common: they were all reinforcements, replacements who went to Vietnam as individuals or small groups rather than in battalions. They didn't train and bond with the hundreds of men around them as did the men who were shipped over in complete units. As replacements they invariably stepped into gaps left by men who had been killed or wounded. This sometimes caused resentment, irrational hostility or indifference in their fellow soldiers. It was rare that a replacement was made to feel welcome. Replacements were invariably only partly accepted by the rest of the battalion who had trained and embarked together, giving them a feeling of loyalty and belonging to each other and their battalion.

When the platoon members returned to Australia they found they were not recognised as the unit involved in the action at

Thua Tich. They were told their unit didn't even exist. This caused a frustrating bureaucratic Catch 22. To get a pension on the basis of PTSD, a veteran has to cite the stressful action which caused the PTSD. A 2nd D&E Platoon member couldn't cite the Thua Tich ambush as there was no record of them being there because there was no record their unit existed.

The Defence Force chief psychiatrist between 2005 and 2008, Len Lambeth, told a 2009 ABC Four Corners program on veterans' PTSD this sort of situation could end up having an even bigger impact. He said:

> It's vital if you've been through a traumatic event or series of events and your experiences are not validated by those that you deem important – and that includes Defence personnel, politicians, family, friends – then you are much more prone to developing some mental health problems as a result.[4]

A total of 521 Australians were killed during the Vietnam War and another 3000 were wounded. But the combined research has now made it very clear that those figures don't show the true casualty list. Nor do those figures show the numbers of suicides and early deaths among veterans. You have to add 80,000 veterans whose lives have been afflicted by mental illness caused by the Vietnam war; men who are constantly haunted by a war that will not leave them alone, even after 40 years.[5]

The war's long reach also extends to the families of Vietnam veterans. Studies have found that children of fathers suffering

PTSD are at a greater risk of developing emotional and behavioural problems. They have a bigger likelihood of doing poorly at school, breaking the law and substance abuse. A 2006 report showed that suicide among veterans' families was three times higher than expected and that one in six veterans reported their children suffered from an anxiety disorder or other psychological problem. This extended even to the grandchildren of afflicted veterans.[6]

The 2009 Dunt Review of mental illness in the military found 18 per cent of soldiers who served in Iraq were expected to develop PTSD. The rate for Afghanistan veterans is estimated at 11 per cent. But when a high deployment rate was added to the mix, a much bigger impact on mental health became apparent. A 2008 study of American troops in Iraq and Afghanistan by the Rand Corporation found one in every ten soldiers who completed a single combat deployment developed a mental ailment; that rate jumped to 1 in 5 with a second deployment and nearly 1 in 3 with a third.[7]

Australian troops deployed to conflicts since Vietnam should be far better prepared to cope with the mental anxiety caused by war. Troops sent to the wars in Afghanistan and Iraq as well as policing operations in East Timor and Rwanda were all regular army, far more highly trained and generally older than those sent to Vietnam. The Defence Department is now acutely aware of the risks to the mental health of the soldiers sent to these conflicts – wars very similar to Vietnam in that they were fighting against guerilla forces hidden in the surrounding local community, they were not welcomed as liberators, and back at home support for the war was divided.

Despite claims by Defence and Veterans' Affairs that they are now far more understanding of the effect of war on mental health, the experiences of men returning from the wars in Iraq and Afghanistan indicate nothing much has changed. Bureaucrats are still bureaucrats and make soldiers jump through hoops to get their entitlements. Money that was easily available and plentiful to send men to war is hard to come by for the men who come back wounded, not just in body but in spirit. The afflicted are still treated with scorn and suspicion by some of their officers and NCOs.

Governments are now having to pay bills for the mental trauma caused by war for many decades. The Department of Veterans' Affairs has 600 veterans from the East Timor operation on benefits because of PTSD, 500 from the first Gulf War, Rwanda and Somalia combined, 300 from Iraq and Afghanistan, and 1500 from other conflicts.[8] More than 140 troops suffering mental breakdowns were discharged from the army after serving in Iraq and Afghanistan – 42 per cent of all those who were discharged for medical reasons.[9]

The level of mental health problems among service men and women in Iraq and Afghanistan so shocked the Department of Defence that they removed transcripts of interviews conducted by military researchers from a research website. Pilots were taking Stilnox 'like smarties' to help them sleep. One soldier said there were six suicides in his troop and 22 men discharged on mental-health grounds. The soldier quit the army. Two years later he was diagnosed with PTSD.[10]

It should be no surprise, then, that a large proportion of the young men that politicians send to fight in conflicts overseas, particularly conflicts which present no immediate threat to the security of Australia, come back suffering mental health problems. The entire basis of their military training is to take them out of their world of peaceful communities surrounded by loving families and turn them into trained killers. They are broken down and rebuilt to follow orders, to kill when ordered. Most psychologists say it is not a natural state for a human to cold-bloodedly kill another human without motive unless he is defending family or home. There is an innate resistance to kill that has to be overcome by training, conditioning or desperation. Yet for Vietnam veterans there was no training and preparation to help them return to a peaceful community.

Jane Nursey, a senior clinical specialist at the Australian Centre for Posttraumatic Mental Health at Melbourne University, says despite the advances in treatment it was still unusual for Vietnam veterans to be cured of PTSD, 'particularly if they have been suffering in silence for many years'.[11]

Rather than a cure, therapists treating veterans with PTSD hope for improvements such as a drop in substance abuse, nightmares receding, better sleep, better mood and an improvement in relationships. It usually takes more than three months of treatment to see some some positive change. 'There will be some who actually get worse for a while during and after treatment,' says Nursey. Therapy methods include imaginal exposure, a treatment for people who have avoided thinking about traumatic incident. The aim is to get them to reflect on the trauma in a supportive way, without it overwhelming them. It helps the sufferers make better sense of what happened to them, and their reaction to it.

Nursey has treated hundreds of veterans. She's found that the likelihood of contracting PTSD depends not only on the trauma faced in war, but also the make-up of the individual, their environment as they grew up, and the degree of support from their family and friends. A group of soldiers who faced the same traumatic incident wouldn't necessarily react in the same way, nor would they all develop PTSD. And if some of them did develop PTSD, none would exhibit exactly the same symptoms.

However, Nursey, explains, 'One typical symptom of a Vietnam vet with PTSD many years after the war is that their life will have shrunk – they will have constricted family life and little social life, they withdraw from friends and family, they have poor relationships with their children, they have frequent partner break-ups, poor sleep and are incessantly troubled by nightmares. They can constantly relive an event and have the same nightmare every night. Often it wakes them up at the same point. They will hide under beds or attack their wife. A critical time is around anniversaries or birthdays, especially when their kids turn the age they were when they were at war.'

Retirement is a dangerous time for veterans. They can find themselves with time on their hands and reflect on their life, some veterans developing PTSD even in their 60s and 70s. Nursey says PTSD is a disorder of fear. Sufferers become highly suspicious of the motives of other people; they distrust everyone and see conspiracies everywhere, particularly among government organisations.

'That suspicion of government and organisation is worse among Vietnam veterans,' said Nursey. 'They know about Agent Orange and suspect a lot of other things happened to them that they were not told about. They want someone to blame, and it's often out of proportion. They feel the need to focus their anger on something or someone.'

The number of soldiers turning up with PTSD who served in Iraq and Afghanistan is alarming. Nursey says these cases are far more acute than veterans of Vietnam and earlier wars, 'probably because the trauma is so recent. Defence is getting better at referring service people for treatment for mental health problems, but people are better educated about PTSD and can recognise what may be going on.'

Former SAS major Peter Tinley, who was elected to the West Australian parliament in 2009 as a Labor MP, warned there was a potential 'tsunami of psychological problems' coming from soldiers who had been sent to Afghanistan on multiple deployments. His comment was prompted by the death of commando Sergeant Todd Langley, 35, killed in action during his fifth tour of duty to Afghanistan on 4 July

2011. Langley was the 28th soldier killed over ten years of Australian deployment.

Tinley told *The Australian* that special forces lived to do their job and mental health problems did not show up while they were in the 'surrogate family' of their regiment. 'But I've seen men as hard as teak turn to custard once they separate from the service,' Tinley said. 'A soldier's only option if he does not want to go to Afghanistan is to resign from the army. They'll keep going back until they die. Often, when a man's bottle is full he doesn't know it. We need to watch it.'[12]

What research has uncovered in the past 20 years is that, for veterans, the consequences of war last for the rest of their lives. The damaging effect is often passed on to the next generation, and even the one after that. But politicians don't like to talk about that. As they send young men off to war, they prefer to give speeches about noble sacrifice and the glorious Anzac spirit.

Sixty thousand Australians were sent to the Vietnam War between 1962 and 1972. According to the department of Veterans' Affairs, 47,500 Vietnam veterans were alive as at 31 December 2010. The department has 22,500 of those veterans registered as having PTSD – a staggering 47.4 per cent of them. And that's a conservative estimate. It doesn't include veterans with PTSD who are registered with different but more overwhelming health problems.

It also doesn't include the veterans with PTSD who have since died or committed suicide. The 521 men killed during the war, as well as the 12,500 veterans who have died since the war – one in five of the 60,000 who served – have all been removed from the government-held records for veterans and their health statistics. No one knows how many of those 12,500 veterans died from war-related problems or suicide.

15

WE ALL DIED IN THAT WAR

It's a half-hour bus ride from the centre of Newcastle upon Tyne to Jim Riddle's flat on the outskirts of the working-class city in northern England. Newcastle is a spirited, gutsy city and visiting Australians are taken aback at the sight of a mini version of the Sydney Harbour Bridge over the river Tyne. It's midwinter and bitterly cold when I arrive to interview Riddle. Frost and snow cover the footpaths and lawns, trees are bare and stark. Low thick cloud permanently blankets the sky, throwing a damp grey pall over everything. Through the wet condensation on the bus window, row upon row of neat, white two-storey apartment blocks line the road.

Next to the bus stop in front of Riddle's apartment is a low stump of chunky stone bricks. A sign above it says it is

Hadrian's Wall, built by the Romans almost 2000 years ago. This was the northernmost border of the Roman Empire, built to keep out marauding Picts. It was a desolate, miserable posting for soldiers who were stuck for years in this remote, forgotten frontier outpost. Most weren't even Romans, but recruits from conquered lands. As the Roman Empire collapsed and the wall was abandoned, many simply walked away from the army and the war.

In a way it's appropriate the one-time fearless soldier Jim Riddle settled in this place. The name Riddle has Germanic origins. It's likely he is descended from the Angle, Jute and Saxon mercenaries from northern Germany and Denmark who were brought in by local warlords to keep out the marauding Picts once the Roman legions left. Like those ancient warriors, Riddle sought battles in far-off lands only to be dumped when he was no longer needed.

Jim Riddle greets me at the door of his sparsely furnished flat slumped in the wheelchair he is condemned to remain in for the rest of his life. His left side is paralysed after several strokes and his left eye droops until it's almost closed. His left arm is in a sling to stop it flopping down beside the wheelchair where it could hit tables and walls as he propels himself around the small apartment.

Riddle has to wear heavy boots on his swollen feet, otherwise he'll damage them when his wheelchair hits door frames as he struggles to get through. They're just not wide enough for the wheelchair, which he manoeuvres with an electronic control stick with his right hand. Every day is a battle. He has difficulties getting his right hand to do what he wants. He is a shell of the man he once was, but he still has an inner toughness, a wicked sense of humour and a determination to tell his story. He wants Australians to know what happened to the ordinary Aussie rank and file in the Vietnam War. He wants them to know how sick he gets whenever he thinks of the people dressed in black pyjamas that he and other diggers shot, killed and maimed.

'They were just defending their country,' he says, staring out the window as snow flurries drift down. 'What would we do if we had a foreign army marching through our streets, burning our houses and killing our people? That's all they were doing.'

When Riddle found out the army refused to admit the 2nd D&E Platoon had existed, he was furious. It was only 33 of the 734 days he spent fighting for the Australians in Vietnam, but it was the only time he led an entire platoon. It grated on him that credit for that action had been taken away from him and the men.

He stews in anger over his treatment since the war. It has consumed him for decades, but he can't afford to waste energy on that now. It takes all his strength just to accomplish his everyday physical needs. He's cared for by his daughter-in-law, Lucy, who copes with his teasing, bad jokes and occasional frustrated outbursts with good grace. She makes sure no alcohol gets into the house, and that has probably saved his life. She confides that as the date for my visit and interview crept closer, his nightmares got a lot worse.

The night after my first day of talking with Riddle, Lucy got a desperate phone call from him at three in the morning. He'd fallen out of bed and was in a lather of sweat. When she got there Riddle was still weeping, partly out of frustration with his condition, but also because the nightmare was back, the one he thought had left him. When I next saw him I asked him to describe the nightmare. He took a deep breath. During our talks I offered several times to steer away from matters that upset him. But he insisted; he wants the story told. He wants Australians to know how the army and the government neglected the ordinary private soldier, the incompetence of many officers, how their lives were fed into a big war machine for nothing and how people mustn't let it happen again. He wants Australians to know about the reality of war, how ordinary good men can do terrible things in the heat of battle, things that will torment them for the rest of their life.

The nightmare was the same one he'd had for decades. He is captured by the Viet Cong in battle, and can't escape to help save the younger men in his unit. He is struggling and fighting his captors to get back into the fight, but they are holding him down and he is screaming to let him go. But that's not all that has come back to haunt him in recent years. The fight for recognition of the 2nd D&E Platoon by the Australian army and military historians caused huge divisions within sections of the veteran community, and Riddle has felt the sting.

'I do feel sad as everything that happened is coming back to haunt me. A lot of the diggers I was with have turned on me, accused me of being a liar, stabbing me in the back. They say it wasn't like that.'

Riddle insists he never asked to be called a hero, that he'd rather government minister Mike Kelly hadn't singled him out for praise for his courage and leadership at Thua Tich. The irony is that in that moment of triumph for the men of the Ghost Platoon, just when they'd finally won recognition, the criticism of them as individuals by other veterans increased.

'It's the tall poppy syndrome,' Riddle says with a snarl. 'They want to chop me down. All the diggers who come back from war are heroes in their own minds. They don't want to be reminded about the mistakes made, about things that were done that look terrible once you are out of it. They don't want those things talked about in the cold light of day where civilians can hear it.'

From his wheelchair Riddle gazes out onto the road and the stump of Hadrian's Wall. His three grandchildren are coming by after school with Lucy. He loves them dearly, but he finds it hard at times to have them around when they squeal and argue with each other. The high-pitched noise whisks him straight back to Vietnam. 'Sometimes they sound just like screaming Vietnamese women . . . and it gets to me,' Riddle says.

'Look, I really wish I didn't have these stories to tell you. I'd rather just quietly watch TV and try to forget. I'm stuck in this bloody wheelchair now, and life is shit, quite frankly. But it's important for people to know what happened. It's vital you tell this story. A lot of people would rather not know. They'd prefer it just stay buried. They say "Why stir all this up now?" But if you don't get it out in the open then it'll continue to haunt everyone involved.'

•

The ghosts of war haunt many people. An article in *The Australian* detailed how the Vietnamese believe the spirits of those whose fate is unknown, or those who die violently without being properly buried, are condemned to walk the earth forever. They are known as 'wandering souls'. Australia and America have gone to great lengths to recover the bodies of their servicemen who fell in the Vietnam War. With the considerable help of Vietnamese authorities, the remains of the last two missing Australian servicemen were recovered in 2009 and brought home to be buried with full military honours. Their families were finally able to put them to rest.

Forty years after the war, the US is still searching for around 1700 of their missing servicemen. The search is ongoing, and there is now a great deal of cooperation between the former enemies to find the remains of the missing. Every few months Vietnamese authorities announce they have found human remains and a special US team conducts DNA tests to try to identify them. Then, once they're identified, with great solemnity they are flown back to the US to be handed back to their family and buried in a dignified military ceremony.

Unfortunately the task facing the Vietnamese is far greater. The Hanoi government estimates there are between 300,000 and 400,000 Viet Cong and North Vietnamese regular soldiers still missing in action for whom there is no known burial site.[1] Australian troops were supposed to bury enemy soldiers where they fell and mark the position on a map but this didn't always happen. Australian military researchers have appealed to Australian veterans to help locate these makeshift burial sites so that Vietnamese authorities can search for them. They then notify relatives and comrades to give them a proper burial.

The Australian mission to help the Vietnamese locate the remains of their missing soldiers is called Operation Wandering Souls. Veterans who kept items from enemy bodies such as photographs, letters, award certificates, or other personal items have been encouraged to return them so that they can pass them on to relatives. The team has identified the names and burial sites of more than 120 Vietnamese troops killed by Australian and New Zealand forces.

Many Australian veterans came out of the war believing there was something far more real to the wandering souls belief than just a psychological need to put loved ones to rest. In 2010 I joined a group of men and the relatives of their mates killed in the war on a trip back to Vietnam and the battlefields where they fought. One of the men was Ray Knapp, who served 391 days in Vietnam as a conscript in the 5th Battalion, Royal Australian Regiment, earning himself a lance corporal's stripe. A knockabout level-headed bloke, Ray admitted he found it emotionally difficult to return to some of the places he'd been during the war and he was relieved to be doing it with his old 5RAR army mates. Their tour included a quiet spot in a copse of woods in the Phuoc Tuy province where two of his mates had been blown up right beside him by mines. Ironically, they were Australian mines which had been dug up and stolen by the Viet Cong and laid in cool, shady areas where unsuspecting Aussie troops might stop for a rest.

After a week touring the province, and over many cold Tiger beers, Knapp told me an eerie story. Toward the end of his tour he was part of a patrol that ambushed and killed three VC. The sergeant in charge of the patrol searched the bodies and handed Knapp a watch he'd taken from one of them. 'You're about to go home and you've never taken a souvenir, have you Ray?' the sergeant said. Knapp hadn't ever kept anything, but the sergeant insisted he keep the watch as a memento. So Knapp pocketed the watch, and when he got home he put it in a drawer and largely forgot about it.

Then the nightmares started. They were always the same. Knapp said he'd hear several men moving around the house, going from room to room as though they were looking for something. He'd be frozen, unable to get out of bed. Then three men, small wraithlike figures, would come into his room. One of them seemed to be the leader and would stand at the foot of his bed and just stare at him. Knapp couldn't make out their faces, but they were dressed in loose black clothes like the Viet Cong.

The nightmare figures kept visiting him for years. The years rolled into decades, and still they came. Knapp married, moved house, had children, but still the nightmare returned, three men searching for something, then coming to the foot of the bed and staring at him. Every time he'd scream in his sleep. His wife would wake him and hold him as he shook in a lather of sweat.

Finally, when Knapp returned to Vietnam for the first time in 2000, he brought the watch with him. He wanted to give it to the dead owner's family, but he had no idea how to find them. He left it with a Vietnamese bar owner in Vung Tau, a woman who'd fought with the Viet Cong. Some weeks later she took it to a watchmaker who opened the back of the watch and found an inscription with a man's name and a dedication from his wife. With that information, she managed to track down the man's relatives and hand them the watch. They were thrilled and very thankful the Aussie digger had gone to the trouble of returning it.

'I'd been back home from the trip for about three weeks when the nightmare came again,' said Knapp. 'The men were moving around the house. My wife said I was yelling and screaming out in my sleep, "Run, run!" She woke me up and I was sweating and shaking. Then, over her shoulder, I saw them – three shadows in the doorway staring straight at me. They just stood there. Then the one in the middle just kind of nodded, and they disappeared. It was the last time I ever had the nightmare.'

Knapp isn't the only one who's managed to lay the ghosts of war to rest. Sisters Vickie Barnes and Karen Kennedy were 11 and 10 years old on 15 June 1969 when their father Corporal John Joseph Kennedy was blown up by a mine right next to Ray Knapp. Kennedy was 29 and had volunteered to go back to Vietnam on a second tour as he needed the money for his large family of seven children. Vickie and Karen had always felt guilty about that. Their father left for the war without saying goodbye to them as he'd had a row with their mother. She didn't want him to go, and told him he should be home for the children. He rang from the base to say he was leaving for Vietnam early the next morning.

In 2010 the sisters travelled with Knapp and the 5RAR veterans to the exact place beneath the trees where their father and Private Peter Jackson, 22, were killed on that hot summer's day in 1969. Knapp and the other veterans stood in the woods and described the moment, pointing to where each of them had stood, how their bodies twisted in the explosion, who ran for help and the path they took. They described the terrible condition of the bodies of those who were killed and wounded. The sisters cried as Knapp and the others described it in simple straight soldier's language, sparing them nothing. As they talked and the tears flowed, sunlight filtered down through the branches and I watched two black and gold butterflies flitter around behind the small gathering. Afterwards the sisters said they felt enormous relief that they finally knew their father's death had been swift, and that he had died surrounded by his mates who cared for him.

'It's wonderful, finally we were able say goodbye to Dad,' said Karen. 'All these years we've felt something was missing because we never said goodbye. Now we've stood on the spot where he died, and we felt close to him. We said goodbye. We hope he's at peace.'

A day later, two veterans and mates of Kennedy secretly returned to the spot in the woods. At the foot of a big tree they buried a small memorial the sisters had brought with them from home. It was a piece of plastic piping containing a copy of their father's wedding photo, a picture of his seven adult children and numerous grandchildren all wrapped in a small Australian flag. I took photos of the quiet ceremony to give to the sisters. As I watched, another black and gold butterfly settled on a branch overlooking the veteran burying the cylinder. The other veteran saw the butterfly and remarked that it was uncanny – 5RAR was known as the Tiger Regiment, and their colours were black and gold. Later, when I gave the sisters the photographs and told them about the butterflies, they were overjoyed. They don't necessarily believe in ghosts, but they thought maybe, just maybe, the butterfly was a sign their father's spirit was happy, too.

'I know his body was brought home and we have his grave to visit. But that was where he was killed, that's where his spirit was released from his body,' said Vickie. 'Now he knows he is not forgotten, he knows his family miss him and love him. The photos are now with him so he can see how his children have grown and that they had children of their own. In a way, he lives on in them. He isn't alone anymore in those trees in a strange land.'

•

It's only with honest acknowledgement of the past that the horror of war can be left behind – for everyone. In 2009 the military attaché at the Australian Embassy in Hanoi, Colonel Stuart Dodds, appealed to all Vietnam veterans for any information they might have on the location of burial sites of enemy soldiers. Colonel Dodds contacted veterans from the units recorded in the archives as having killed 11 enemy soldiers at the ambush at Thua Tich. This included members of the 2nd D&E Platoon, which had only been formally recognised 12 months earlier as the infantry unit in that action.

Once again Don Tate sparked a furore among veterans by declaring to *The Sun-Herald* they would never find the bodies from Thua Tich. 'This has been a bullshit cover-up for 40 years and it is now finally coming out in the open,' Tate told the Sunday paper. 'They will never find the graves as there aren't any.'[2]

Despite the abuse and threats he'd copped over the years for publicly talking about the treatment of dead bodies after the ambush at Thua Tich, Tate declared there was simply nothing left for the researchers to find. He said most of the bodies had been blown to bits, while others were dragged by the heels into the village as a warning to Viet Cong sympathisers. He also said the heads fell off the bodies during the convoy to Xueyn Moc. 'God knows where they ended up.'

Tate went on, saying that the platoon members were acting under orders. 'To cover that atrocity up, the military establishment has wiped the official record of 39 Australian diggers, denying some of them access to military pensions. Finally the truth can come out.'

A spokesman for the Australian War Memorial told the paper there was 'no official view' of what happened at Thua Tich. 'Operational records and veterans' accounts indicate conflicting views over the manner of disposal of enemy bodies.' It was a major concession by the AWM as official record keepers of the Vietnam War. For the first time they conceded theirs wasn't the only view of what happened at Thua Tich.

On top of that the platoon now had support from two senior army officers. Brigadier George Mansford, who had been a captain in the highly respected Australian Army Training Team, which won four Victoria Crosses in Vietnam, told *The Sun-Herald* it was best for all veterans to drop the matter. 'Some things are best left alone. If what we hear is true then it would certainly be rubbing salt in the wound.'

Retired Brigadier Neil Weekes was a lieutenant in Vietnam and won the Military Cross. He was a member of the Prime Minister's Advisory Council on Ex-Services Matters and had joined the platoon veterans when they met Kelly in Canberra in 2008. Weekes told the paper Tate's allegations of an atrocity being committed was a controversy that 'needs to be resolved at a pretty high level.'

The story sparked another storm among a section of veterans. Tate came in for a pasting from his anonymous critics on the website Australian Veteran Matters, as did Weekes and Mansford. Online abuse increased. They threatened the publisher of Tate's book with a boycott by veterans unless they withdrew it from circulation, demanding as well that the Australian War Memorial ban the book from sale at its shop. Tate also received threats to his family, which he took to the police.

Weekes, too, had gone to police over threats made against him. 'I was accused of being a dangerous radical conspiracy theorist just because I supported the platoon members in their campaign to get recognition that they had existed.' The retired brigadier said the critics see themselves as custodians of the reputations of the fabled bronzed Anzacs. He believes they had a wider agenda of stamping out any criticism of the conduct of Australian soldiers in the Vietnam War.

Brigadier Mansford said he was only trying to appease the two groups of veterans and stop them ripping into each other. He feared it was violent, unpleasant and aggressive and causing divisions among veterans. He thinks allegations of atrocities should no longer be aired. 'It isn't going to bring them back. There is nothing to be gained by it. We have good relations with Vietnam now. The past is the past.' He said dragging enemy bodies behind APCs and tanks was not unheard of in Vietnam, although it was done by Americans rather than Australians. 'Don't forget the Yanks threw them out of choppers. It was an ugly war and terrible things happened.'

Mansford believes the members of the platoon and their critics are all suffering from post-traumatic stress disorder. 'The displays of obsession, suspicion and belligerence against each other are all symptoms of it. I am very concerned that threats and aggression can lead to actual violence and pressure to commit suicide. I think everyone just needs to back off.'

But Tate is not one to back off. In early 2011 he compiled a thick dossier of the long struggle to get recognition for the 2nd D&E Platoon and those who had opposed it. He sent the dossier to Canberra politicians he hoped might listen – the Independent and Green MPs. Tate demanded a Royal Commission or parliamentary inquiry into what he said was corrupt behaviour by the Australian military. He asked the parliamentarians to 'right a terrible wrong' that has affected the lives of many Vietnam veterans for four decades. He argued the platoon had been deleted from all histories of the Vietnam War. This, he said had caused considerable angst as well as compromising their service histories and war pensions.

Tate appealed for the parliamentarians to mount an official inquiry as there were 'much deeper and darker issues involved . . . Evil has been done here. There appears to have been a criminal conspiracy to cover up improper and illegal actions of senior commanders in the handling of troop numbers, field operations and of atrocities committed in the field – all to protect the reputations of those officers involved.'

He said the government's 2008 recognition that the 2nd D&E Platoon had existed should not be the end of the story.

He wanted an inquiry to investigate why the existence of the platoon was denied for so long, and why official recognition was opposed by historians at the Australian War Memorial and the Army. He argued the treatment of enemy bodies after the ambush at Thua Tich amounted to a contravention of the Geneva Convention, and this may have been the reason to cover up the existence of the platoon that was involved in the fighting.

On January 11 2011, three weeks after he revealed to the veteran community that he was sending the dossier to the parliamentarians, Tate was strolling outside his home on the south coast of New South Wales when a car suddenly pulled up beside him. A burly man got out and belted Tate. Tate went down, and then a second man jumped from the car. Together they kicked and punched Tate 10 to 20 times while he was down on the ground. Tate was left with bad cuts and bruises to his face, and he had photos taken of his battered face to prove it.

Tate's wife rushed him to the local hospital. He told police but nobody has been arrested for the attack. Tate doesn't know who they were, but he reckons he was being sent a strong message to quit his campaign. It didn't work. As soon as he got out of hospital he posted the dossier to the parliamentarians. Tate believes the bashing was part of an ongoing campaign by a small group of veterans to suppress anyone who might tarnish the golden image of the Anzac legend.

'Most veterans know our military "history" is bullshit,' Tate said as he recovered from the bashing. 'The breast-beating and shiny medals on parade by veterans marching on Anzac Day masks an underbelly of self-aggrandisement and corruption of military history and records to further the careers and civic ambitions of senior officers.'

The furore has led to most members of the platoon not wanting anything to do with a public investigation into what happened to them and raking up the past of Thua Tich. This was something I heard time and again from the dozens of veterans I interviewed for this book. Some spoke openly and without qualification of their experiences. A few spoke to me only on condition of anonymity. Some spoke freely with me, then a few days later rang or emailed to withdraw everything they'd said. Nearly all are still battling the effects of the war. Most confided they drank far too much – or their wives whispered it as I left. Men like Don Moss and Bob Secrett admitted alcohol ruined their lives as they tried to cope after the war. They said they were better after therapy, which provides hope that it might work.

Photographer Denis Gibbons, who arrived in the helicopter with Brigadier Pearson the morning after the ambush at Thua Tich, was the longest serving war correspondent in the Vietnam War – an intense six years. He was wounded six times. Now, he likes to spend time in a darkened, windowless room in his house watching old movies from Hollywood's golden era. He doesn't like modern movies; he says there's too much swearing, action and violence. His photographs, which capture some of the most memorable images of the war, hang from walls. Others, images from past exhibitions, are stacked up together. He has many boxes full of diaries, notes and photos he kept from the war, but he refuses to allow access to them by historians or archivists. He doesn't want to have to see them again. He had a falling out with the Australian War Memorial over the issue of copyright, and most of his war photographs have been taken off their website.

When members of the platoon came to ask for his support in their campaign for recognition, Gibbons sent them packing. He remembers the action differently to them. He is adamant the bodies were buried properly, and he believes the platoon veterans were only after a better pension. 'They were doing a lot of damage to good guys who went to Vietnam and did a damn good job,' Gibbons told me. 'They came home to all that hatred from the public, and now there is shit like this being thrown at them. I told them to piss off.'

Sandy Pearson, the brigadier in charge of the Australian force in 1969, said Gibbons was one of the few war correspondents who did their job properly. Speaking to me in 2010, Pearson didn't remember Gibbons being at Thua Tich, though he clearly was because Gibbons took photographs of the aftermath of the ambush. Pearson was also annoyed at Tate and the platoon members. He felt they had tried to ambush him at an Anzac Day march by having a film crew pretending to be from SBS suddenly ask him questions about Thua Tich.

Pearson insisted nothing untoward happened at Thua Tich. He said he was never told of any Australian troops mistreating enemy bodies during the war; that Thua Tich was just one of many ambush operations at that time. He landed in the helicopter and stayed only about 15 minutes. 'I saw the bodies on the road and gave orders to bury them.'

Pearson admitted that he knew in 1969 the war could not be won. 'I never did think it could be. In 1965 when we first sent combat troops I said to the commander that if the Americans are going we have to go, but we can't win. It's like Afghanistan – we can't win that either. But having gone in we can't pull out, because if we do pull out the other side has won. It's like beating your head against a brick wall.'

His tactic in 1969 was simply to hold the line. It was a war of attrition. Pearson said Canberra virtually ignored the Vietnam command. 'I got no orders at all about how to conduct the war or what sort of casualties were acceptable.' He thought 521 Australians killed in the war was 'not bad' as a result.

I asked Pearson whether, 40 years after the Vietnam War, he believed it was worth the lives of the 521 men who were killed. The troop commander gave a disturbing answer: 'Oh yes! Look what happens on the roads. Are you going to ban cars because 2000 a year are killed in car smashes? I knew the war could not be won, but if we pulled out it would be lost.'

•

War is ugly. Especially so when lessons are not heeded and history suppressed. There are important things our military can learn from our veterans – but not if they are denied a voice.

The last thing Jim Riddle told me as I prepared to leave him after a long and intense week of interviews will stay with me forever. I was saying goodbye and putting on my coat to head out into the cold, when Riddle grabbed my arm with his one shaky hand and pulled me closer.

In a firm, angry voice, he whispered: 'You know, we all died in that fookin' war – some of us are just taking longer to stop breathing.'

EPILOGUE

The Smoking Gun

Just after completion of the manuscript for *Ghost Platoon*, I received a message from a dogged, diligent archivist at the National Archives of Australia (NAA). For months they had been trying to track down the 1976 report written by Major Gordon Pound about the alleged atrocities committed at Thua Tich.

The archivist was determined to find the report. After all, the Department of Defence had rejected my Freedom of Information application to see the report on the grounds that all files from that period had already been transferred to the National Archives of Australia, a distance of about three kilometres, on the other side of Lake Burley Griffin.

In my application I had also asked the department for 'all Defence documents, files, inquiries and notes relating to allegations of atrocities committed at the Thua Tich ambush', specifically the blowing up of enemy bodies, the towing of enemy bodies behind an APC to Xuyen Moc and the shooting on civilians on the road to Xuyen Moc. But as with the Pound Report, Defence reported back that the papers from that era had all been transferred to the National Archives.

The Pound Report was integral to the story of the Ghost Platoon. It stemmed from allegations raised publicly in 1976 by one of the members of the platoon that these incidents had definitely occurred. The ex-soldier felt he had to unburden himself and tell the story publicly. The army's response was to send Major Pound to investigate. Pound's report concluded the allegations couldn't be proved, so nothing could be done about it.

Members of the Ghost Platoon suspected Major Pound's report was a whitewash. No member of the platoon had ever been interviewed about the incident. No troops in the cavalry unit who had been there were asked about it. Photographs had existed to back up the allegation, but as discovered when researching this book, these photographs had been destroyed or buried in Canberra back in 1969.

In 2008, when the Labor government pressed the Defence Department for answers about the Ghost Platoon, Defence relied on the 1976 Pound Report to tell the Minister, Mike Kelly, that the allegations had already been investigated by the army and 'there was no evidence of wrong doing'.

Despite my best efforts, and the efforts of archivists at the National Archives, the Pound Report and papers relating to the Thua Tich allegations could not be found. It wasn't in any of the documents and files Defence had transferred to the National Archives in the decades since the Vietnam War.

At first the archivist thought the report must be buried somewhere in the pile of boxes containing material about the Vietnam War that Defence had handed over. Not all of them had been examined and catalogued by the National Archives. But after months of frustrating searches, the NAA archivist asked fellow archivists on the other side of the lake at Defence if they happened to have any remaining files at all relating to the 1969 ambush at Thua Tich and the 1976 allegations of atrocities committed at the ambush.

A few weeks later I received a message from the archivist, who had received a thin file from Defence titled 'Atrocity Allegations – South Vietnam, 3 Cav. Regiment'. It had been stamped 'Confidential'. This was the Army's third highest secrecy classification behind Top Secret and Secret. It means the file contained 'material the unauthorised disclosure of which would cause damage to the interests of the nation.'

Inside were several papers.

The first was a cable sent in August 1976 from the Darwin army base to Brigadier Butler at Army HQ in Canberra. It was Major Gordon Pound's account of his interview with former Sapper Robert Jon Enright, who had left the army in 1973. A few days earlier Enright had talked to the *Northern Territory News* and been interviewed by a Sydney radio station about atrocities he had been involved in during the war in Vietnam, including the ambush at Thua Tich while Enright had been a member of the 2nd D&E Platoon.

His story, headlined 'Vietnam Veteran: I Shot Women in Ambush' appeared on the front page of the *Northern Territory News* on 9 August 1976. Enright said it took place while he was in a platoon with the 9th Infantry Battalion in late 1969.

Enright told the paper nobody gave the order to fire when a small boat carrying four women and steered by a man floated down a river they were watching. But before the platoon had set out on patrol, they were told to shoot anybody who came down the river. Enright was the first to fire. He killed the man and swept his fire along the boat. He saw his bullets slam into the women. Other members of his platoon then joined in the shooting until all the Vietnamese on the boat were dead. Enright said he was only 19 at the time and 'full of glory and all that crap.' Enright then mentioned the ambush at Thua Tich while he was in the D&E Platoon. He wasn't involved in the shooting, but was positioned north of the village gates with other members of the platoon and several APCs during the night ambush.

He also told his story to radio announcer Greg Grainger on Sydney based radio station 2UE, giving Enright's story a much wider audience.

Major Pound visited Enright several days later and asked Enright to give him details of the matters he discussed with the *Northern Territory News* and 2UE. According to Pound's cable to Army HQ, Enright decided to tell his story to the press after he heard Defence Minister Jim Killen on the ABC rejecting claims by anonymous ex-soldiers that Australian troops had shot unarmed civilians during the Vietnam War. Killen said he would not order an investigation into the allegations until he had the names of the former soldiers making the allegations, but the ABC would not hand Killen the names.

'The things he [Killen] said made me feel pissed off and while I was at work I kept thinking about it,' Enright told Pound. Enright told the major he rang the *Northern Territory News* and spoke to a female reporter called Terry Dahlenberg. She was very interested in his story, and asked him to come into the newsroom with some evidence he had fought in Vietnam. Enright got his discharge papers from home and went in to see her.

Pound's cable to HQ said Enright told him: 'The bodies were left out until the afternoon. Then we had to drag them into a bomb crater. We put their weapons and ammo in as well and the sappers blew them. An APC dragged, I think it was four bodies, by the feet on the end of a rope back to Xuyen Moc. The bodies included a young woman who had a new AK-47 and a medical pack.'

Enright said they were ambushed by Viet Cong on the way to Xuyen Moc and they killed five of them. After that firefight, they continued on towards Xuyen Moc with the bodies dragging behind the APCs.

'On the way the APC fired at villagers in the fields who ran away at the sight of the bodies. They fired until the villagers stopped. I think they fired over their heads. By the time we got to Xuyen Moc the bodies were in a bad way. We left them in the main square.'

'It has been worrying me for the last couple of years. I told the story because people have been saying that such things did not happen. I say they did.'

Another significant paper in the Defence Department file was a four-page document handwritten in pencil. Curiously, it contained no cover page saying who wrote it and on whose authority it was written. The signature page was also missing. This is highly unusual in military record-keeping. The cover was either deliberately removed from the file, or was somehow lost. It may have been a draft but importantly it had been buried in the Defence files – until now.

As I discovered, this document is the smoking gun, the record that verifies all the allegations made by the members of the Ghost Platoon about what really happened at the Thua Tich ambush and during the convoy to Xuyen Moc. Even though there is no signature to identify the author of the paper, it's clear it was an internal army report responding to the 1976 Thua Tich allegations, and was written by an unidentified senior military officer.

It's not too big a leap to propose that the author of the anonymous report was Major Pound, following up his interview of Enright. The report's author had interviewed a Colonel Rooks, who at the time of the 1969 incidents was the major in charge of B Squadron, 3rd Cavalry. Rooks was also the senior officer of Captain Arrowsmith, who was in charge of B Squadron's 2 Troop unit at the Thua Tich ambush.

The report's author did not interview Captain Arrowsmith. Rooks had arrived at the Thua Tich ambush site the morning after the ambush, flying in on a helicopter with Brigadier Sandy Pearson. On board were also the photographers Bellis and Gibbons. Rooks and Pearson stayed only a short time before flying out again. The report appears to be based solely on what Rooks had to say.

The handwritten report begins by recounting the ambush at Thua Tich on 29 May 1969. It says Captain Arrowsmith laid out his force around the Thua Tich gate with a section of D&E soldiers hidden several hundred metres down the road. It says they opened fire with machine guns and Claymore mines on the VC column which had well in excess of 50 enemy soldiers.

The report appears to be trying to answer criticisms that the ambush was conducted beyond the range of artillery support, something that was deemed essential after artillery fire saved the surrounded Aussies at the Battle of Long Tan. It notes the ambush site was:

> well outside of artillery range and although they had a section
> of mortars under command, HQ 1ATF took the following
> precautions:
> a. A spooky aircraft armed with mini guns was tasked to
>   give fire support to the troop.

    b. Tango Force [elements of the tank squadron] which was operating in the adjacent district of Duch Tan was put on notice to move to help 2 Troop if that proved necessary.

    c. A section of 105 mm guns was warned to be ready to move from Nui Dat base to within gun range.

The fire effect from the Spooky was effective and it was not necessary to move Tango Force or the section of 105mm guns.

All this confirms that Jim Riddle had good reason to be concerned about his exposed position at the forward post hundreds of metres down the road from the APCs during the ambush. By the time tanks or artillery could be moved to a position where they could support the Australians, his isolated post could well have been overrun by the vastly superior numbers of troops in the enemy column.

The report notes that after the ambush, HQ at Nui Dat received a radio request from the district chief of Xuyen Moc to have enemy bodies from the ambush delivered to Xuyen Moc and that 'this request was approved by the SO2 Ops HQ 1ATF.' The report goes on to say that, after the convoy was ambushed on the road south to Xuyen Moc, it continued on as quickly as possible to reach the town. Tellingly, it also reports that:

As they left Route 328 another group of people was sighted in long grass. The troop leader was not certain that they were VC so machine guns were fired over their heads. The group turned out to be women and children from Xuyen Moc collecting grass.

The report says some time after the convoy reached Xuyen Moc with the bodies, Major Rooks was told by Command 1TF 'to investigate how the bodies had been carried to Xuyen Moc' but that 'Colonel Rooks cannot remember why he was asked to carry out the investigation, except that it was related to bodies being towed by APCs.'

It's highly likely that this order came directly from Defence HQ in Canberra. By then the photographs of the bodies being towed taken by army photographer Chris Bellis would have arrived and set off a chain reaction of inquiry.

The report goes on to say that, because Arrowsmith had:

> wanted to leave Thua Tich as quickly as possible to avoid being attacked, he destroyed all bodies and equipment of use to the VC, except for about four bodies which were not badly cut about. The bodies not destroyed were tied on to the back [here the report's author later added in the word 'top'] of the APCs. The captured weapons were not destroyed but placed inside an APC.
>
> The bodies had not been dragged from Thua Tich. During the ambush on 30 May the tactical manouvres of the APCs caused the bodies to fall off the APCs. The troop leader was not prepared to risk the lives of his men to lift the bodies back on to the APCs. The troop was still at considerable risk of being ambushed again. The bodies were dragged for the remainder of the move to Xuyen Moc.

The report ends by saying that Rooks repeated Arrowsmith's explanation to the commander of the Task Force, and that no further action was taken except that Rooks told the Cavalry Squadron that from now on: 'VC bodies were not to be carried on APCs without his personal approval, and in future all VC bodies were to be buried.'[1]

Despite the Army's continued insistence for the past four decades that nothing irregular or improper had occurred at Thua Tich and on the way to Xuyen Moc, this report clearly states that it did.

It confirms that, after the ambush, enemy bodies were blown up rather than buried.

It confirms that enemy bodies were towed behind APCs into Xuyen Moc.

It confirms that the APC convoy fired on innocent Vietnamese civilians – women and children – on the way to Xuyen Moc.

Yet as late as 2008 the top ranks of the Army were still maintaining that there was no evidence to support the claims being made by members of the Ghost Platoon. To support their position, the Army cited Pound's initial 1976 report, a document they still cannot produce, and which is at odds with the handwritten account eventually found in the wayward file.

Further, the Army can't claim they didn't know about this file. It has been accessed 13 times since 1976. At least, that's the number of times the file has been officially signed out of its box. The file was begun in 1976, examined six times in the 1980s, four times in the 1990s, and then once in March 2011, shortly before it was finally sent to the National Archives. There is nothing to indicate whether the file is complete, or how many papers had originally been held inside it.

It's hard not to conclude that a lot of effort has gone into suppressing this report over the years. Instead of supporting their former diggers who had risked their lives fighting for their country, the Army dismissed their concerns out of hand.

Instead of choosing to properly investigate the claims by Riddle, Tate and others that something stank about the Thua Tich ambush, the Defence Department, top-ranking generals and taxpayer-funded military historians all chose to pull the shutters down and hide behind bureaucratic semantics.

Instead of doing the right thing and seriously looking into the allegations which were causing decades of distress and anxiety to these former soldiers, the Defence establishment chose to do nothing.

But many veterans do want the truth to come out and sympathise with the plight of the men of the Ghost Platoon. After the publication of the first edition of this book, several Vietnam veterans contacted me to confirm the account told in this book of what happened at Thua Tich and Xuyen Moc.

Don Greentree, the soldier in the hat in the foreground of the photo on the cover of this book, said he personally placed mortars and explosives under the pile of enemy bodies dropped into a pit close to the gate over the road after the ambush. He was in the last APC to leave the site.

We were in a hurry to get away from the explosion and the driver stalled the APC. So we were only 20 yards away when they were blown up. We saw bits of bodies blown high into the air. If you dug around the gates today you would find bits of bone from the bodies we blew up.

Greentree also confirms seeing enemy bodies being tied by the heels to the rear door of an APC. He confirms the bodies were dragged into Xuyen Moc after they came loose during the second ambush. He confirms the lead APCs fired on civilians in the fields on the way to Xuyen Moc.

We were at the end of the column and when we went past I saw some people lying on the ground. But I'm sure they hadn't been hit. Their bodies weren't twisted and bent like they would be if they'd been hit by 50 calibre fire.

Donald Campbell worked in Army public relations HQ in Saigon. He remembers seeing the photo Sgt. Chris Bellis took of three battered enemy bodies being towed behind an APC into Xuyen Moc. 'I numbered them in chronological order and sent them all on to Canberra,' he said. 'If there is now no gap in the chronological order of the photos, then someone in Canberra changed the numbers.'

That confirms there was a concerted effort by Defence PR in Canberra in 1969 to obliterate all trace of the photo Bellis took of the APC dragging bodies behind it.

It's hard for people with no experience of active service or the military to understand why there has been such vitriol and venom among the veterans over whether a single unit existed for a few weeks in 1969.

Certainly, what happened at Thua Tich and on the way to Xuyen Moc wasn't the worst thing that happened during the ugly war that was Vietnam. It was no My Lai. If civilians were hit by fire as the convoy broke clear from the jungle after nearly 36 hours of tension and action, it was an accident. There is no suggestion that innocent women and children were deliberately targeted. All accounts describe it as a very short burst of fire when it was understood the figures in the grass could be Viet Cong about to launch yet another attack. As soon as they were tagged as innocent civilians, the firing stopped immediately.

Certainly it's true that enemy bodies were mistreated after the ambush. This was a breach of the Geneva Convention. But they were already dead. It was unsavoury and unpleasant, but it was war. The Australians were in hostile country, and needed to get out quickly before a larger enemy force could rally and launch a counterattack.

It wouldn't have done the Army any harm to have given a more reasoned and sympathetic response to the former members of the platoon when they raised the matter publicly long after the war was over. The Army could have investigated their claims properly, and unearthed the file which proves the veterans were right. They could have issued an apology for the way the Australian soldiers were treated, and recognised their contribution to the service of their country.

But it appears the Department of Defence, the military establishment and a core of veterans are more intent on trying to preserve the glossy image of the bronzed Anzac – the dashing, fearless Aussie digger who can do no wrong; the irreverent larrikin who fights honourably. It denies the fact that war is hell and that honour is not always the first thought when facing down an enemy.

But the myth serves the military well. How else can the politicians and military establishment continue to find recruits for pointless wars, wars where there is no direct threat to Australian territory? One of the greatest betrayals of World War One veterans has been the building of the myth that they died at Gallipoli and Flanders Fields defending our freedom, that Australia was born in the cauldron of blood of their noble sacrifice. The truth is they died in vain, fighting in horrific conditions against a force that posed no threat whatsoever to Australia. Many diggers knew this, writing home to urge younger brothers not to join up.

The same happened with the Vietnam War: it was started on a lie, fanned by politicians who themselves preferred the safe corridors of Parliament House, and maintained by leaders who knew the war was already lost, who then turned their backs on the damaged men returning home. Now it continues with Australian troops sent to Iraq and Afghanistan. Already hundreds have come home suffering mental wounds only to receive inadequate help from the military. History is repeating itself.

What happened to the men of the Ghost Platoon has happened time and again to men of many units in many wars. In a way, all those who fight in wars are members of the Ghost Platoon, burdened by their dark memories of war on a long march that never ends.

MEMBERS OF THE GHOST PLATOON

Those who served in the 2nd D&E platoon as identified by platoon members who searched documents and fought for the unit's recognition. The following men were all listed as privates in the Headquarters Company Roll Book for May–June 1969. The ranks listed are those they had when they finished service in Vietnam. Not all were at the Thua Tich ambush on 29 and 30 May. Names with an asterisk (*) indicate platoon members on leave at the time of the ambush.

Pte. Peter Denzil Allen
L/Cpl. Richard Henry Appleby
Pte. John Louis Arnold
Pte. Melville Leonard Bann
Pte. Robert Stanley Belgrove

L/Cpl. Richard Alan Bigwood

Pte. Desmond John Blazely

Pte. Hugh Gray Browning

Pte. Ronald Frederick Bryant*

Pte. Robert Joseph Cairns

Pte. Raymond James Clark

Pte. Edward William Colmer

Pte. Cecil Roley Ebsworth

Cpl. Leonard Ellcombe

L/Cpl. Ray Charles Ellis

Pte. Robert Jon Enright

Pte. Colin James Fahy

Cpl. Johannes Cornelius Fleer*

L/Cpl. Richard Brian Howie

Pte. Graham John Hyde

Cpl. Kevin Godfrey Lloyd-Thomas

Cpl. Dennis Noel Manski

Pte. Dennis James McGregor

Pte. Athol Evan Millar

Pte. Peter Stuart Morgan

Pte. Donald Richmond Moss

Pte. Steven Francis Paterson

Pte. Ian Raymond Ramadge

Pte. Brian 'Jock' Rennie

L/Cpl. James Bertram Riddle

Pte. Allan James Roach

Pte. Owen William Schuler

Pte. Robert Stanley Secrett

Pte. Anthony Seychell

Pte. David Halliday Simpson

Pte. Terry John Slattery

Pte. Donald William Tate

Pte. William Harold Whitney*

Pte. Geoffrey Clynton Williams

ENDNOTES

CHAPTER 3   AMBUSHING THE AMBUSHERS

1 *Before I Forget*, Allan Stanton, Sid Harta Publishers, Melbourne, 2009, page 77.

CHAPTER 7   THE FRAGGING OF LIEUTENANT CONVERY

1 *War Without Fronts – The USA in Vietnam*, Bernd Greiner, Bodley Head, London, 2009, page 286.
2 *Vietnam – The Australian War*, Paul Ham, HarperCollins, Sydney, 2007, page 512.

CHAPTER 8   THE COVER-UP BEGINS

1 'The general rule – try to shoot the messenger', Ian McPhedran, *The Daily Telegraph*, 22 September 2010.

CHAPTER 10   HOMECOMINGS

1 'Coming home', Michael Cordell, *The Sydney Morning Herald*, 25 April 1987.

2   *The War Within*, Don Tate, Pier 9, Sydney, 2008, page 395.

3   'Courage after fire', Don Tate, *The Sydney Morning Herald*, 15 August 1997.

CHAPTER 13   SPOILING FOR A FIGHT

1   'Diggers spoiling for fight', *The Daily Telegraph*, 8 April 1969.

2   'Australians kill Reds in ambush', *The Daily Telegraph*, 9 April 1969.

3   *Vietnam – The Australian War*, Paul Ham, HarperCollins, Sydney, 2007, page 412.

4   13 March 1968, Cabinet Minute – Allegation of breaches of Geneva Convention during interrogation of Vietnamese woman prisoner by members of the Australian Task Force, A5872 National Archives of Australia.

5   'Confession of a Digger', Toni McRae, *Fraser Coast Chronicle*, 17 April 2010.

6   'Conscript ruled fit after twice failing medical', *The Australian*, 17 August 1970; 'Inquiry call on "blind conscript"', *The Daily Mirror*, 17 August 1970.

7   *Malcolm Fraser – The Political Memoirs*, Malcolm Fraser and Margaret Simons, The Miegunyah Press, Melbourne, 2010.

8   'Afghanistan like Vietnam quagmire says former prime minister Malcolm Fraser', *The Herald Sun*, 26 August 2010.

9   'Howard defends Vietnam War', *The Herald Sun*, 22 November 2006.

10 Interview with Dick Cheney by George Wilson, *The Washington Post*, 5 April 1989.

11 *War for the Asking*, Michael Sexton, Penguin, Sydney, 1981.

CHAPTER 14   NO ONE IS EVER CURED

1   'Judge gives Army part of blame for killing', *The Sydney Morning Herald*, 26 August 1970.

2   'The cost of PTSD in Australia's Vietnam veteran community', Professor Graeme Hawthorne, Department of Psychiatry, University of Melbourne, August 2010. www.psychiatry.unimelb.edu.au/centres-units

3   *On Killing,* Colonel Dave Grossman, Black Bay Books, New York, 2009, page 3.

4 'The war within', *Four Corners*, ABC TV, 30 March 2009.

5 'Review of mental health care in the ADF and transition through Discharge', Professor David Dunt, initiated by the Minister for Defence, Science and Personnel and the Minister for Veterans' Affairs, Australian Federal Government, January 2009.

6 'Australia's Vietnam Veterans – a review', Hedley Peach, *Australian Family Physician*, Vol 35, No.8, August 2006.

7 'An Rx for the US Army's wounded minds', *Time* magazine, 16 August 2010.

8 Department of Veterans' Affairs response to questions by the author, 2011.

9 'Diggers scarred by war', *The Daily Telegraph*, 5 August 2010.

10 'Soldiers' hidden trauma and despair confront Defence', *The Weekend Australian*, 10–11 July 2010.

11 Jane Nursey interview with author, 2011.

12 'Forces face "tsunami of illness"', Brendan Nicholson, *The Australian*, 8 July 2011.

CHAPTER 15 WE ALL DIED IN THAT WAR

1 'Vietnam vets find "wandering souls"', *The Australian*, 20 July 2010.

2 'Phantom force secrets – Vietnam's grave request to reveal war atrocities', Matthew Benns, *The Sun-Herald*, 12 July 2009.

EPILOGUE THE SMOKING GUN

1 'Atrocity allegations – South Vietnam – 3 Cav. Rgt', File no. A4090, National Archives of Australia.

BIBLIOGRAPHY

Caulfield, Michael, *The Vietnam Years*, Hachette Australia, Sydney, 2007.

Cosgrove, Peter, *My Story,* HarperCollins, Sydney, 2006.

Fraser, Malcolm and Simons, Margaret, *The Political Memoirs*, The Miegunyah Press, Melbourne, 2010.

Greiner, Bernd, *War Without Fronts – The USA in Vietnam*, Bodley Head, London, 2009.

Grossman, Dave, *On Killing*, Back Bay Books, New York, revised edition 2009.

Ham, Paul, *Vietnam – The Australian War,* HarperCollins, Sydney, 2007.

Hersh, Seymour, *Cover-Up – The Army's Secret Investigation of the Massacre at My Lai*, Random House, New York, 1972.

McNamara, Robert, *In Retrospect – The Tragedy and Lessons of Vietnam*, Times Books, New York, 1995.

Tate, Don, *The War Within*, Pier 9, Sydney, 2008.

Sexton, Michael, *War for the Asking*, Penguin, Sydney, 1981.

Stanton, Allan, *Before I Forget*, Sid Harta Publishers, Victoria, 2009.

PAPERS AND NEWSPAPER, MAGAZINE AND JOURNAL ARTICLES

'Afghanistan like Vietnam quagmire says former prime minister Malcolm Fraser', *The Herald Sun*, 26 August 2010.

'American B-52s use Viet truce for big raids on Laos', *The Australian*, 3 June 1969.

'An Rx for the US Army's wounded minds', *Time* magazine, 16 August 2010.

'Australia's Vietnam Veterans – a review', Hedley Peach, *Australian Family Physician*, Vol 35, No.8, August 2006.

'Australians kill Reds in ambush', *The Daily Telegraph*, 9 April 1969.

'Bloodbath in Vietnam', *The Sunday Observer*, 14 December 1969.

'Coming home', Michael Cordell, *The Sydney Morning Herald*, 25 April, 1987.

'Confession of a digger', Toni McRae, *Fraser Coast Chronicle,* 17 April 2010.

'Conscript ruled fit after twice failing medical', *The Australian*, 17 August 1970.

'Courage after fire', Don Tate, *The Sydney Morning Herald*, 15 August 1997.

'Digger counts the dead', *The Australian*, 3 June 1969.

'Digger had his say at rally', *The Courier Mail*, 9 May 1970.

'Diggers scarred by war', *The Daily Telegraph*, 5 August 2010.

'Diggers spoiling for fight', *The Daily Telegraph*, 8 April 1969.

'Forces face "tsunami of illness"', Brendan Nicholson, *The Australian*, 8 July 2011.

'Howard defends Vietnam War', *The Herald Sun*, 22 November 2006.

'Inquiry call on "blind conscript"', *The Daily Mirror*, 17 August 1970.

Interview with Dick Cheney by George Wilson, *The Washington Post*, 5 April 1989.

'Judge gives Army part of blame for killing', *The Sydney Morning Herald*, 26 August 1970.

'Phantom force secrets – Vietnam's grave request to reveal war atrocities', Matthew Benns, *The Sun-Herald,* 12 July 2009.

'Private facing murder charge', *The Sydney Morning Herald*, 10 January 1970.

'Review of mental health care in the ADF and transition through discharge', Professor David Dunt, initiated by the Minister for Defence, Science and Personnel and the Minister for Veterans' Affairs, Australian Federal Government, January 2009.

'Soldiers' hidden trauma and despair confront Defence', *The Weekend Australian*, 10–11 July 2010.

'The cost of PTSD in Australia's Vietnam veteran community', Professor Graeme Hawthorne, Department of Psychiatry, University of Melbourne, August 2010. www.psychiatry.unimelb.edu.au/centres-units

'The general rule – try to shoot the messenger', Ian McPhedran, *The Daily Telegraph*, 22 September 2010.

'This dirty war', *The Sydney Morning Herald*, 26 February 1966.

'Vietnam veteran: I shot women in ambush', *Northern Territory News*, 9 August 1976.

'Vietnam vets find "wandering souls"', *The Australian*, 20 July 2010.

'Vietnam vet "officially forgotten"', *The Illawarra Mercury*, 7 September 1992.

'Viet vet reprisal threat', *The Illawarra Mercury*, 28 April 1987.

MATERIAL SOURCED FROM THE NATIONAL ARCHIVES OF AUSTRALIA

'Allegations of Australian atrocities in Vietnam', file no. A1209 – 1976/1905.

'Allegations of torture of Viet Cong spy', file no. A432 – 1969/461.

'Alleged breaches of the Geneva Convention by Australian forces in Vietnam', file no. A5619 – C35.

'Atrocity Allegations – South Vietnam – 3 Cav Regt', file no. A4090.

Prime Minister's Department Cabinet Minutes 13 March 1968, file no. A5872 – 73.

Transcript of court martial of Private Allen, Peter Denzil, 8–15 January 1970, file nos. A471, B2458.

Parliamentary question regarding war atrocities in Vietnam – Mr Hayden, file no. A463 – 1971/1189.

MATERIAL SOURCED FROM THE AUSTRALIAN WAR MEMORIAL

1969 photographic record book assembled by Defence Public Relations.

'Impressions: Australians in Vietnam; photography, art and the war', online essay by Simon Forrester.

DOCUMENTS OBTAINED UNDER FREEDOM OF INFORMATION LAWS

Dept of Army briefing to Minister Kelly.

Ministerial representation: Mrs Jennie George MP re formal recognition of 2nd D&E Platoon, 27 March 2008.

Various letters from Minister Kelly to Jennie George MP.

Dept of Army briefing to Minister Kelly: Supplementary advice on the possibility of formalising 2nd D&E Platoon 22 May 2008.

Numerous emails between Army History Unit and historians at Australian War Memorial discussing 2nd D&E Platoon.

Emails between Army History Unit and Central Army Records Office concerning 2nd D&E Platoon.

Copies of Australian Military Forces Headquarters 1st Australian Task Force Vietnam Daily Situation Report covering the period of the formation of the 2nd D&E Platoon and the Thua Tich ambush in May 1969, as well as log sheets.

Letters in 2007 from Veterans' Affairs Minister Bruce Billson to Jennie George MP about the 2nd D&E Platoon.

DOCUMENTARY AND TELEVISION AND RADIO BROADCASTS

'Defence reveals Vietnam War "ghost unit" did exist', Brendan Trembath, *AM*, ABC Radio, 31 May 2008.

'Ghost Platoon fights for recognition', Lisa Whitehead, *The 7.30 Report*, ABC TV, 8 July 2008.

The Fog of War – Eleven Lessons from the Life of Robert S. McNamara, directed by Errol Morris, Sony Pictures Classics, 2003.

'The war within', Nick McKenzie, *Four Corners*, ABC TV, 30 March 2009.

PRIVATE ARCHIVES

'A call for a parliamentary enquiry or royal commission into corrupt behaviour by the Australian military' and attachments (prepared by Don Tate and sent to various Federal MPs).

Movie footage filmed by Don Tate during his tour of Vietnam.

Movie footage filmed by Peter Board during his tour of Vietnam, in particular the aftermath of the ambush at Thua Tich.

WEBSITES

Australian Veteran Matters: www.austvetmatters.net

Department of Veterans' Affairs: www.dva.gov.au

VVCS Veterans and Veterans Families Counselling Service: www.dva.gov.au/health_and_wellbeing/health_programs/vvcs/Pages/index.aspx

Australian War Memorial: www.awm.gov.au

Vietnam Veterans Association of Australia: www.vvaa.org.au

Australian Centre for Posttraumatic Mental Health: www.acpmh.unimelb.edu.au

Lifeline (crisis support, suicide prevention, mental health support):
www.lifeline.org.au
24-hour phone around Australia: 13 11 14

ACKNOWLEDGEMENTS

My thanks go to the many Vietnam veterans and the men of the Ghost Platoon who agreed to talk to me about their war and the incidents recounted in this book. It wasn't easy for them to bring up memories they would rather leave buried. Most are very damaged men, still suffering the impact of the war on their bodies, minds and souls. They showed enormous courage in facing their demons once again to recount in vivid detail what they saw, and what happened. For some it brought back nightmares, and I am sorry for that, but many said they were glad to be able to tell their story as they believe Australians should know the truth.

I am particularly indebted to Jim Riddle, who struggled with his physical disabilities to spend day after day telling me his amazing story. In graphic detail he went through his memory of the Thua Tich ambush, sparing no detail in his tales of the horror of war. He didn't shy away from matters that were embarrassing to him. Even when dredging up these memories brought on nightmares, he insisted on continuing. His wicked sense of humour keeps him going. Riddle told his story as a warning to the current young generation not to believe everything politicians say when they wrap themselves in the flag and send young men and women to war.

Don Tate was very generous in providing me with access to the large amount of documents, papers, emails and photographs he had gathered in the course of his research into proving the existence of the 2nd D&E Platoon. He has gone through hell ever since that bullet slammed into his hip in a jungle clearing in Vietnam, and he poured his energy and writing skills into telling Australians the reality of life for veterans since the Vietnam War. He was the force behind the push to get the platoon acknowledged by the government and win a decent war pension for Jim Riddle. He's faced death threats and abuse from a small section of the veteran community, but not even a street bashing by mysterious attackers has silenced this warrior.

I thank platoon members Don Moss and Bob Secrett for telling their stories. I thank Peter Allen for breaking his silence of 40 years to try and explain what led him to murder his senior officer. Several ex-soldiers chose to talk only if their names weren't used. I thank them and understand their position. I respect those who agreed to talk, then withdrew all they had said. I appreciate it isn't easy to go public, and I'm sorry if I caused them anxiety.

I thank two members of the cavalry who were present at the Thua Tich ambush for talking to me, despite suspicion from their army mates that bringing it all up would not be good. Peter Board talked openly about the impact the ambush still has on him. Allan Stanton demonstrated true courage in pulling back the cloak of silence thrown over the difficult matter of blowing up enemy bodies and towing bodies into the nearby town. Barry Parkin and Sandy Pearson were gracious in answering my questions. I thank Chris Bellis for initially talking to me, and I appreciate the pressure he must have felt to withdraw his cooperation.

I would also like to thank a small group of veterans from 5RAR who had nothing to do with Thua Tich, but with whom I travelled around Phuoc Tuy province in 2010. I thank Peter Taylor, Ray Knapp, David Judd, Barney Simpson, Ken Aspinall, Arnold 'Dutchy' Lockrey, Vickie Barnes and Karen Patterson for sharing their stories. Special thanks go to Monkey Bridge Tour leader Walter Pearson, also a 5RAR veteran, for his help in getting to the gates of Thua Tich. Thanks also to Kevin McMillan for his help at Xuyen Moc. As a non-military man they provided tremendous insight for me into their lasting cameraderie. They told their stories of war quietly and with dignity, and I hope their return to the scene of their battles helped them to finally find peace within themselves.

Several non-military people were essential for this book to come to fruition. Fellow journalist and author Matthew Benns tipped me off to the larger story behind his 2009 newspaper article on the Ghost Platoon. He then proceeded to distract me with online chess as we wrote our respective books.

Vanessa Radnidge, my publisher at Hachette Australia, immediately saw the power of the story of the Ghost Platoon. I thank editor Roberta Ivers for her perceptive mind and eagle's eye in brushing up my efforts into a presentable form. Thanks also to proofreader Katie Stackhouse for skilfully picking up my inconsistencies; however, any errors that made it through are mine. I thank two journo mates, my brother Peter and Terry Smyth, for proofreading and suggesting how I could improve the raw copy. Jane Nursey, the senior clinical specialist at the Australian Centre for Posttraumatic Mental Health, was an enormous help in explaining PTSD and its impact on war veterans.

Archivists toil away anonymously in the world of conserving and locating files and documents. Their skills and dedication are all too often unappreciated. I thank Bill Edwards at the National Archives of Australia for his bloodhound-like determination to track down key papers. Joanne Smedley and Amanda Burrows at the Australian War Memorial's photographic archives were very helpful. Caroline Quinn at the Department of Veterans' Affairs helped with statistics and contacts. Theresa Stinson in the Freedom of Information section of the Defence Department helped me through the maze of bureaucracy to get the papers I needed.

Finally I'd like to thank my family for their support in this, my second non-fiction book on the Vietnam War. It's been a long hard road, and I couldn't have done it without them.

To contact me about this book, please email me at ghostplatoonbook@gmail.com.

Frank Walker

INDEX

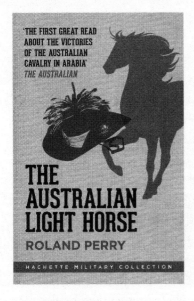

'THE FIRST GREAT READ ABOUT THE VICTORIES OF THE AUSTRALIAN CAVALRY IN ARABIA'
THE AUSTRALIAN

THE AUSTRALIAN LIGHT HORSE

ROLAND PERRY

HACHETTE MILITARY COLLECTION

The true story of the Australian Light Horse – the men from the bush who played a decisive role in World War I as they rode and fought their way into history.

Commanded by the brilliant Sir Harry Chauvel, they survived the hell-hole of Gallipoli, repulsed the Turkish invasion of Egypt, and achieved great victories in the Sinai, Palestine and Syria – culminating in the last great cavalry charge in our military history, the taking of Beersheba in 1917.

'A history book that deserves a place in every suburban home library ... the story of an extraordinary generation of Australians who created an enduring legend while changing the course of history'

—*West Australian*

'This is an enthralling and absorbing tale'

—*Good Reading*

'A compulsive read'

—*Newcastle Herald*

'Thrillingly described'

—*Sun-Herald*

'Briskly written, well-researched'

—*The Age*

AN ELITE FIGHTER
INSIDE AUSTRALIA'S
TOUGHEST AND
MOST SECRETIVE
COMBAT FORCE

Clint Palmer
SAS INSIDER
ROBERT MACKLIN

HACHETTE MILITARY COLLECTION

Clint Palmer always had a driving ambition to join the army. After enduring the toughest of tough training, he was accepted into the elite Australian SAS as it developed into the highly skilled and supremely effective fighting force it is today.

Thirty years of service later, Palmer shares the story of this adrenaline-fuelled world and how it became a lifelong commitment. He takes us to Iraq and Afghanistan – where he was at the heart of some of the worst fighting in Operation Anaconda – and tells what it was like to witness the bravery, the confusion, and the price paid by some men for the mistakes of others.

A true story of the SAS – Australia's elite fighting force – and a man who has spent a lifetime in its service.

'A high tempo ride through a soldier's life at the sharp end'
—*Australian Defence Magazine*

SAS
OPERATION STORM

THE SAS UNDER SIEGE, NINE MEN AGAINST FOUR HUNDRED

ROGER COLE &
RICHARD BELFIELD

HACHETTE MILITARY COLLECTION

SAS Operation Storm is a page-turning account of courage and resilience. Mirbat is one of the least-known and yet most crucial battles of modern times. *SAS Operation Storm* is the inside story – told by those who took part – of the greatest secret war in SAS history. The tipping point was Mirbat, a secret battle which defines the world we all live in today.

Roger Cole, one of the SAS soldiers who took part, and writer Richard Belfield have interviewed every SAS survivor who fought in the battle from the beginning to the end – and the first time every single one of them has revealed their experience.

SAS Operation Storm is a classic story of bravery against impossible odds, minute by minute, bullet by bullet.

'The time is now right for their bravery, at long last, to be properly recognised'

—Lord Ashcroft, KCMG, *Sunday Times*

'The SAS's finest hour'

—*Daily Mail*

'A MARVELLOUS
AND ORIGINAL BOOK'
SIR JOHN KEEGAN

TANK MEN
THE HUMAN SIDE OF TANKS AT WAR
ROBERT KERSHAW

HACHETTE MILITARY COLLECTION

The First World War saw the birth of an extraordinary fighting machine that has fascinated three generations: the tank.

In *Tank Men*, ex-soldier and military historian Robert Kershaw brings to life the grime, the grease and the fury of a tank battle through the voices of ordinary men and women who lived and fought in those fearsome machines.

Drawing on vivid, newly researched personal testimony from the crucial battles of the First and Second World Wars, this is military history at its very best.

'I thought *Tank Men* was a triumph . . . it really is a fine piece of work'
—Richard Holmes

'Some of the eye witness accounts Kershaw has collected for this comprehensive review of tank warfare have the power to chill the reader to the bone. This is warfare at the sharp end'
—*Nottingham Evening Post*

'A turret eye perspective of tank fighting from British, German, Russian and American tankies . . . Former Para Kershaw has compiled a very human history from interviews, letters and diaries'
—*Soldier Magazine*

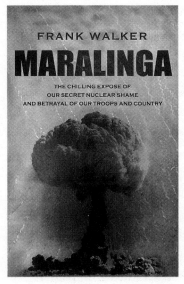

FRANK WALKER

MARALINGA

THE CHILLING EXPOSE OF
OUR SECRET NUCLEAR SHAME
AND BETRAYAL OF OUR TROOPS AND COUNTRY

The facts are shocking. The treachery is chilling. The fallout ongoing.

Investigative journalist Frank Walker's *Maralinga* is a must-read true story of the abuse of our servicemen, scientists treating the Australian population as lab rats and politicians sacrificing their own people in the pursuit of power.

During the Menzies era, with the blessing of the Prime Minister, the British government exploded twelve atomic bombs on Australian soil. RAAF pilots were ordered to fly into nuclear mushroom clouds, soldiers told to walk into radioactive ground zero, sailors retrieved highly contaminated debris – none of them aware of the dangers they faced. But it didn't end with these servicemen.

This chilling exposé drawn from extensive research and interviews with surviving veterans reveals the betrayal of our troops and our country.

'An original and compelling account that succeeds in exposing the subterfuge and myopia of both British and Australian governments'
—*Saturday Paper*

'Demonstrates powerfully why, regardless of the context in which the testing took place, the emotional legacy of Maralinga will linger in the Australian psyche'
—*Weekend Australian*

'Excellent examination of a dark chapter in Australian history'
—*Australian Defence Magazine*

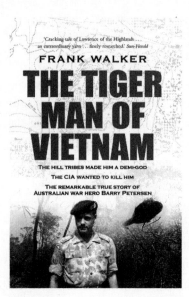

'Cracking tale of Lawrence of the Highlands . . . an extraordinary yarn . . . finely researched.' *Sun-Herald*

FRANK WALKER

THE TIGER MAN OF VIETNAM

THE HILL TRIBES MADE HIM A DEMI-GOD
THE CIA WANTED TO KILL HIM
THE REMARKABLE TRUE STORY OF AUSTRALIAN WAR HERO BARRY PETERSEN

In 1963, Australian Army Captain Barry Petersen was sent to Vietnam. It was one of the most tightly held secrets of the Vietnam War: long before combat troops set foot there and under the command of the CIA, Petersen was ordered to train and lead guerrilla squads of Montagnard tribesmen against the Viet Cong in the remote Central Highlands.

Petersen successfully formed a fearsome militia, named 'Tiger Men'. A canny leader, he was courageous in battle, and his bravery saw him awarded the coveted Military Cross and worshipped by the hill tribes. But his success created enemies, not just within the Viet Cong. He was lucky to make it out of the mountains alive.

The Tiger Man of Vietnam reveals the compelling true story of little-known Australian war hero Barry Petersen.

'One of those great untold stories ... Walker tells it with verve and excitement and with meticulous attention to detail'

—*Sydney Morning Herald*

'Walker's finely researched book goes beyond the biographical account of an Australian war hero'

—*Sun-Herald*

'It's been suggested Petersen was the model for the character of Colonel Kurtz in the film Apocalypse Now. But this remarkable true story is much richer and more compelling than anything Hollywood could conjure'

—*West Australian*

hachette
AUSTRALIA

If you would like to find out more about Hachette Australia,
our authors, upcoming events and new releases you can visit
our website, Facebook or follow us on Twitter:

hachette.com.au
twitter.com/HachetteAus
facebook.com/HachetteAustralia

Frank Walker has been an Australian journalist for forty years and this is his second non-fiction book. He has been a foreign correspondent in the United States and Europe, covered wars in Afghanistan, terrorist attacks in Indonesia and military coups in the South Pacific. His first book – *The Tiger Man of Vietnam* – revealed more uncomfortable truths about Australia's actions in the Vietnam War. It was a bestseller and went into several printings. His third bestselling book – *Maralinga* – lifted the veil of secrecy still hanging over the British atomic-bomb tests in Australia in the 1950s and 60s. His upcoming book – *Commandos* – examines the heroism of Australians and New Zealanders in the most daring raids of World War II. He can be reached through his website: www.frankwalker.com.au